CRIMINAL
JUSTICE
HISTORY
AN INTERNATIONAL ANNUAL

Board of Editors

CRIMINAL JUSTICE HISTORY

AN INTERNATIONAL ANNUAL

Volume IV

1983

Meckler Publishing
520 Riverside Avenue, Westport, CT 06880, USA

3 Henrietta Street, London WC2E 8LU, UK

ISBN: 0-930466-70-5
ISSN: 0194-0953

Manufactured in the United States of America.

Contents

Local Jurisdictions and Judgment of Death in Later Medieval England

J. B. Post
Public Record Office, London

Maitland judged that in the thirteenth century the summary justice of local jurisdictions was ridding England of more malefactors than the king's courts could hang.[1] Certainly, when the landholders of England defended their franchises before the justices of Edward I, many of them claimed rights and duties in the local administration of justice, but it is often unclear whether a claim to criminal jurisdiction was notional, or gave a fair representation of current practice. In the thirteenth century, and for much of the fourteenth, criminals must have entertained "considerable uncertainty as to who would have the privilege of indicting or hanging them,"[2] and the patchwork of local liberties, varying widely in their powers and in the exercise of them, forces the historian to sympathise with this general uncertainty.[3] It is nevertheless possible to get a detailed impression of the part then played by local and private jurisdictions in the trial and execution of felons, and to chart provisionally the stages whereby the crown, in the shape of quarter sessions and assizes, gained in the fifteenth century an effective monopoly in the hearing and determining of causes touching life and member.

There was no single term—nor, indeed, any single concept—by which king, lord, or lawyer could designate jurisdiction over felony; instead, it was defined by two patterns, one of courts and one of pleas. Although the county court was a customary court of considerable status that long retained vestiges of criminal jurisdiction as the court of first instance for appeals of felony and as the forum for exaction to outlawry, it was not the preeminent local court of criminal justice; very probably its geographical immediacy was inadequate for that function. In the thirteenth century, as long before, the standard unit was the hundred or wapentake, whose three-weekly or monthly sessions for private litigation and minor business were varied, twice a year, by a great hundred or lawday, at which serious criminal business was treated and view of frankpledge was taken. Although view of frankpledge

1

was in essence a review of the tithing system of mutual local pledges,[4] it came to be associated so closely with criminal jurisdiction at the same sessions that *view of frankpledge* became the normal term for a hundredal court of first instance, and *leet*, the term which ultimately came to predominate for this purpose,[5] was, as Maitland pointed out, the word with which a fourteenth-century lawyer would have translated *visus franciplegii*.[6] This lawday was held (if the hundred was in the king's hand) by the sheriff or his surrogate at his tourn,[7] or, if not, by the steward of a lord to whom the hundred had been granted—with, in theory at least, the king's serjeant or the hundred bailiff in attendance. The relatively simple hundredal model, however, was complicated by the various terms on which hundreds had been granted into private hands. The hundredal model was complicated further by the similarly diverse grants of quasi-hundredal liberties, with exemption from hundredal jurisdiction and the grant of an independent view of frankpledge, to great numbers of smaller units: portions of hundreds, manors, portions of manors. It was upon this background that the crown was superimposing, increasingly and with varied experiments, local justices and exclusive criminal jurisdiction.

The powerful and growing family of crown pleas was already old. Well before the Conquest, particular types of plea were reserved to the jurisdiction of the crown, initially in fiscal reservation of forfeitures and mulcts, but also in assertion of a royal interest in serious crime as a breach of the king's peace.[8] By the early twelfth century the compiler of the *Laws of Henry I* could assemble a large ragbag of items, judicial and fiscal, "which," he claimed confidently, elaborating the secular dooms of Cnut, "are the rights which the king of England has alone and above all men."[9] Thenceforward it was increasingly recognised that the crown had a proper interest in any plea which might involve judgment of death or mutilation. Moreover, the introduction and development of new presentment procedures, over which the crown could exercise prerogative from the start,[10] fostered these reservations. The encroachment of crown pleas upon judicial practice was fitful, especially in the face of disparate local customs,[11] and was partly countered by grants of specified jurisdictions or their profits to local lords. Nevertheless, from the twelfth century onwards, any exercise of felony jurisdiction implied a claim to a licensed or recognised exemption from a royal monopoly.

The county court had very little call for this exemption. Appeals of felony (the customary mode of prosecution, by the victim or next of kin) were normally brought in the county,[12] but there was no general practice of determining them there;[13] in 1286 the county of York argued that appeals should be "begun, pleaded, and held" there, without mentioning judgment,[14] and the sheriff's roll of appeals for Norfolk in 1271 shows pleading and process only.[15] It is also clear that in the early decades of presentment for the crown, the county was used to review or record cases from hundred courts,[16] but it is unlikely that this function extended to trial or execution. Confession was irrebuttable,[17] and a confessed felon thereby stood "convict and condemned";[18] yet counties which dared to execute such a convict, despite the presumable presence of coroners to record the matter,[19] were amerced.[20] Since the counties pertained to the crown, and their judicial administration was heavily dependent upon the sheriff and the coroners, the reservation of their crown pleas to appointed crown agencies would have been straightforward; it was only because of exceptional status as a marcher liberty that the men of Chester could even claim, in 1325, that they and their predecessors, from time immemorial, had "rendered judgments and decisions of the county both in pleas of the crown and in all other pleas whatsoever."[21]

Although the hundred was the standard unit of local criminal jurisdiction, its powers were, by the thirteenth century, customary and hence rarely defined. It seems likely, however, that from the tenth century onwards the range of hundredal justice was severely limited,[22] and that with the possible exception of communal accusations before the Assize of Clarendon in 1166,[23] the hundredal and quasi-hundredal courts were competent to determine only noncapital causes, infangthief excepted.[24] Certainly, the sorts of jurisdiction attributed to hundreds, whether royal or private, in the thirteenth century suggest such limitations. In 1231 Bullingdon hundred, for example, was said to have view of frankpledge, attachments of pleas of the crown, and amercements otherwise due to the sheriff.[25] Whorwellsdown, according to an agreement three years later, had view of frankpledge and of assizes of bread and ale, attachments, and jurisdiction over crimes of violence "in which felony is not imputed."[26] A review of the Wiltshire hundreds, c. 1251, attributed to none of them any jurisdiction greater than that enjoyed by the sheriff in his tourn.[27]

It was "enquiry of the articles of which the sheriff enquires at his tourn," together with view of frankpledge, by which the holders of franchises most frequently sought to define their criminal jurisdictions.[28] The sheriff's powers at the tourn had been defined and circumscribed on four occasions. In 1166 the Assize of Clarendon required, although it did not introduce,[29] presentment by jury of robbery, larceny, murder, and reset; the sheriff was responsible for the enquiry at hundredal level. In the Assize of Northampton, ten years later, presentment procedure was formally extended, perhaps in accordance with current practice, to forgery, arson, and "other serious felony."[30] It was further laid down that suspects arrested on this procedure or on any other should be kept in custody by the sheriff for trial before the royal justices.[31] In 1215, Magna Carta emphasised, perhaps of necessity, that "no sheriff, constables, coroners, nor other of our bailiffs, shall hold pleas of our crown,"[32] and the 1217 reissue limited the hundredal tourn to twice a year, with view of frankpledge at one of those sessions.[33] These limitations of the tourn—presentment of felonies, and, by implication, full jurisdiction over noncapital offences—tally well with the business stipulated for private leets in the earliest of their articles of enquiry,[34] and contemporaries regarded the private leet and the sheriff's tourn as exact equivalents.[35] The claim of parity with the sheriff's tourn thus did not of itself imply any jurisdiction over felony save the taking of presentments.

The solitary point of full felony jurisdiction customarily enjoyed by the hundred—and commonly conveyed with grants of liberties—was infangthief, with its habitual companion, outfangthief—rights, variably defined, over the handhaving thief, the thief caught with the mainour or booty upon him. Jolliffe suggested that infangthief as a hundredal jurisdiction may have developed as a substitution of legal procedure (however rudimentary) for the more ancient idea that a manifest criminal was an outlaw and could be killed outright with impunity.[36] This suggestion is consistent with the evident extension of the concept, both by the blurring of definition and by the elaboration of associated procedures. The *Laws of Henry I*, in saying that "theft not punished by death" (*furtum morte impunitum*) was reserved to the crown, presupposed a normally summary treatment of thieves,[37] and the author of *Glanvill*, possibly looking back in time, saw theft as a serious crime over which the sheriff might nonetheless have jurisdiction.[38] Definitions became progressively less consistent and more confused. A twelfth-century compiler quoted the standard, and narrowest, description of infangthief: judgment "of one's own man taken on one's own land."[39] But a ruling of 1230 defined infangthief as "one's man taken on someone else's land" and outfangthief as "an outsider taken for theft on one's own land."[40] In 1253, a royal charter, issued in clarification of vernacular terms, defined infangthief as "judgment of thieves taken with the mainour within one's liberties";[41] and in 1233, the disputants over judgment of thieves in a Kentish hundred did not trouble to distinguish infangthief from outfangthief.[42] At quo warranto the archbishop of York claimed infangthief to be the right of judgment on felonies committed within his liberties and outfangthief as the right to execute his tenants who had been condemned in other courts.[43] In 1303, an inquisition found that the Fitz Stephen family (who at quo warranto had disclaimed pleas of the crown) had the following among the customary pleas of their hundredal manor of Ermington: "[I]f any person be taken with stolen goods at the suit of any in that manor, he will be hanged or delivered by judgment of the court."[44] The broadest claim came from the prior of Bodmin in 1302: "[W]e say that infangthief extends to the case of a thief being taken with the mainour at the suit of anyone, and that if he will submit to the court we may hold the plea, and may proceed to judgment if he be condemned."[45] Lawyers and administrators came to regard a set of definitions, however aberrant, as a useful item to include in any compilation of precedents or practice.[46]

An element of trial is suggested by some of these definitions, and it is likely that formal testimony, and perhaps the ordeal, were used against even the most obvious thieves at an early date:[47] the abbot of St. Edmunds traced his judgment of crown pleas to the right of ordeal before 1215.[48] This supposition is supported into the later period by other evidence. In the early thirteenth century, though probably not much later, coroners sometimes attended such judgments of death,[49] which indicates a special rather than an impromptu hearing. Other instances of extraordinary sessions occur. The charter of Quarr abbey granted exemption of suit "at any hundred save *hundredum latrocinii*," and similar terms were granted by the bishop of Ely and by the abbot of Ramsey.[50] A tenant of the abbot of Beaulieu claimed in 1231 exemption from fortnightly suit at Faringdon, attending only "when a thief is to be judged" and "for afforcement of the court at the law hundred."[51] In the 1280s, the steward of the bishop of Norwich resummoned the liberty court of South Elmham to try a thief locally accused,[52] while the prison at Yardley Hastings, which before 1353 "used to be the prison of the lordship by reason of the liberty of infangthief and outfangthief," shows that summary justice upon thieves was not necessarily hasty or informal.[53] The heyday of these procedures is perhaps represented in precedents given in two treatises on franchise courts—probably composed in the third quarter of the thirteenth century, but with conservative models in mind—which set out the trials of handhaving thieves by local juries.[54]

It was probably the self-evident guilt of the handhaving thief which allowed infangthief to persist as an exception to the reservation of crown pleas; manifest guilt was, under rather limited circumstances, a justification for summary executions in other cases. Hundredal officials were competent to witness confessions,[55] as subsequently were coroners,[56] and testified to the confessions before royal justices.[57] On occasion, however, the local court took the confession in lieu of a judgment (whether or not that judgment would have been within its competence) and proceeded to execution. In 1195, one of the Aylesbury hundreds hanged on confession to one felony a prisoner arrested for another;[58] more than a century later, four Cheshire townships witnessed a confession to larceny and acted upon it, without exciting adverse comment.[59] In 1272, the abbot of St. Albans claimed that the right to have a private coroner conveyed jurisdiction over confessed felons.[60] The effect of confession before local officers was apparently an extension, as was infangthief, of the legitimate reaction to felons caught in the act and killed by the hue or by the victim. Such summary execution, traditionally by beheading, was common at least until the end of the thirteenth century, despite some royal efforts to contain it,[61] and in 1348 it was ruled, from numerous precedents, that no pardon was required for killing a robber, burglar, or thief who would otherwise escape arrest.[62] Even in 1396 the crown accepted that a local posse had believed it lawful to behead an outlaw.[63]

Beyond these limited areas of summary justice, some few franchises had recognised powers to determine crown pleas. Four great ecclesiastical liberties — Ely, Glastonbury, Ramsey, St. Edmunds — are known to have had full criminal jurisdiction, with the appointment of omnicompetent justices and the disposal of rights to subsidiary liberties,[64] in the thirteenth century and later.[65] These may have had their origins in courts over several hundreds and centred on royal burghs, of which the very few granted into private hands before the Conquest were the only survivors.[66] In a greater number of cases, liberties which may once have exercised full criminal jurisdiction came, with the development of the eyre in the twelfth century, to have the modified privilege of exemption from the jurisdiction of the eyre, having instead a special session within the liberty, at which its ministers held court with the attendance or participation of an eyre justice. This, again, was characteristic of great ecclesiastical liberties. Tenants of the fee of the archbishop of Canterbury, for example, if arrested or indicted on a crown plea, could be tried in a royal court, but the archbishop's bailiffs could then have the case transferred for judgment to the liberty court with royal justices in attendance.[67] Similar sessions were enjoyed by the archbishop of York, the abbot of Battle, and the abbot of Reading,[68] but there were secular claimants as well: Corfe castle had a town court where all pleas of the crown could be determined before the king's justices.[69]

Secular claims to full independence of jurisdiction were rare, and tended, significantly, to come from areas at the fringes of royal governance. The sweeping claims of Cheshire have been mentioned already.[70] The county of Hereford declared in 1281 that Archenfield hundred had an immemorial right to hold crown pleas before the sheriff.[71] In Cumberland, the miners of Alston had full criminal jurisdiction in their own court held before a coroner and a king's serjeant,[72] while the honor of Cockermouth castle had comprehensive rights of criminal justice, with the exception of final exaction to outlawry.[73] It may well have been easier to acknowledge such rights than to enforce the alternative so far from Westminster; the countess of Norfolk had no difficulty in arrogating crown pleas from Richard II to her court in the Welsh march for several years.[74] Under such circumstances the crown's acknowledgement at least put the holders of exemptions in the positive role of royal delegates.[75]

These patterns of courts and pleas were necessarily only a background to the exercise of justice; they suggest who might legitimately have tried or hanged a felon, but they do not show who normally did so. The evidence of claims and claimants, indeed, itself often gives the impression that, fiscal considerations apart, the lords of franchises took little interest in felony jurisdiction. Complaints about encroachments upon liberties tend to dwell on the financial losses of amercements and felons' chattels, rather than on problems of conflicting jurisdictions, and the intruder was often a royal official.[76] More telling is the evidence of claims to gallows. Possession of gallows did not imply the right to judge capital causes; a lord might simply have the right to execute the judgments of royal courts[77] and to keep the felons' forfeit chattels. On the other hand, the lack of gallows would be inconsistent with any effective claim to judgment of death. Occasionally, special circumstances, such as the execution of judgments at the eyre given far from the relevant liberty, might require the loan of a gallows,[78] and the borrowing of instruments of justice was not unknown at a lower level;[79] but the frequent disclaimer of gallows at quo warranto suggests a lack of use for them.[80] Even more, the desuetude of gallows bespeaks a decline in the exercise of a liberty which was once observed. Time and again the claim of gallows was accompanied by the admission or proof that the gallows had decayed from disuse. Philip Marmion and his ancestors "anciently had gallows on their own land. . .which were demolished a long time ago"; the abbot of Leicester's bailiff erected a gallows on one specific occasion, "but no one can remember that any thief was ever taken or hanged there before or since"; John St. John's gallows had fallen into disrepair.[81] Fulk Lucy erected gallows in Shrewley, apparently as a means of staking a territorial claim,[82] and instruments of punishment were used widely as symbols of local jurisdiction: in 1223 Ralph Moyne and the abbot of Cirencester disputed the gallows at Shipton, where the local penalty was only loss of an ear;[83] in 1367 the abbot's successor found that the gallows at Eastleach Turville were merely the symbolic focus of Bruern abbey's efforts to avoid hundredal suit.[84] Later still, the judicial instruments of Chipping Walden were defended only "for preserving the liberty of the town."[85]

It was hardly surprising that lords should fail to erect or maintain gallows. Despite their proliferation (there were about a hundred gallows in Gloucestershire and Worcestershire),[86] the amount of possible custom was limited, and as Maitland emphasised, they could never have been very useful.[87] A stronger disincentive was the crown. When the abbess of Romsey, whose gallows had fallen down from disuse, said she dare not set it up again without the king's leave,[88] she was pointing to a very real opponent. Possibly she, like others later,[89] wanted to enjoy the profits of the king's judgments rather than exercise her own. The town gallows of Hereford had to be erected specially when the eyre was due.[90] Even the bishop of Ely, roundly and with some precedent claiming "imprisonments, attachments, judgments, and executions of judgments of malefactors" within all the manors of the liberty, conceded that his bailiffs usually took offenders for trial by the justices in eyre.[91] In all these cases, the need and the enthusiasm for felony jurisdiction do not seem very marked, and this in itself may have encouraged the crown to experiment with supplementary courts of its own.

Despite the evidence of disclaimer or disuse, many local courts remained active in the trial and judgment of felony throughout the thirteenth century and later; the articles of the eyre, enquiring "of felons hanged and condemned elsewhere than before the justices for all pleas," expected as much.[92] The evidence for county courts, as already indicated, is sparse and suggests little in the way of criminal business, although the attempt by the sheriff and jurors of Yorkshire to represent judgment of an appeal of homicide as the hanging of a handhaving thief shows that they expected to have the latter allowed.[93] The sheriff of Bedfordshire and Buckinghamshire certainly took no part in felony proceedings, beyond appeals at first instance, in the 1330s.[94] But hundreds and quasi-hundredal liberties were active, and not solely in the matter of infangthief. Hundredal judgment of the handhaving thief, taken and prosecuted at suit of the victim, was taken for granted on the Ramsey estates in the mid-thirteenth century.[95] The suitors of Buxted in Sussex, less sure of themselves, judged to death a thief taken with mainour, but mainprised each other "for the observance of the king's peace"—prudently, since the thief's widow tried to appeal them of homicide.[96] In the same year, 1277, Ralph Tony's steward at Walthamstow, who hanged a man there without suit, was indicted before the keepers of the peace for infringing the hundredal rights of the abbess of Barking.[97] Well into the next century, a Cornish hundred heard and judged an appeal of robbery.[98]

Over a similar period and longer, the evidence for liberty courts, great and small, is plentiful, although it comes mainly from the records of superior courts and is often brief. An appeal of wounding was heard in the court of St. Edmunds in 1231, and the right to hear it was defended.[99] Handhaving thieves, however, were the staple of judgments within liberties: in 1242 at the bishop of Bath's hundredal liberty of Cheddar;[100] in 1248 at the abbot of Cirencester's court at East Hagbourne (where the forfeit chattels seem to have gone to the crown);[101] in 1267 in Sir John Burgh's court at Rayne in Essex;[102] and throughout the reigns of Edward I and Edward II at Wakefield.[103] In the fourteenth century such evidence declines — partly, no doubt, for want of the general eyre to record. But some liberties continued in the customary way: in 1381, a thief convicted on appeal before the bishop of Lincoln's steward at Louth was sent to the county gaol because he had pleaded clergy.[104] In the next year, an appeal of larceny was determined before the bishop of Salisbury's bailiff;[105] and in 1387, John Beauchamp of Powick's steward was indicted in king's bench for incompetence in failing to execute a thief tried by jury before him.[106] Such evidence shows that the trial of felony was by no means unknown in local courts in the quo warranto period and later.

More important, the evidence above suggests that the dearth of references to such trials in the records of private courts cannot be taken at its face value. It is not that the trials were surreptitious; more probably, the dearth of records reflects the purpose for which the records were prepared. The felony business of a private court was exceptional, not only in its rarity among the minor and private cases which occupied most of the proceedings, but also in the likelihood that the court would have to answer for it elsewhere by accounting at the eyre for felons judged, or forwarding indictments with prisoners for gaol delivery. The need to transmit the record of particular types of cases, and the need for indictments at least to be authenticated by seal or indenture,[107] argued for keeping such records distinct from the routine enrolment, filing them until needed, and subsequently keeping only the counterparts, if any. At worst, therefore, the records of felony proceedings would be drafted in a single copy for transmission. A more careful steward or clerk would keep counterparts either loose or perhaps sewn to the court roll until their usefulness was past; and only the most laborious would transcribe the entry from the roll to the slip, or vice versa. The Wakefield rolls already cited are examples of this last practice, while the early fourteenth-century court rolls of Minchinhampton, where the abbess of Caen claimed leet and gallows,[108] bear authenticated counterpart schedules recording felony cases proceeding elsewhere and handhaving thieves tried by jury and hanged in the manor.[109] Most local rolls, however, fall into the earlier categories and give no indication whether or not the court dealt with felony. Thus, the crown's need for individual records probably caused the loss of an unknowable proportion of them.

In fact, the direct evidence of hundredal business in the fourteenth and early fifteenth centuries suggests that these courts were vigorous enough in small, private causes (hundred and tourn were still vexatious among the Paston acquaintance in 1460),[110] but that their effectiveness for criminal business at any level was dwindling.[111] Before 1300, the Lancastrian hundred of Appletree, in Derbyshire, was dealing at every session—not merely at the leets—with bread and ale offences,[112] public works, bloodshed, affray, concealments of hue, and defaults by frankpledges. In the course of the fourteenth century, fewer and fewer peacekeeping matters arose, and the evidence of defaulting suitors increased; only bread and ale offences recurred undiminished. By the early decades of the fifteenth century, breaches of the peace, however trivial, were exceedingly scarce, and by the middle of the century had disappeared altogether.[113] Other hundreds showed the same or less concern for criminal business. Penwith in Cornwall saw only private litigation at its ordinary sessions in 1333;[114] Milton in Kent had the same balance in the 1280s;[115] and there is no evidence that Highworth exercised infangthief among its small turnover of petty crime.[116] The manorial hundred of Crondal in Hampshire, at much the same date, concentrated substantially on tenurial transactions and land trespasses.[117] Shrieval tourns were evidently following a similar general pattern, although peacekeeping continued to occupy some of their time. A Yorkshire tourn in 1381 included a few felony presentments among many for public works;[118] Devon tourns in 1400 noticed only assaults and bread and ale offences.[119] Warwickshire and Leicestershire tourns dealt with a broader range of business, but the offences presented were all trifling, and peacekeeping functions evidently declined in the second quarter of the fifteenth century.[120] This is also true of Wiltshire tourns in 1439.[121] Despite, therefore, possible gaps in the enrolment of felony proceedings, it seems that the normal criminal business at the hundred was minor at the beginning of the fourteenth century and declined thereafter.

This does not necessarily mean that the pattern of the larger, better organised, or royal hundreds was shared by the generality of leets and franchises, but there are powerful reasons for supposing that the criminal jurisdiction of most local courts was in decline—erratically, varying in chronology from place to place, but always giving ground. The crown was providing two major inducements to such decline: sustained hostility to the exercise of crown pleas jurisdiction by anyone but its own justices, and the provision of regular and effective courts as practicable alternatives.

From the reign of Henry II onwards there is much evidence that the reservation of pleas and procedures which was propounded in law was applied, and where possible, extended in practice, so that in the thirteenth century even the traditional summary justice of the hundreds came under attack: Geoffrey George, amerced in 1188 because "he made a man abjure the realm, without warrant";[122] Limpsfield township, amerced in 1191 for hanging a woman without view of the king's serjeant;[123] Roger Cook, amerced in 1196 "for a man hanged without view of the justices and sheriff";[124] and the men of Romney, amerced two hundred marks in 1233 for holding a duel on an approver's appeal.[125] These were not punishments for lawlessness, but for arrogating justice at levels or in particulars to which royal supervision had now—and by implication, recently—penetrated. The attack was frequently on a procedure rather than a substantive jurisdiction. Confession to felony was a matter of crown record and hence a reserved procedure, whatever the status of the felony. Hanging a confessed homicide taken with mainour was found in 1225 to be beyond the competence of the court of the abbot of Reading,[126] and in 1229 the archbishop of Canterbury's court was in mercy for judging a confessed thief.[127] The tendency to act on confessions persisted, but the countervailing doctrine was maintained and elaborated. In the Kent eyre of 1313 it was ruled that a steward could not proceed to judgment of a handhaving thief taken, and confessing, within a liberty with infangthief, nor put him on the country, "because a court baron does not bear record of confession."[128]

Proceeding to judgment was also tricky. Hanging a man without judgment was penalised at an early stage,[129] and the prior of St. Swithun found in 1234 that a notorious thief killed resisting arrest was not regarded as convicted of larceny.[130] The right to judge handhaving thieves was acknowledged in due cases well into the fourteenth century,[131] and it is perhaps significant that, in the lists of forfeitures prepared in 1357, the "thieves" were already hanged while other "felons" were fled, outlawed, or otherwise accounted.[132] Yet even this right was increasingly circumscribed. The charter of Kingston upon Hull, in 1279, made it clear that the grant of gallows and of summary jurisdiction was merely a delegation of royal authority.[133] Moreover, any delay in executing summary judgment was taken to forfeit the right to do so. In the Kent eyre, the justices allowed three days for convening a private hundred to judge a thief,[134] and in the Cornish eyre of 1302, the vill or tithing was allowed one night of custody before sending a prisoner to the king's gaol,[135] but a prevailing judicial opinion held that summary justice should be exercised outright or not at all.[136] By the early fourteenth century this opinion was widely shared or accepted. The hundredal suitors of the Isle of Wight in 1283 envisaged no capital trials at their courts,[137] and the author of *The Mirror of Justices* maintained that no leet could hear or determine felony.[138] In wrangling over the franchise of the city of Canterbury it was accepted that statutory offences were not within the competence of private justice[139] — a point later extended to cover common-law offences which had been treated in statutes[140] — and by 1355 Thorpe could rule against the great liberty of Ely that "life and member pertain to the king and no one else, and lords have nothing but custody."[141] When the mayor of Dartmouth unlawfully burned a woman for petty treason in 1390, he showed a quite remarkable ignorance of, or disregard for, the progress made by crown pleas over the previous hundred years.[142]

More effective than the mere assertion of exclusive crown rights was the development of royal courts which could compete with franchise and customary courts. Throughout the thirteenth century and into the fourteenth, much faith was placed in the general eyre, but its pattern of minutely exhaustive and fiscally rapacious local enquiries, coupled with sessions of civil litigation, and all conducted at the highest judicial level, was too cumbersome and protracted to be a readily effective means of keeping the peace.[143] Consequently, there were frequent attempts to modify or extend the range of judicial resorts; of these, the trailbaston proceedings after 1304 were perhaps the most successful, but they, too, were cumbersome and oppressive, and the general oyer and terminer commissions of which they were a variant did not persist on a broad scale.[144] There was, however, an important component of local crown jurisdiction already at hand. The king's county gaols, in the custody of the sheriff, were periodically delivered by trial of the prisoners before royal justices commissioned for the purpose. From an early date it was sometimes found convenient to give this duty to the justices assigned to deal regularly, county by county, with the possessory assizes. By Henry III's reign, this dual function was accepted as a standard, though not invariable, practice.[145] The regularity and frequency of gaol deliveries was uneven, but one or two sessions a year gave considerably greater opportunity than did the eyre for trying before royal justices felons arrested and indicted elsewhere. On this basis gaol delivery, eventually borrowing its common title from the elder session, became, as "assizes," the normal jurisdiction for the trial of felony.[146]

Gaol delivery, however, was merely a system for dealing with prisoners; it did not provide a court of first instance, and did not therefore compete directly with the private courts. It was in commissions of the peace that the crown eventually found a satisfactory complement to gaol delivery. Local gentry under royal commissions as keepers of the peace gradually increased their police functions, hearing trespass presentments in Edward I's time and determining these and other cases, according to their fluctuating competence, from the beginning of the fourteenth century.[147] Within sixty years, the addition of jurisdiction over labour laws and economic regulations, and the elevation of keepers into justices, made peace sessions the established royal alternative to any other court of first instance for felony.[148] This experiment had two particular advantages. First, the lords and gentry who maintained private courts were the typical recipients of commissions of the peace, and were thus far less likely to resist this encroachment of royal justice in their localities.[149] Indeed, the swollen peace commissions which became customary in the course of the fifteenth century show that inclusion in the commission was a desideratum, and it is not difficult to see why. The afforcement of private authority by royal delegation might be desirable in itself (justices sometimes dealt at quarter sessions with offences within their private franchisal competence),[150] but a justice of the peace could act over a wider area than his own property rights could ever allow, and, increasingly, he could act individually out of session,[151] so that his commission became essential to the assertion and defence of his status in the country. Second—and this can hardly have been coincidental—the establishment of peace sessions as quarter sessions, made statutory in 1351 but probably an older habit,[152] enabled them by their frequency alone to preempt much of the business which might otherwise have gone to the half-yearly leets. The permanence of the innovation, however, and the extensive investigations which modern scholars have made among the peace rolls[153] give a misleading impression that quarter sessions themselves eliminated competition and, once firmly established in the mid-fourteenth century, had no rival.

Gaol delivery records show very plainly that the customary and franchise courts, whether under duress or for their own convenience, were passing much of their business to the royal justices well before the end of the thirteenth century. At the Warwickshire eyre of 1285, the presentments of summary justice done upon handhaving thieves were heavily interspersed with those of thieves, suspects, and homicides sent for trial at gaol delivery,[154] and the gaol delivery rolls subsequently illustrate developments. Many handhaving thieves were sent to the king's gaol for delivery, some from liberties with infangthief,[155] and the rest of the prisoners were arrested by local officials, appealed, or indicted at tourns, leets, or coroners' inquests.[156] The appearance of prisoners indicted at peace sessions was rare before 1350,[157] and it was not until the last quarter of the century that they came to predominate over those from other agencies.[158] The last franchise indictment came from the Black Prince's steward in 1371,[159] the last tourn indictment in 1379.[160] Warwickshire, moreover, was a county of relatively simple judicial structure; all four hundreds pertained to the crown, and the supersession of their criminal jurisdiction under the sheriff, by royal courts which he served, cannot have been inconvenient. Similar arguments apply to Huntingdonshire, where Ramsey abbey held one hundred and the crown two or sometimes three.[161] Again, peace sessions indictments occurred only from the 1350s onwards, with tourn and leet indictments persisting until the end of the century;[162] but the great liberties were falling into line: a prisoner of the bishop of Ely, consistent with earlier practice, was sent to gaol delivery in 1355,[163] while Ramsey's independence had dwindled to a special gaol delivery by the county justices (resembling the special eyre formerly enjoyed by other liberties) by Richard II's reign.[164] Other counties with few hundreds, such as Leicestershire, Worcestershire, and Staffordshire, also show a great predominance of peace sessions indictments by the early decades of the fifteenth century.[165]

The establishment of a virtual monopoly by quarter sessions took considerably longer in counties where hundredal courts abounded. In Hampshire, where only fifteen of the forty-one hundreds pertained to the crown, the justices of the peace gained ascendancy only in the middle of the fifteenth century; at the end of the fourteenth, private courts accounted for half the indictments at gaol delivery, with coroners' inquests and tourns accounting for many of the remainder.[166] And the decline of the tourn in the second half of the fourteenth century, anticipating that of the private hundred, can be seen in the increasing tendency for the sheriff to hold fewer tourns for larger areas.[167] Correspondingly, the justices of the peace were less careful to enquire hundred by hundred where this meant summoning large numbers of juries, and the work of hundredal courts was not therefore exactly duplicated. This delay in the triumph of quarter sessions occurred in other complex counties: Gloucestershire gaol delivery, for example, still saw tourn and leet business under Henry V,[168] while in Lincolnshire the tourn was particularly active into the following reign.[169] When in 1461 the Commons complained of shrieval abuses and secured the transfer of tourn indictments to quarter sessions before process could issue,[170] the death-blow was given to a living if moribund jurisdiction, and, even at the leet, presentment of felony became rare.[171]

Not until the mid-fifteenth century, therefore, did indictment at quarter sessions and trial at assizes become the normal procedure by which felony was prosecuted. Steadily from Henry II onwards, the crown was able to effect and extend the reservation of its pleas and procedures, at first from the jurisdiction of the sheriff, but progressively from the customary and private courts as well. By the end of the thirteenth century the lords and stewards of liberties were in general accepting trial of felons by royal justices as a normal and convenient alternative to the hazards of administering their own criminal justice, save in the most traditional and limited instances. Yet leets and tourns persisted thereafter as courts of first instance for felony, despite declining criminal business of all kinds, and the keepers of the peace had been justices for a hundred years before they came into their own.

Notes

This paper has benefited greatly from criticisms by Dr. R. F. Hunnisett and Professor L. A. Knafla, sundry references kindly provided by Dr. P. A. Brand, Miss M. M. Condon, and Mr. A. J. Prescott, discussion with Dr. M. C. Carpenter, comparison with an as yet unpublished paper generously lent by the late Professor R. B. Pugh, and a now ancient correspondence with the late Mr. G. D. G. Hall. Persistent defects are the fault of the author.

All unpublished documents cited are in the Public Record Office, London.

1. F. Pollock and F. W. Maitland, *The History of English Law before the Time of Edward I*, 2d ed. reissued with addenda by S. F. C. Milsom (Cambridge, 1965), II, 579.
2. B. H. Putnam, "The Transformation of the Keepers of the Peace into Justices of the Peace, 1327–80," *Transactions of the Royal Historical Society*(hereafter cited as *T. R. H. S.*), 4th series, XII (1929) p. 21.
3. For good county surveys of medieval liberties, see G. C. Baugh, "The Franchises," in *Victoria County History* (hereafter cited as *V. C. H.*) *of Shropshire*, III (London, 1979), pp. 33–53; and G. A. J. Hodgett, "Feudal Wiltshire," in *V. C. H. Wiltshire*, V (London, 1959), pp. 44–71, especially pp. 53–68.
4. W. A. Morris, *The Frankpledge System* (London, 1910), or more especially, D. A. Crowley, "Frankpledge and Leet Jurisdiction in Later Medieval Essex" (Ph.D. diss., University of Sheffield, 1971).
5. "Leet" seems originally to have designated a territorial unit of jurisdiction, below hundredal level, in the Danelaw: D. C. Douglas, *The Social Structure of Medieval East Anglia*, Oxford Studies in Social and Legal History, IX (Oxford, 1927), pp. 189–202; B. A. Lees, "The Statute of Winchester and Villa Integra," *English Historical Review* (hereafter cited as *E. H. R.*) 41 (1926):102.
6. F. W. Maitland, ed., *Select Pleas in Manorial Courts* (Selden Soc., II, 1888) p. lxxiii.
7. For *leta* used in 1294 by the undersheriff of Cambridgeshire to indicate a tourn, see G. O. Sayles, ed., *Select Cases in the Court of King's Bench*, III (Selden Soc., XLVIII, 1939), p. 8 (no. 4). Cf. *Calendar of Inquisitions Miscellaneous* (London: H. M. S. O., 1916–1969), IV, no. 193 [1382].
8. P. Vinogradoff, *English Society in the Eleventh Century* (Oxford, 1908), pp. 111–14.
9. L. J. Downer, ed.,*Leges Henrici Primi* (Oxford, 1972), pp. 108–9 (X.1); cf. II Cnut, 12: F. Liebermann, ed., *Die Gesetze der Angelsachsen* (Halle, 1898–1916), I, 317.

10. N. D. Hurnard, "The Jury of Presentment and the Assize of Clarendon," *E. H. R.*, 56 (1941): 397–98.

11. G. D. G. Hall, ed., *The Treatise on the Laws and Customs of the Realm of England commonly called Glanvill* (London, 1965), p. 147 (XII, 23).

12. For the customary procedure, see J. M. Kaye, ed., *Placita Corone* Selden Soc.,(Supplementary Series, vol. 4 1966), p. 1.

13. W. A. Morris, *The Early English County Court* (Cambridge, 1926), pp. 112–15.

14. *King's Bench*, I (Selden Soc., LV, 1936), pp. 163–4 (no. 108).

15. Coroners' Rolls, JUST 2/266, m. 40.

16. *Pipe Roll 32 Henry II* (Pipe Roll Soc., old series, XXXVII, 1915), p. 47; *Pipe Roll 7 Richard I* (ibid., new series, VI, 1929), p. 143.

17. Assize of Northampton, c. 3: *Select Charters...*, ed. W. Stubbs, 9th ed., revised (Oxford, 1921), p. 179.

18. Bracton, *On the Laws and Customs of England*, ed. G. E. Woodbine, revised and translated by S. E. Thorne (Cambridge, Mass., 1968–), I, 430 (f. 152).

19. R. F. Hunnisett, *The Medieval Coroner* (Cambridge, 1961), pp. 1–4.

20. *Curia Regis Rolls* (H. M. S. O., 1923), VI, 10 [Rutland, 1210]; Assize Rolls, etc., JUST 1/956, m. 42d [Warwickshire, 1285].

21. Chester Plea Rolls, CHES 29/37, m. 10, quoted and discussed by R. C. Palmer, "Lawyer and Doomsman in the Old English County Court" (Ph.D. diss., University of Iowa, 1977), pp. 65 and 396.

22. J. E. A. Jolliffe, "The Origin of the Hundred in Kent," in *Historical Essays in Honour of James Tait*, ed. J. G. Edwards, V. H. Galbraith, and E. F. Jacob (Manchester, 1933), pp. 161–62. See also H. R. Loyn, "The Hundred in the Tenth and Early Eleventh Centuries," in *British Government and Administration: Studies Presented to S. B. Chrimes*, ed. H. Hearder and H. R. Loyn (Cardiff, 1974), pp. 1–15.

23. Cf. the evidence adduced by Hurnard, "Jury of Presentment," pp. 391–93.

24. N. D. Hurnard, "The Anglo-Norman Franchises," *E. H. R.*, 64 (1949) :433, 444–46, for infangthief, see further below.

25. F. W. Maitland, ed., *Bracton's Note Book* (Cambridge, 1887), no. 513.

26. Ibid., no. 1110.

27. Miscellanea of the Exchequer, E 163/26/3.

28. *Placita de Quo Warranto* (London: Record Commission, 1818), passim, e.g., 294 (Balliol), 296 (Segrave).

29. Hurnard, "Jury of Presentment," especially pp. 380–82.

30. *Select Charters*, pp. 170 (c. 1), 179 (c. 1). The texts have been vindicated by J. C. Holt, "The Assizes of Henry II: The Texts," in *The Study of Medieval Records: Essays in Honour of Kathleen Major*, ed. D. A. Bullough and R. L. Storey (Oxford, 1971), and more closely by D. J. Corner, "The Texts of Henry II's Assizes," in *Law-making and Law-makers in British History*, ed. A. Harding (Royal Historical Soc., Studies in History, no. 22, 1980), pp. 7–20.

31. *Select Charters*, pp. 170–71 (Assize of Clarendon, cc. 4–8).

32. Ibid, p. 296 (c. 24); cf. J. E. A. Jolliffe, *The Constitutional History of Medieval England from the English Settlement to 1485* (4th ed., London, 1961), p. 193; and Hurnard, "Franchises," pp. 439–40.

33. *Select Charters*, p. 343 (c. 42).

34. Several sets of articles from the thirteenth and fourteenth centuries are analyzed and contrasted in F. J. C. Hearnshaw, *Leet Jurisdiction in England* (Southampton Rec. Soc., 1908), cc. IV–V.
35. E.g., *Rotuli Parliamentorum* (London, 1783–1832), I, 293 (no. 24) [1314/5].
36. Jolliffe, "Hundred in Kent," pp. 162–64.
37. *Leges Henrici Primi*, pp. 108–9 (X.1.).
38. *Glanvill*, p. 177 (XIV, 8).
39. "Laws of Edward the Confessor," c. XXII; *Select Charters*, p. 128.
40. *Curia Regis Rolls*, XIV, no. 135.
41. *Calendar of Charter Rolls* (London: H. M. S. O., 1903), I, 423.
42. *Bracton's Note Book*, no. 821.
43. *Plac. Quo Warr.*, p. 221; cf. similar claims by the abbot of Byland: ibid., p. 223.
44. *Cal. Inq. Misc.*, I, no. 1914; *Plac. Quo Warr.*, p. 174.
45. A. J. Horwood, ed., *Edward I Year Book 30–31* (London: Rolls Series, 1863), pp. 501–3. The case also occurs in F. W. Maitland, L. W. V. Harcourt, and W. C. Bolland, eds., *Year Book of the Eyre of Kent, 6 & 7 Edward II (1313–1314)*, I (Selden Soc., XXIV, 1909), pp. 104–5.
46. E. g., the Coventry priory cartulary: E 164/21, f. 81.
47. Hurnard, "Franchises," p. 292, n. 1 and pp. 436–7; J. M. Kaye, "The Sacrabar," *E. H. R. 83* (1968): 744–58, assembles much evidence for procedures upon handhaving thieves.
48. *Bracton's Note Book*, no. 592.
49. Hunnisett, *Medieval Coroner*, p. 6. For a late instance, in 1275, see W. P. Baildon, J. Lister, and J. W. Walker, eds., *Court Rolls of the Manor of Wakefield*, I (Yorkshire Arch. Soc. Record Series, XXIX, 1900), p. 103. Cf. M. Bateson, ed., *Borough Customs*, I (Selden Soc., XVIII, 1904), p. 54.
50. Hurnard, "Franchises," pp. 448–49, n. 2; Douglas, *East Anglia*, p. 141.
51. *Bracton's Note Book*, no. 655.
52. *Cal. Inq. Misc.*, I, no. 2311.
53. Ibid., III, no. 145.
54. F. W. Maitland and W. P. Baildon, eds., *The Court Baron* (Selden Soc., IV, 1890), pp. 62–64, 65–66, 73–74.
55. Assize of Northampton, c. 3: *Select Charters*, p. 179.
56. Hunnisett, *Medieval Coroner*, pp. 68–69.
57. E.g., F. W. Maitland, ed., *Select Pleas of the Crown (A.D. 1200–1225)* (Selden Soc., I, 1887), nos. 111, 140, 194.
58. F. W. Maitland, ed., *Three Rolls of the King's Court in the Reign of King Richard the First* (London: Pipe Roll Soc., old series, XIV, 1891), p. 143.
59. Palmer, "Lawyer and Doomsman," pp. 61–64.
60. Hurnard, "Franchises," p. 454, n. 4.
61. For discussion and numerous examples, see H. N. Schneebeck, "The Law of Felony in Medieval England from the Accession of Edward I until the Mid-Fourteenth Century" (Ph.D. diss., University of Iowa, 1973), pp. 157–220.
62. A. Fitzherbert, *La Graunde Abridgement* (London, 1577), Coron 179; cf. Coron 288–290 and 330.
63. *Calendar of Patent Rolls 1396–9* (London: H. M. S. O., 1909), p. 62.
64. Cf. *Placitorum . . . Abbreviatio* (London: Record Commission, 1811), p. 22

[St. Edmund's, 1199]; *Plac. Quo Warr.*, p. 297 [Ramsey].

65. Hurnard, "Franchises," pp. 316–20; M. D. Lobel, "The Ecclesiastical Banleuca in England," in *Oxford Essays in Medieval History presented to H. E. Salter* (Oxford, 1934), pp. 128–33.

66. Hurnard, "Franchises," pp. 446, and 447, n. 9.

67. *Bracton's Note Book*, no. 277 [1228]. Cf. Hurnard, "Franchises," pp. 452–59.

68. Lobel, "Banleuca," pp. 126–27; S. Reynolds, ed., "Pleas in the Liberty of the Abbot of Battle at Bromham, 1289," in *Collectanea*, ed. N. J. Williams (Wiltshire Arch. and Nat. Hist. Soc., Records Branch, XII, 1956), pp. 129–41; M. T. Clanchy, ed., *The Roll and Writ File of the Berkshire Eyre of 1248* (Selden Soc., XC, 1972–73), xxxi and no. 1001.

69. *Cal. Inq. Misc.*, IV, no. 147 [1380].

70. Cf. n. 21 above.

71. *King's Bench*, I 82–3 (no. 60).

72. *Calendar of Close Rolls 1354–60* (London: H. M. S. O., 1908), p. 281; *Cal. Inq. Misc.*, III, no. 222 [1356].

73. *Cal. Inq. Misc.*, VI, no. 50.

74. *Cal. Inq. Misc.*, IV, no. 373.

75. Cf. H. M. Cam, "Suitors and Scabini" [reprinted from *Speculum* 10 (1935)] in *Liberties and Communities in Medieval England* (London, 1963), pp. 59–60, and "The Evolution of the Medieval English Franchise" [reprinted from *Speculum* 32 (1957)] in *Lawfinders and Lawmakers in Medieval England* (London, 1962), pp. 37–39.

76. *Rot. Parl.*, I, 192 (no. 5) [1306], 318 (no. 127) [1314]; II, 141 (no. 38) [1343]; III, 276 (no. 10) [1389].

77. E.g., R. F. Hunnisett, ed., *Bedfordshire Coroners' Rolls* (Bedfordshire Hist. Rec. Soc., XLI, 1960), no. 263 [1303].

78. E.g., Hurnard, "Franchises," p. 460, n. 3; H. M. Cam, "The King's Government as Administered by the Greater Abbots of East Anglia" [reprinted from *Cambridge Antiquarian Society Transactions*, XXIX, 1928] in *Liberties and Communities*, p. 203.

79. E.g., *Plac. Quo Warr.*, p. 294 [Stukeley].

80. E.g., ibid., pp. 293–94 [prior of St. John], pp. 295–96 [William Engayne], p. 297 [John Engayne].

81. *Plac. Quo Warr.*, pp. 780, 782, 766.

82. Ibid., p. 785.

83. *Bracton's Note Book*, no. 1651. This penalty occurred elsewhere, e.g., *Curia Regis Rolls*, XIII, nos. 2783–4, 2786; JUST 1/778, m. 59d.

84. C. G. Crump, "What Became of Robert Rag, or Some Chancery Blunders," in *Essays in Medieval History presented to T. F. Tout*, ed. A. G. Little and F. M. Powicke (Manchester, 1925), pp. 335–47.

85. Crowley, "Frankpledge," p. 51.

86. R. H. Hilton, *A Medieval Society* (London, 1966), pp. 230–34.

87. Pollock and Maitland, I, 577.

88. *Cal. Inq. Misc.*, I, no. 275 [1263]; grant of gallows: *Cal. Pat. Rolls 1258–66*, p. 276.

89. Cf. *Cal. Inq. Misc.*, I, no. 1851, and *Cal. Pat. Rolls 1292–1301*, p. 580.

90. Historical Manuscripts Commission, *Thirteenth Report* (London, 1892),

Appendix IV, p. 295 [1292].
91. Coram Rege Rolls, KB 27/1, m. 22.
92. *Statutes of the Realm* (London: Record Commission, 1810–28), I, 234.
93. Hunnisett, *Medieval Coroner*, p. 108 [1218–19].
94. G. H. Fowler, ed., *Rolls from the Office of the Sheriff of Beds. and Bucks., 1332–1334* (Beds Hist. Rec. Soc., Quarto Memoirs, III, 1929), e.g., p. 42 (nos. 126, 128, 131), p. 46 (no. 183).
95. W. O. Ault, ed., *Court Rolls of the Abbey of Ramsey and of the Honor of Clare* (New Haven, Conn., 1928), pp. 41–42.
96. KB 27/1, m. 23.
97. H. M. Cam, ed., "Some Early Inquests Before 'Custodes Pacis'" [reprinted from *E. H. R.* 40 (1925)] in *Liberties and Communities*, p. 167.
98. Court Rolls, SC 2/161/74, m. 18 [1333].
99. *Bracton's Note Book*, no. 592.
100. C. E. H. Chadwyck Healey, ed.,*Somerset Pleas*, I, (Somerset Rec. Soc., XI, 1897), no. 785.
101. *Berks Eyre*, no. 916.
102. *Cal. Inq. Misc.*, I, no. 590.
103. *Wakefield Court Rolls*, I, 103, 212; ibid., III (Yorks Arch. Soc., LVII, 1917), p. 136.
104. Quaere, when the lord was the ordinary? Gaol Delivery Rolls, JUST 3/167, m. 26d. The bishop claimed gallows and view of frankpledge: *Plac. Quo Warr.*, p. 429.
105. C. Gross, ed., *Select Cases from the Coroners' Rolls A.D. 1265–1413*(Selden Soc., IX, 1895), p. 107.
106. JUST 1/977, m. 3.
107. An established practice confirmed by statute in 1327: *Rot. Parl.*, II, 11–12 (no. 41); *Statutes of the Realm*, I, 257 (1 Edward III.2, c. 17).
108. V. C. H. *Gloucestershire*, XI (London, 1976), 190; *Rot. Hundr.*, I, 178; *Plac. Quo Warr.*, p. 254.
109. SC 2/175/83 and 84B.
110. N. Davis, ed., *Paston Letters and Papers of the Fifteenth Century* (Oxford, 1971–), II, no. 618.
111 Cf. Crowley, "Frankpledge," pp. 237–40 and appendix B.
112. The assumption that these were presented once or twice a year is, for many leets, mistaken (cf. Hilton, *Medieval Society*, p. 237, and *Rot. Parl.*, II, p. 357 (no. 195)); but the generalization persists, e.g., J. B. Post, "Manorial Amercements and Peasant Poverty," *Economic History Review*, 2d ser., 28 (1975): 306. In 1376 the commons complained that bailiffs required presentments at every hundred (*Rot. Parl.*, II, p. 357, no. 195), while in 1381, at a session of Essex justices against the rebels, one complainant included in his petition a demand that there be no court in any vill "save the king's leet once a year": King's Bench Recorda, KB 145/3/6/1, unnumbered membrane.
113. Duchy of Lancaster Court Rolls, DL 30/43/482, 488, and 498; DL 30/44/509; DL 30/45/526; DL 30/48/562, 570, and 578.
114. G. D. G. Hall, ed., "Three Courts of the Hundred of Penwith, 1333," in *Medieval Legal Records Edited in Memory of C. A. F. Meekings* (London: H.M.S.O., 1978), pp. 169–96.
115. SC 2/181/74.

116. As claimed by B. Farr, editor, in *The Rolls of Highworth Hundred 1275–1287* (Wilts Arch. and Nat. Hist. Soc., Records Branch, XXI–XXII, 1965–6), I, 11; cf. I, 53, 59, where the matters are essentially fiscal. Professor Pugh stated that none of Stratton's manors entertained pleas of theft or other crown pleas: R. B. Pugh, ed., *Court Rolls of the Wiltshire Manors of Adam de Stratton* (ibid., XXIV, 1968), p. 8

117. F. J. Baigent, ed., *A Collection of Records and Documents relating to the Hundred and Manor of Crondal*, I (Hampshire Rec. Soc., 1890), pp. 142–55.

118. E 163/5/24. The process marks of acquittal against a thief and his accessory do not indicate trial at the tourn; the case was seven years old and presumably already tried elsewhere.

119. SC 2/351/7.

120. SC 2/207/7A; E 199/45/2; E 199/45/11.

121. J. E. Jackson, ed., "The sheriff's turn, Co. Wilts, A.D. 1439," *The Wiltshire Magazine* 13 (1872): 105–18.

122. *Pipe Roll 34 Henry II* (Pipe Roll Soc., old series, XXXVIII, 1925), p. 197.

123. *Pipe Roll 3 and 4 Richard I* (ibid., new series, II, 1926), pp. 134–35.

124. *Pipe Roll 6 Richard I* (ibid., new series, V, 1928), pp. 90–91.

125. Pipe Rolls, E 372/76, r. 13d.

126. JUST 1/36, m. 2, cited by Hurnard, "Franchises," p. 443, n. 2.

127. *Curia Regis Rolls*, XIII, no. 2274.

128. *Eyre of Kent*, I, 133; similarly Fitzherbert, *Abridgement*, Coron 237 [1348].

129. E.g., *Pipe Roll 12 John* (Pipe Roll Soc., new series, XXVI, 1949), p. 213 [1210].

130. *Bracton's Note Book*, no. 1114: "convictus ad latronem."

131. *Eyre of Kent*, I, 61, 107, 128–29.

132. For the terms of the grant of felons' chattels, see *Calendar of Fine Rolls* (London: H. M. S. O., 1911–1963), VII, 44–6, 63–4. For examples of returns, see Subsidy Rolls &c., E 179/211/27 [Yorks, North Riding], E 179/202/54 [Yorks, E.R.], E 179/195/15 [Westmoreland], E 179/192/17 [Warwicks]; cf. Accounts, Various, E 101/506/14 [Yorks liberties, Edward I to Edward III].

133. *Cal. Charter Rolls*, II, 475.

134. *Eyre of Kent*, I, 147.

135. *Year Book 30–31 Edward I*, pp. 506–7.

136. *Beds Coroners' Rolls*, no. 78; Schneebeck, "Felony," pp. 182, 193–94, and cf. pp. 204–20.

137. *King's Bench*, I, 128 (no. 85).

138. W. J. Whittaker, ed., *The Mirror of Justices*, with introduction by F. W. Maitland (Selden Soc., VII, 1893), p. 41.

139. *Eyre of Kent*, I, 130–31.

140. Fitzherbert, *Abridgement*, Leete et Hundred, 10 [1429], 3 [1491].

141. Ibid., Coron 462.

142. *Cal. Pat. Rolls 1388–92*, p. 253.

143. For the decline of the eyre, and its experimental competitors, see A. Harding, *The Law Courts of Medieval England* (London, 1973), c. 3, and references there.

144. Introduction to A. Harding, ed., "Early Trailbaston Proceedings from the Lincoln Roll of 1305," in *Medieval Legal Records; Calendar of London Trailbaston Trials under Commissions of 1305 and 1306*, ed. R. B. Pugh (London: H.M.S.O., 1975), pp. 1–2, 41–43.

145. *Bracton's Note Book*, no. 1716 [1226]; cf. R. B. Pugh, *Imprisonment in Medieval England* (Cambridge, 1968), c. XII, especially 257.

146. J. S. Cockburn, *A History of English Assizes 1558–1714* (Cambridge, 1972), c. 1.

147. A. Harding, "The Origins and Early History of the Keeper of the Peace," *T. R. H. S.*, 5th ser., 11 (1960): 85–109.

148. Putnam, "The Transformation," especially pp. 41–47; J. B. Post, "The peace commissions of 1382," *E.H.R.* 91 (1976): 98–101.

149. Harding, *Law Courts*, p. 92.

150. E.g., JUST 3/197, m. 5d [John Beauchamp of Holt, 1414].

151. B. H. Putnam, ed., *Proceedings before the Justices of the Peace in the Fourteenth and Fifteenth Centuries* (Cambridge Mass.: Ames Foundation, 1938): cvii–cxi.

152. *Statutes of the Realm*, I, 313 (25 Edward III.2, c. 7). Cf. *Kent Keepers of the Peace 1316–1317* (Kent Records, XIII, 1933), p. 109.

153. *Proceedings before the Justices of the Peace* is the most extensive of many published texts.

154. JUST 1/961, mm. 1d–12.

155. E.g., JUST 3/96, m. 43 (liberties of John Hastang and the prior of Coventry: *Plac. Quo Warr.*, pp. 777, 778) [1296].

156. JUST 3/89, 91–92, 95–97, 99, 214/1, 101–102, 105, and 133; JUST 1/966.

157. KB 27/264, Rex mm. 5–5d [two indictments, 1326]; none in JUST 3/133 or KB 27/296, Rex mm. 13d, 22–22d, 25.

158. JUST 3/137A-137B, 140, 146, 32/2, 149, 142, 157, 159–160, 162, 167, 67/2, and 67/4–6; KB 27/368, Rex mm. 26, 50.

159. JUST 3/142, m. 15d.

160. JUST 3/67/2, m. 6d.

161. *Victoria County History: Huntingdonshire*, III (London 1936), 131–32.

162. JUST 3/110, 139, and 164.

163. JUST 3/169, m. 10.

164. JUST 3/164, m. 13.

165. JUST 3/197 and 203.

166. JUST 3/130, 174, 179, 194, 61/3.

167 At the Wiltshire eyre of 1281 extra-hundredal indictments at the tourn had been forbidden: JUST 1/1001, m. 24.

168. JUST 3/197.

169. JUST 3/203.

170. *Rot. Parl.*, V, 493–4 (no. 42); *Statutes of the Realm*, II, 389–91 (1 Edward IV, c. 2).

171. Cf. Crowley, "Frankpledge," pp. 223–24.

Middle-Class Crime in Nineteenth-Century England

Rob Sindall

University of Leicester

I

It is unfortunate that most of the literature on the subject of nineteenth-century crime dwells almost entirely on the acts of the lower socio-economic groups, which the Victorians identified as "dangerous" or "criminal" classes, and theories of crime causation only took these classes into account. However, a study[1] of the calendars of prisoners appearing before the Quarter Sessions and Assize Courts[2] of the two major cities, London and Birmingham, reveals that the middle classes exhibited as many criminal tendencies as the lower classes. These courts were established to hear more serious cases than those before Petty Sessions and there is evidence of a tendency for middle-class crimes to be of a greater magnitude, in monetary terms, than the crimes of the other groups. The study shows that middle-class crime was closely associated with occupation and may be explained by modern theories of criminal behaviour.

For the purposes of the study the definition of middle class was based on the occupation followed, using the Registrar-General's classification of 1921. Social class I (Upper and Middle) consisted of members of the professions, managers, company directors, bankers, stockbrokers, insurance officials and journalists. Social class II (Intermediate) included proprietors of retail and wholesale premises, civil service officials, teachers, veterinary surgeons, departmental managers and commercial clerks. Although the Registrar General's classifications are open to criticism they are still a widely used classification for the ordering of nineteenth-century material, and that of 1921 is the nearest comprehensive and reliable social classification to the period under review.[3]

During the second half of the nineteenth century there was a general decline in the number of people per 100,000 population appearing before the courts of England and Wales so that by 1890 the rate of indictable offences was down to a rate considerably lower than that prevalent today.

Middle-class crime followed the same downward trend as crime in general. The decline, however, was not so marked. In absolute terms, middle-class crime was on the increase while general criminal statistics showed a diminution during this period. This is partly explained by the rise in numbers of the middle classes, but the evidence shows that this group was exhibiting greater criminal tendencies over time relative to the rest of society. This is evident from the figures in Table 1 drawn from the sample.

Table 1. Percentage of social groups committed for trial.

	% Middle Class	% Other Groups
Middlesex 1855–65	2.1	2.8
Surrey 1855–65	1.0	1.4
Middlesex 1878–88	1.2	1.2
Surrey 1878–88	0.7	0.4
Birmingham 1880–1900	3.3	1.3

These figures point to two conclusions. Firstly they show that by the end of the period the middle classes showed a greater criminality than the rest of the population. Secondly, we must conclude that this was not always so as the figures show a distinct change over time. In all cases the percentage of both groups who were committed for trial fell. However, the middle-class percentage fell less quickly than the other groups causing a reversal in their relative criminality. Prior to circa 1870 it would seem that the other groups showed a greater criminality than the middle classes. Post circa 1870 the middle classes show a greater tendency to commit indictable offences than other categories. The first conclusion raises the question of whether the rest of the population may have contained a small "criminal class." It is possible that the rest of the population contained small groups which displayed greater criminality than the middle classes as a whole, but this is unlikely in terms of large social groupings or on a class level. As the sample only contained two upper-class court appearances and given that the upper classes formed such a small proportion of the population, it may be assumed that the category of "other groups" fairly reflects the criminality of the lower classes.

Within the lower classes it is difficult to assess whether the tendency to commit crime was evenly spread throughout the various sub-groups or whether, as the Victorians themselves believed, there was a "criminal class." As no person would state his occupation as "criminal" the onus lay with the annual police returns which showed the estimated number of "known thieves" in each police district. Such returns were made from September 1858 onwards, but the definition of a "known thief" varied from district to district, and the returns, which were based on the extent of police knowledge and distorted by police prejudices, were of dubious value. The preoccupation with "thieves" as a basis for a criminal class also made the concept less credible. For all groups, including the middle classes, larceny was amongst the most common of crimes but did not account for the largest monetary losses. Thieves were "small fry" but there were many of them from all social classes and so it was easy for the police to talk of a criminal class and hint at a social conspiracy in crime. That there were professional criminals is beyond doubt and it would be correct to say that they formed a small hardcore of the criminal statistics, but to attribute to them the qualifications of a criminal class would be entirely wrong. We are still left with the conclusion that the middle classes displayed greater criminality than other social ones.

There are several explanations of the second conclusion that, after 1870, the criminality of the middle classes relative to that of the lower classes increased. As we shall see, post circa 1870 crime was becoming a more attractive proposition to the middle classes and less attractive to the lower groups. As the commercial and service sectors of the economy expanded so did the opportunities for the middle classes to commit crimes. Meanwhile, between 1860 and 1875 the lower-class criminal suffered several setbacks. For a variety of reasons the "age of the pickpocket" was fast disappearing. The introduction of reformatory schools led to an increase in the number of committals of juveniles while a change in fashion, bringing closer fitting clothes, made the art less simple both in terms of accomplishing the theft and also of concealing the proceeds about the person. The Education Act of 1870 helped to diminish the number of "nimble fingers" which could wander the streets. Some adult lower-class criminals, with less pickpockets to work for them, resorted to "garrotting," a form of violent street robbery involving the strangulation of the victim until unconscious, but this was quickly terminated by the police aided by the Security from Violence Act of 1863 which allowed for long prison sentences and reintroduced flogging for such offences.

It is likely that the increasing efficiency of the police and the introduction of detective forces also made the perpetration of crime by the lower classes a more dangerous proposition. The middle-class criminals were less affected by the increase in the number of police because the types of crime in which they specialised occurred inside offices, away from police observation. The police, for example, would have no deterrent effect on embezzlers or the perpetration of fraud.[4]

The increasing tendency of the middle classes to commit crimes went unnoticed by the Victorians and even by modern social historians, largely because of the low numbers of middle-class persons, in absolute terms, being committed for trial. Much of the literary evidence on crime was produced by middle-class Victorian philanthropists and social reformers[5] who were convinced of the existence of a criminal class and so concentrated their attentions on the acts of those criminals who fitted their stereotype image of members of such a class. However, as can be seen from Table 2, after 1870 the percentage of middle-class committals equalled or exceeded the percentage of the middle classes in the population. These figures demonstrate that criminality amongst the middle classes exceeded that of other categories.

Table 2: The middle class as a percentage of population and percentage of committals post 1870.

	% Population	% Committals
Middlesex 1878–88	4.9	4.7
Surrey 1878–88	5.0	8.3
Birmingham 1880–1900	3.1	7.2
Manchester 1882–84	4.2	7.9

Source: Sessions' records and 1881 Census

It is not only the quantity of middle-class crime which is of interest but also its quality. The sample points to the conclusion that the higher the court or the more serious the offence, the higher the percentage of middle-class committals to trial. The serious nature of the criminality is shown by the results of two three-year samples of those prisoners appearing before the Central Criminal Court. In the earlier period (1857–59) the middle classes accounted for 9.2 per cent of the cases while in the later period (1881–83) this figure had risen to 15.5 per cent. Conversely, small numbers of the middle classes appeared before Summary Courts which dealt with minor offences. The Lancashire Police Charge books (Manchester division) showing those appearing before the Petty Sessions between 1843 and 1854 are mainly filled with cases of drunkenness, petty assault, petty theft, bastardy arrears and such like. Of 10,732 charged in this period only sixty-four were listed as following middle-class occupations and of these ten were noted as being unemployed at the time.

Two tentative explanations of the more serious nature of middle-class criminality may be offered. Firstly, it is likely that the middle-class criminal was intelligent enough to realise that crime was a gamble and that the price of losing was some months or years in prison, the loss of one's job and with it, the loss of one's social position. As the sentence rarely seemed proportionate to the amount of depredation it was, perhaps, wisest to gamble for high stakes.[6] It is likely that the middle-class criminal had a wider vision than his lower-class counterpart and was more capable of thinking in terms of very large sums of money without over-awing himself—he knew how to spend one hundred thousand pounds; his counterpart did not. Secondly, and more importantly, the middle-class criminal had greater opportunities to commit large crimes. Months of planning and considerable personal risks led to the Great Bullion robbery in 1855 which netted a mere twelve thousand pounds.[7] The middle-class criminal could often sit at his desk and embezzle several times this amount during the course of his work. The growing world of shares, accounts and limited liability gave a greater and more lucrative opportunity to commit crimes than could be committed without resort to violence and so would tend to appeal to the better educated.

The tendency for the higher social classes to commit the most serious offences is further revealed in a social-class breakdown of the sample. Of the total of middle-class committals, 7 per cent followed occupations listed by the Registrar-General as reflecting social class I. In the more serious cases of the Central Criminal Court, 33 per cent were class I. This shows a proportionately greater participation by class I in the more serious cases than in those tried at ordinary Quarter Sessions and Assizes.

In terms of the actual crimes committed social class I displayed a distinctive pattern of criminal behaviour compared to the rest of the Sessions' sample. In the whole sample the most common crime with which middle-class defendants were charged was larceny (24.5 per cent), followed by fraud (14.7 per cent), embezzlement (12.3 per cent), larceny from the person (5.7 per cent), larceny by a servant (5.2 per cent), and receiving of stolen goods (5.0 per cent). Amongst the defendants in social class I the most common charge was fraud (26.7 per cent), followed by larceny (18.2 per cent), common assault (8.6 per cent), indecent assault (7.2 per cent), embezzlement (5.4 per cent), and larceny in a dwelling house (4.0 per cent). The high percentage of common assaults and indecent assaults would imply that for many in social class I satisfaction of physical desires (both violent and sexual) was more important than the acquisition of monetary gain which, their social position would imply, they were quite capable of achieving by non-criminal methods with a large degree of success. The analysis below of occupational groups reveals that the group of independent gentlemen who controlled enough wealth not to require an occupational income were those most likely to perpetrate such "physical" crimes.

Although the sentences imposed on criminals of social class I were similar to those imposed on the rest of the sample, 28.5 per cent of social class I indictments were found "Not Guilty" compared to 18.5 per cent of social class II demonstrating, perhaps, that juries could be influenced by the social class of the defendant or by a good defence lawyer which only this social class could afford.

II

In order to investigate the relationship between the type of occupation and the type of criminal activity the middle-class sample was divided into six occupational groups. These were:

Group 1	Independent Gentlemen
Group 2	Professions (military, law, medicine and church)
Group 3	Quasi-professional and businessmen (managers, surveyors, architects, accountants, pharmacists etc.)
Group 4	Clerks
Group 5	Wholesalers
Group 6	Retailers

The three most common crimes committed by the different occupational groups are shown in Table 3.

It would appear that the type of crime committed was largely a result of the opportunities afforded by the type of occupation followed, and that only the unoccupied but comfortably-off members of Group I could indulge in non-acquisitive violence. This tradition of "violence for fun" amongst higher social groups was not a new phenomenon. Although the Mohock outrages of 1712 were probably politically motivated rather than a result of hooliganism, this earlier period had been marked by "younger members of the nobility . . . indulging in the nocturnal habit of assaulting in the streets harmless passers-by."[8] In the first quarter of the nineteenth century the "Bucks" were reported as "louts, most of them members of the aristocracy [who] took their manners from the least respectable of the lower orders."[9] Similarly, in the closing decades of the century there was a revival of the Hell-fire rowdyism of the eighteenth century amongst the middle classes.[10]

The occupations of the professional, quasi-professional and whole-saling groups (groups 2, 3 and 5) allowed them to perpetrate frauds with greater ease than the clerks of group 4 who concentrated on embezzling from their masters. That occupation determined the type of crime committed is most clearly demonstrated by the members of group 6

Table 3:

The three most common crimes committed by different middle-class occupational groups.

	Larceny	Fraud	Embezzle-ment	Common Assault	Indecent Assault	Receiving Stolen Goods	Keeping a Bawdy House
Group 1	16.7%	19.5%	—	22.3%	—	—	—
Group 2	18.9%	26.1%	—	8.7%	—	—	—
Group 3	24.3%	22.8%	—	—	8.5%	—	—
Group 4	24.1%	13.2%	22.1%	—	—	—	—
Group 5	30.0%	16.7%	8.8%	—	—	—	—
Group 6	19.0%	—	—	—	—	11.1%	29.5%

Source: Sessions records

amongst whom it seemed quite common practice to use their retail premises as fronts for bawdy houses and the receiving and selling of stolen goods.

The fabled stringencies of Victorian domestic sexual morality seemed to have taken their toll of the business and professional world of groups 1, 2 and 3 who committed a large proportion of sexual offences (e.g., Indecent assault accounted for 9.8 per cent of group I crimes, 5.8 per cent of group 2 and 8.5 per cent of group 3). It was, perhaps, their poor domestic experience which led them not to commit any offences of bigamy, an act, it would appear from the sample, only committed by group 6.

For the sample as a whole embezzlement and fraud are the crimes that stand out as the specialities of the middle classes. As with most crimes favoured by the middle-class group, embezzlement was not the sole preserve of the middle-class criminals although they succeeded in acquiring larger sums of money by means of such crimes than criminals of other social classes. Embezzlement accounted for less than 4 per cent of total committals to trial but over 12 per cent of the committals to trial of the middle classes.

Nearly 70 per cent of embezzlements were executed by members of other social classes, but the middle classes managed to acquire about that proportion of the receipts. In Birmingham between 1880 and 1900, embezzlement cases involving a total of £2,007 were heard by the Sessions and Assize courts of which £1,981 had been appropriated by middle-class criminals and only £26 by criminals of other social classes. In Surrey between 1878 and 1888 a total of £1,623 was embezzled of which £1,153 went to the middle classes. In Surrey between 1855 and 1865 a total of £809 was divided between middle-class embezzlers and those of other classes in the ratio of £412 to £397. This figure is more impressive when it is known that the ratio of embezzlers was 64 to 204.

The average embezzlers receipt for the whole sample showed that the middle-class embezzler received at least three times the sum received by his counterpart from other social classes. The occupations of many of the middle classes would daily bring them into contact with large and relatively easily embezzled amounts of money, whereas much of the lower-class embezzlement was by domestic servants absconding with errand money or "fiddling" housekeeping accounts. In Surrey the lower-class figures are affected by several tram conductors prosecuted by the London Tramway Company for embezzling the fare of one penny. These cases provide a good example of the disproportionate sentencing cited above as a possible encouragement to the middle-class criminal to risk larger crimes. The conductors all received between nine and twelve months imprisonment for their crime.

An analysis of fraud cases revealed similar results to that of embezzlement. Middle-class participation was numerically lower than that of other social classes but the amounts misappropriated were far greater. Average receipts fradulently gained by middle-class criminals (with the figure for other social classes in brackets) were:

Surrey 1855–65	£9	(£1)
Surrey 1878–88	£15	(£6)
Birmingham 1880–1900	£62	(£7)

These figures do not include any of the major frauds of the period. As with embezzlement, the famous large-scale frauds portray clearly the ability of certain middle-class criminals to obtain sums of money which would probably exceed the receipts of all the crimes committed by the lower classes. A brief review of some of these major crimes reinforces the conclusion that it was the quality of their crimes rather than the quantity that made the middle-class criminals such a major force in the redistribution of wealth by illegal means.

During the 1850's the more serious cases of fraud and embezzlement began to appear in the court rooms and receive limited publicity although few observers managed to discern the growing trend in middle-class crime to which these cases were pointers. Between 1844 and 1850, Walter Watts, while employed as a check-clerk in the cashier's department of the Globe Assurance Company, systematically embezzled between £71,000 and £80,000. In 1849 alone his illegal income from the company was circa £18,000. In 1855 the case of Strahan, Paul and Bates revealed that they had embezzled almost three-quarters of a million pounds from customers of the Temple Bar bank over a period of four years. William Robson, as chief clerk of the Crystal Palace Company, was discovered in 1856 to have systematically embezzled £27,000. In 1902, Thomas Goudie, as a clerk for the Bank of Liverpool, was discovered to have embezzled £162,000 by means of forged cheques.

A.R. Barrett, writing in 1894, on depredations of banks in the United States noted, "statistics show that during the past ten years, bank-wreckers, embezzlers and defaulters have robbed the people of this country of over one hundred million dollars," and that where banks were concerned:

> there seems to be more danger from the trusted officer and the employee than from the burglar. . . now it is the skilled financier or bank clerk who coolly and quietly abstracts or misapplies the funds, falsifies the accounts, and makes away with millions where the burglar got thousands.[11]

A.T. Craig[12] implied that the American experience was reflected in Britain. He noted the embezzlement of £1,000 annually for thirty years by a clerk at the Cardiff Savings Bank; the embezzlement of £17,000 from the

Sudbury Trustees' Savings Bank by its actuary; the appropriation, stock-exchange speculation and loss of £200,000 worth of securities held by the River Plate Bank by its London manager; the embezzlement of £19,000 by the manager of the Woodford branch of the London Joint-Stock Bank; and the Vagliano case which involved a systematic fraud by a bank clerk in the 1880's using forged letters of advice and bills by which he had embezzled £71,500.

In 1857 the London and Eastern Banking Corporation was forced into liquidation when it was found that one of the directors, Colonel W. Petrie Waugh, with the connivance of the manager, was indebted to the bank for £244,000 — only £6,000 less than the entire subscribed capital of the bank. On liquidation the shareholders found themselves liable and Waugh fled to Spain where he started a mining company. A similar case occurred in 1878 involving frauds on the City of Glasgow bank by its directors to the extent of £300,000, although the real loss to investors amounted to six million pounds. The case provided another example of the disproportionate sentencing previously mentioned as an encouragement to middle-class crime as the guilty directors were sentenced to terms of imprisonment not exceeding eighteen months.

The cases of R.F. Pries in 1853 and J.W. Cole in 1854 resulting from the use of duplicate dock warrants often involving transactions which were large enough to cause fluctuations in the price of grain, were further evidence that the middle classes produced criminals, the magnitude of whose crimes were capable of rocking the financial and trading institutions of the world's leading commercial and trading nation. The public eye, however, remained firmly directed towards the petty crimes of a "criminal class" whose existence as a class was doubtful and whose main motivation was thought to be drink.

III

The theories of the classic nineteenth-century criminologists[13] were disturbing in their absence of reference to middle-class crimes. It was as if middle-class criminologists felt that they would have been betraying their class if they were to admit to and account for the existence of middle-class criminals. Modern theories of criminology, although more sophisticated, are based on twentieth-century data and so, to a large extent are limited in their applicability to modern social situations which, in many ways, differ considerably from the nineteenth century. However, arguably, two modern theories do assist in the understanding of the activities of the nineteenth-century middle-class criminal.

Firstly, in 1949 Edwin H. Sutherland completed a study of white-collar crime which he defined as "a crime committed by a person of respectability and high social status in the course of his occupation"[14] and concluded that the hypotheses of differential association and social disorganisation may be applied to white-collar crimes as well as crimes of the lower classes. The hypothesis of differential association is the concept that criminal behaviour is learned in association with those who define it favourably and in isolation from those who define it unfavourably. Differential association on an individual level is paralleled on a social level by the concept of social disorganisation which may appear in the form of a lack of standards or a conflict of standards. Secondly, in 1953 Donald Cressey's study of the social psychology of embezzlement concluded that in all cases of trust violation the violator was faced with a non-shareable problem. This is a financial problem which it is felt could not be shared with those financially capable of solving it. According to Cressey that which constituted a non-shareable problem depended on the psychological makeup of the person involved and that although all trust violators have non-shareable problems, not everyone with a non-shareable problem becomes a trust violator. Thus some individuals could daily lose considerable amounts of money at the race track but the loss, although a problem, might not constitute a non-shareable problem. Others might define the problem as one which had to be kept secret and private and so it would be viewed as a non-shareable problem. Similarly a failing bank or business might be considered by some individuals as presenting problems to be shared and discussed with business associates and members of the community while others would conceive it as a non-shareable problem.[15] It is especially pertinent to this study of middle-class crime based on occupations of the criminals, that the person who has a non-shareable problem must also have the opportunity to commit a crime before he becomes a criminal. For the middle classes this opportunity would often present itself during the course of their work.

Before relating concepts of differential association, social disorganisation, non-shareable problems and occupationally determined crime to the experience of the Victorian middle classes, it must be considered to what extent such concepts are being taken out of context. Sutherland's study was concerned with the twentieth century, the United States and was limited to business managers and executives. These are the three main points of departure from this study of nineteenth-century England and all persons following middle-class occupations.[16]

Sutherland has claimed that his hypothesis is universally applicable with regard to social class and so the differing width of the occupational sample should have no adverse effect. As nineteenth-century Britain and twentieth-century North America both experienced a dynamic, materialistic culture characterised by a capitalist economic system based on limited companies with a social system dominated by the middle classes, it may be argued that the cultural contexts of the studies are similar enough to allow the concepts of Sutherland and Cressey to be tested in the historical context of this study of middle-class crime.

It is likely that the major source of non-shareable problems for the Victorian middle classes was the maintenance of the standard of comfort prescribed by the middle classes themselves on what was often little more than a working-class income. However, in a salaried heirarchy only salary indicated level and only display could reflect salary.[17] The increasing cost of such display and its effect on family size has been clearly described by J.A. Banks,[18] and the strain involved was hinted at by G.K. Richards, the Professor of Political Economy at Oxford University. When lecturing on the middle classes to his students in 1853, Richards described "the pressure of needy and energetic aspirants, keeping every path of industry full" which necessitated "a constant effort on the part of those who have attained a comfortable position to maintain it," and that "the difficulty of securing a provision[19] for a family, combined with the dread of sinking to a lower level includes in numerous cases, the postponement of marriage."[20] This "lower level" was referred to by C.F.G. Masterman as the "ghetto" and the "abyss",[21] and these words sum up the awfulness with which the middle classes regarded the prospect of becoming part of the lower social level. The fear of the abyss necessitated constant striving to attain the higher aspirations of the middle classes and such aspirations were nearly always of a materialistic nature and required increased income. The main obstacles to the attainment of these intensified the potential non-shareable problems perceived by the middle classes.

Towards the end of the century the small businessman's ability to make money was hindered as small masters were increasingly squeezed by the growing concentration of capital, the advance of large-scale production and the growth of cartels and monopolies. At the same time the frustrations of the salaried work force increased. As Crossick[22] noted, the ambitious clerk hoped to (1) rise to a partnership in the firm, (2) set up business on his own, or (3) rise by merit in the clerical scale. After 1870 the increased scale of enterprise and capital made (1) and (2) difficult and the practice of multi-level recruitment curbed (3) so that many clerks were placed in an increasingly marginal position with their chances of rising to the employer class diminishing. It is little wonder, therefore, that a percentage of the middle classes, frustrated in their attempt to achieve their monetary ambitions by honest means, should turn to dishonest sources of income to supplement their salaries.

In the late fifties and early sixties the "proper" time to marry was debated at great length in the weeklies and monthlies. In the letter columns of *The Times* of June 1858 a protracted discussion ensued as to whether it was possible to be happily married on an income of £300 per annum—in short, whether the husband could maintain the standard of living of both himself and his partner at that which he had enjoyed as a single man. Professor Banks has shown that the average age of marriage among the upper-middle classes from 1840 to 1870 was between twenty-nine and thirty years of age.[23] It is, perhaps, not just coincidence that the most common age range of the middle-class criminal was between thirty and thirty-five years of age. This was the age when the most common cause of non-shareable problems (i.e. marriage) was most likely to occur and by which the potential criminal would have risen to an occupational position which would have made the commission of a crime more simple.

The concept of differential association seems to be less applicable to the middle classes of Victorian Britain than it is to the lower classes, some sections of which accepted crime as a necessity. For many in the lower classes lack of employment presented the twin options of either entering the workhouse or generating an illegal income through the pursuit of crime. Evidence abounds that the dread of the workhouse was such that crime was perceived as the more acceptable of the two options amongst those members of this class whether employed or not. For those in the middle classes outward respectability was the social requirement of the class, and perpetrators of criminal acts, who were automatically assumed to be members of the lower class, were despised as people who could not fit into the social system which was largely designed around the middle classes and for their benefit. This may be a superficial view as its counterpart on a social level—social disorganisation—was very much in evidence. In 1843, the editor of the *Illustrated London News* warned that, "the agents of our trading and fiscal affairs live, move and breathe, in a perfect atmosphere of fraud. If we progress at the same rate for half a generation longer, commercial dishonesty will become the rule, and integrity the exception."[24] In 1854 Herbert Spencer unwittingly described how railway managers of the period fit perfectly into Sutherland's concept of differential association when he wrote,

> Bearing in mind the comparative laxity of the corporate conscience; the diffusion and remoteness of the evils which malpractices produce; and the composite origin of these malpractices; it becomes possible to understand how, in railway affairs, gigantic dishonesties can be perpetrated by men, who, on average, are little if at all below the generality in moral characters.[25]

S.F. Van Oss agreed with Spencer when referring to all limited companies; he wrote, "Management is, in the majority of cases, utterly corrupt and dishonest, besides being generally incompetent."[26] J.W. Horsley, in analysing the commercial immorality which he believed characterised the period, related it to the development of middle-class values which had led to property rights being the primary rights of citizenship; the indiscriminate respect for wealth; and the belief that poverty was a contemptible thing.[27] Such literary evidence points to the existence of a conflict of standards which permits the conclusion that much of the crime committed by the middle classes in the nineteenth century may well have been the result of differential association and social disorganisation.

Given the source of a non-shareable problem and the fact that the potential criminal had subconsciously acquired the belief, through differential association, that the problem should be solved by the commission of a crime, he still required the opportunity to commit the crime. This opportunity had to occur relatively quickly or the non-shareable problem may have been resolved by other factors. The occupations of the middle classes offered them unique opportunities for the commission of several types of crime, and in many cases this opportunity was heightened by the lack of strict legal, commercial and bureaucratic controls.

The results of this study show that middle-class criminals made use of the opportunity afforded by the type of occupation that they followed to commit a crime. For example in the Birmingham sample from 1880 to 1900 at least 48 per cent of middle-class crimes could only have been committed inside the place of work and many were actually incorporated within the work itself. The examples of embezzlement by clerks, fraud by members of the professional and managerial group and the keeping of bawdy houses and receiving of stolen goods by retailers are all too obvious. It is on this point that the crime of the lower classes differs from that of the middle classes. It is noticeable that the only middle-class group without a set occupation — gentlemen and independent widows — is the group most involved in crimes which would be difficult to commit whilst in occupation (i.e. common assault, sexual assault and riot and assault). Generalisations may well be erroneous as little research of a statistical nature has been made into the crimes of lower-class criminals,[28] but it may be conjectured that the middle classes were afforded more opportunities to commit large crimes of a serious nature during the course of their occupation, and, owing to the length of the working day and the permanent nature of the posts, were offered fewer opportunities to commit crimes outside their working hours. Conversely the lower social classes were engaged in work which afforded lesser opportunities to commit serious (in financial terms) crimes and, owing to periods of under-employment and unemployment, were afforded more opportunities to commit crimes unassociated with their employment.

The commission of many crimes by the middle classes during the course of their occupations was aided by the lack of strict controls of the work involved. This statement applies mainly to the crimes of embezzlement, fraud and falsification of accounts, and the fact that these were among the main crimes of the middle classes adds weight to the hypothesis that the middle-class criminal was encouraged by the opportunity to commit crime afforded by the lax control of his occupation. Alfred Emden, in 1894, believed that the law actually encouraged dishonesty and wrote, "The carrying out of objects which would be more or less fraudulent, and would be impossible in the case of a private individual or a partnership is rendered easy by means of the Companies Acts."[29] Emden later noted the failure of company legislation to alter in order to accommodate new developments in business practice.[30] The Directors' Liability Act of 1890 made directors culpable for the publication of fraudulent prospectuses but it was not until well after the period of this study that balance sheets (1908) or profit and loss accounts (1929) had to be published, and it was not until the Company Act of 1948 and the Prevention of Fraud (Investments) Act of 1958 that investors were afforded real protection. Fraud and embezzlement were both facilitated by the poor accounting methods used during the period. The Company Act of 1844 had stated that auditors had to examine books as a prerequisite of legal sanction to carry out business. However, the auditors were not required to be accountants and the compulsory requirement was dropped in the case of companies formed under the general statutes of 1856 and 1868.[31] Although it was claimed in 1876 that accounts were "generally audited"[32] they were not compelled to be so until 1900.

IV

This survey points to the conclusion that in the second half of the nineteenth century the middle classes had the motives, the moral environment, and the opportunities which encouraged the commission of crime. Ironically, the motives were generated by the middle classes themselves in contrast to the lower-class criminals who were often forced into crime by a social and economic system which was imposed on them from above. The mobile middle class was constantly striving to move socially upwards in the hierarchy and geographically outwards to the suburbs. Hence, one reviewer of the Victorian age, writing in 1897 noted that "an impatient restlessness is socially a note of the period."[33] This restlessness amongst Victorian clerks (the grass roots of the middle classes) is captured in the following letter from John Holt, in the early 1860's, who wrote to his father about his routine clerk's job:

What am I to do? If I stay where I am I have the prospect of a £60 salary which to my ambitious nature is beggary. No! it is money I want and money I must have if I go through fire and water for it. . . . It is not the gold, but the independence it brings and the cares it drives away.[34]

The non-shareable problems appeared to be self-generated but were no less real for that. Their solution through the commission of crime connected with one's occupation seems to have been encouraged by a conflict of standards which accepted acts by corporate bodies which were considered criminal or immoral if committed by private individuals. Hence, during the course of his work the middle-class criminal was in association with those who defined "immoral" acts favourably. The lax control of occupation allowed such people to then perpetrate such immoral acts for their own personal gain, but, when carried out by an individual, society re-defined such acts as criminal.

Throughout the century the numbers of the middle classes grew, and at the same time the criminality of the class rose so that by 1870 their criminality, in terms of indictable crimes, was greater than that of other social classes. In addition, the crimes that they committed were far more extensive than those of other social classes. In noting the crimes of Watts, Redpath and R.F. Pries, Kellow Chesney remarked:

Apart from a few professional forgers and their associates, financial swindling was characteristically the crime of business and professional men. A man who commanded the resources to shake the money market could hardly be considered a member of the "dangerous classes" and it is almost axiomatic that the biggest and most profitable crimes were beyond the reach of the underworld.[35]

Middle-class crimes left no blood on the pavement, no scars, no property damaged, no visible signs. As with shop-lifting from large retail outlets in our modern society, the victim was difficult to identify and seemed to merit little sympathy. Consequently middle-class crime was a social phenomenon which was unremarked, and the rise in criminality of the central social class went largely unnoticed by society. Given the stereotyped image of the respectability of the Victorian classes which has been handed down to the twentieth century reader, the phenomena of a criminal middle class is truly remarkable.

Notes

The place of publication is London unless otherwise stated.

1.   The information for this study was obtained from the calendars of prisoners appearing before the Quarter Sessions and Assize Courts for Middlesex

1855–65, 1878–88, Surrey 1855–65, 1878–88, Birmingham 1880–1900 and Manchester 1882–84. The counties of Middlesex and Surrey included the bulk of the population of London. Two three-year samples of the calendars of prisoners appearing before the Central Criminal Court 1857–59 and 1881–83 were also used. The study covered 106,505 cases of which 5,016 (4.17 per cent) involved charging members of the middle classes. This choice of samples was largely determined by the availability of continuous series of records lying either side of 1870 and the fact that they do relate to large urban conglomerations whose growth was an important facet of the new industrial society of the nineteenth century.

2. Minor offences were treated summarily by a Justice of the Peace at the Petty Sessions. More serious offences were indicted before a grand jury and then sent for trial by jury at an Assize court presided over by a judge or at Quarter Sessions chaired by Justices of the Peace. The allocation of indictable cases between the Assizes and Quarter Sessions was governed after 1848 by the convention that Quarter Sessions tried all indictable offences except those carrying penalties of life imprisonment on first conviction and burglary. In 1834 the Central Criminal Court at the Old Bailey was set up as a special permanent court at which the most serious offences were tried.

3. Armstrong used the classification for his study of York with much success, and many believe that failure to utilise the 1921 survey has led to poor classification and lax definition by other authors. For fuller discussion of the point see, W.A. Armstrong, "The interpretation of the Census Enumerator's books for Victorian Towns," and H.J. Dyos and B. Baker, "The Possibilities of Computerising Census Data," with the ensuing discussion in H.J. Dyos, *The Study of Urban History* (1968).

4. The Metropolitan Police Fraud squad was not formed until 1945.

5. Amongst the best known and prolific of these writers were Rev. John Clay, Mary Carpenter, Henry Worsley and W.D. Morrison.

6. The relationship between intelligence and successful perpetration of crime is a matter for interesting debate. A modern view is that, "Only the simpler and more impulsive crimes are available to the person of low intelligence and even at these he will probably be unsuccessful." Howard Jones, *Crime in a Changing Society* (1965), p. 44.

7. See D. Morier Evans, *Facts, Failures and Frauds* (1959) and Michael Crichton, *The Great Train Robbery* (1975).

8. Max Beloff, *Public Order and Popular Disturbances, 1660–1714* (1938, reprinted 1963), pp. 20, 33.

9. Thomas Burke, *The Streets of London through the Centuries* (1940), p. 94.

10. Richard N. Price, "Society, Status and Jingoism: The Social Roots of Lower-Middle-Class Patriotism, 1870–1900," in Geoffrey Crossick, ed., *The Lower-Middle Class in Britain, 1870–1914* (1977).

11. A.R. Barrett, "Era of Fraud and Embezzlement: Its causes and remedies," *Arena*, 14 October 1894.

12. A.T. Craig, "Frauds in connection with Book-keeping and Methods to be used for their Detection," *Accountant*, February 1898.

13. For example Cesare Lambroso, Paul Broca, Enrico Ferri, Gabriel Tarde.

14. Edwin H. Sutherland, *White Collar Crime* (1949).

15. Donald R. Cressey, *Other People's Money* (1953).

16. Sutherland's study also included "criminals" who were not convicted, and it
     is on this point of definition that he has been severely criticised. See R.G.
     Caldwell, *Criminology* (New York, 1965) and P.W. Tappen, *Contemporary
     Survey of Juvenile Delinquency* (New York, 1952).
17. See Geoffrey Crossick, "The emergence of the lower-middle class in Britain:
     a discussion," in Geoffrey Crossick, ed., *The Lower Middle Class in Britain*
     (1977), p. 117.
18. J.A. Banks, *Prosperity and Parenthood: A study of family planning among the
     Victorian middle classes* (1954).
19. By the second half of the nineteenth century the old professions were reaching
     saturation point. See Harold Perkin, *The Origins of Modern English Society
     1780–1880* (1969), p. 255. "Even with connections and capital, professional
     success was not guaranteed; without either it seems exceedingly difficult for
     men honestly to make a prosperous way." Geoffrey Best, *Mid-Victorian
     Britain 1851–75* (1971), p. 77.
20. Quoted in L.G. Johnson, *The Social Evolution of Industrial Britain* (1959).
21. C.F.G. Masterman, "Realities at Home," in *The Heart of the Empire* (1901),
     p. 13.
22. Geoffrey Crossick, "The emergence of the lower middle class" (1977), pp.
     19–23.
23. J.A. Banks, *Prosperity and Parenthood* (1954), Ch. 3.
24. *Illustrated London News*, 2 December 1843.
25. Herbert Spencer, *Edinburgh Review 100*, October 1854, p. 427.
26. S.F. Van Oss, "The Limited Company Craze," in *Nineteenth Century*, 43
     (1898): 740.
27. J.W. Horsley, *How Criminals are Made and Prevented* (1913).
28. Two good examples, however, are David Phillips, *Crime and Authority in
     Victorian England* (1977) and Howard Zehr, *Crime and Development of
     Modern Society: Patterns of criminality in nineteenth-century Germany and
     France* (1976).
29. Alfred Emden, "The Crying Need for Reforms in Our Company Law,"
     Nineteenth Century XXXV (1894): 1033.
30. Alfred Emden, "Defective Addition to Company Law," *Nineteenth Century*
     (1900): 951–971.
31. See, B.C. Hunt, *The Development of the Business Corporation in England,
     1800–1867* (Harvard 1936), p. 141.
32. C.J. Relton, *Essays on Auditing* (1876).
33. T.H.S. Escott, *Social Transformations of the Victorian Age* (1897,
     Reprinted: Folcraft Library, Pennsylvania 1973), p. 194.
34. Quoted in G.L. Anderson, "The Social Economy of Late Victorian Clerks,"
     in Geoffrey Crossick, ed., *The Lower Middle-Class in Britain* (1977), p. 117.
35. K. Chesney, *The Victorian Underworld* (1972), p. 312.

The Lancashire Constabulary, 1845–1870: The Social and Occupational Function of a Victorian Police Force[1]

W. J. Lowe
State University of New York,
College at Cortland

During the mid-nineteenth century uniformed, full-time police forces became the rule in the United Kingdom. Most people in Great Britain were within the jurisdiction of a police force organized on a county-wide basis. The largest of these was the Lancashire Constabulary. While many of Lancashire's towns had their own local police, the populous urban and suburban areas beyond these borough limits, as well as the extensive rural districts that continued to be characteristic of the urban-industrial North-west, were policed by a force subject to the county magistracy (and later the County Council).

Recent research, particularly by R.D. Storch, shows that the appearance of uniformed police in the north of England during the 1840s and 1850s had a significant impact on working-class life, which was not infrequently manifest in violence against individual constables.[2] The idea of a professional police force was repellent to many British people of all classes because it smacked of the interference, surveillance and repression associated with continental despotism.[3] But property owners generally, and middle-class people in particular, quickly learned to support the police forces, while working-class town dwellers saw them as a very visible restraint on their domestic and social lives. Who were these men who were placed between middle-class respectability and ideas of propriety and the very different, and sometimes threatening, working-class culture? The object of this paper is to shift the focus from questions of crime and disturbances, police establishment and organization, and working-class responses to the presence of the police. Instead, the emphasis is on the members of the Lancashire Constabulary, the Northwest's thin green line. The records of the Lancashire Constabulary, particularly personnel profiles, afford detailed information about the individuals who actually signed on as policemen. Their social and occupational backgrounds; their general conditions of service; and even some of their possible motivations for becoming policemen become clear in the police files.

The first modern police force in England, the Metropolitan Police, was established in London in 1829. Ten years later the Report of the Constabulary Commissioners recommended that uniformed police be extended to the entire country. "The act for the establishment of county and district constables" authorized county or borough magistrates to petition the Home Office for permission to establish police forces, which would then be under local control, though subject to general Home Office regulations.[4] At the Lancashire general quarter session in October 1839 the magistrates were "fully impressed with the conviction that it is of the greatest importance that an efficient police be established throughout the county. . . [particularly] in the more populous parts of Lancashire."[5] By early November it was resolved to apply the new constabulary act throughout Lancashire, except in incorporated municipalities. The appointment of a Chief Constable, Captain J. Woodford, and 500 policemen was authorized on 6 November 1839.[6] By March 1842 the strength of the Lancashire Constabulary had reached 502.

Within two years of its establishment the Lancashire Constabulary was one of the largest police forces in the country. Rather than being a cornerstone of local pride, the large police force, paid for by a county police rate,[7] seemed to some to be too great a burden on the ratepayers. In July 1842 the Lancashire magistrates agreed to a 30% reduction in the size of the force (147 men), which was approved by the Home Office.[8] But the 1842 lay-off in Lancashire serves to emphasize how police forces would be regarded in years to come. Almost immediately after the dismissals the county magistrates were approving, and the Home Office was endorsing, a very steady increase in the size of the Lancashire Constabulary.[9] When Woodford was HM Inspector of Constabulary for the Northwest in 1857, he reported that within a month of dismissing the 147 constables in 1842, "a motion was made and carried for a small augmentation of the force in one of the police districts. From that time similar motions have been carried at ensuing quarter sessions almost without intermission, and frequently, of late years, upon the urgent petitions of ratepayers in various parts of the county." In September 1857 there were 657 men in the Lancashire Constabulary.[10] By 1871 the figure was 942.[11] Clearly, police forces had arrived on a permanent basis even in the early 1840s, and the force reduction of 1842 was an uncharacteristic aberration. Throughout the remainder of the nineteenth century the constabulary was an accessible occupational alternative for workingmen. And for those who could meet the standards and demands of mid-Victorian police life, it offered a secure career.

The police statutes of 1839 and 1840 that dealt with the foundation of police forces set some general standards of conduct which were elaborated by the Home Office and the local forces. Policemen were to be strictly nonpolitical and extra-constabulary jobs ("moonlighting") were prohibited, although receipt of military half pay or other pensions was allowed. Neglect of duty and resignation without a month's notice were punishable by fines, and imprisonment could be imposed for serious matters. The Home Office also prohibited the appointment of men who had been dismissed from other police forces or could not produce certificates of good conduct from their previous police service.[12] Otherwise, standards of eligibility for becoming a policeman were not terribly stringent. Those applying for positions as constables had to be 5 feet 7 inches in height and could be no older than forty years. The prospective constable was required to be "able to read and write, intelligent and active and certified to be free from bodily complaint and of a strong constitution; and recommended as of irreproachable character and connections."[13]

Once enrolled as a constable, the recruit received very little formal training, aside from routine military drill, which emphasizes that the police were regarded as the frontline against disorder in urban areas.[14] The men were expected to learn the details of the job experientially from their superiors and comrades. The Liverpool borough police did have a formal month-long probationary training period,[15] but unsuitable men were weeded out of other forces in the initial period of duty as well. Even though there was little training, the police forces did make a great effort to instill a sense of loyalty and responsibility in their members.[16] Captain Woodford of the Lancashire Constabulary took an early lead in formalizing the individual constable's conduct and duties. Woodford published his *Rules and regulations* in 1842, and it was intended as the policeman's reference handbook. The police were reminded that they "must fully understand that they are placed in a *totally new position on becoming members of the establishment*; they then become Peace Officers."[17]

The life of a policeman was indeed "a totally new position" for any constable who had not come straight from the army. At one time the freeborn English working class was described as "drunk with the cup of liberty,"[18] which is another way of saying that factory-type discipline in social life and at work was much less common than more traditional "irregular labour rhythms."[19] As the industrial organization of labour progressed in England during the eighteenth and early nineteenth centuries, the old, more relaxed work habits were attacked by the division of labour, closer supervision, increasing work by the clock, and propaganda of moralists, businessmen and schoolteachers.[20] Gradually the modern, industrial notions of time, punctuality and steady work took hold among the working class. But by the mid-nineteenth century the new demands of industrial discipline had not been fully assimilated by English workingmen.[21] And the demands on the new police in Lancashire, in terms of discipline, timekeeping, long hours, and personal conduct, were certainly greater than would be experienced in a mill, an engineering shop or perhaps even in the army.

The first thing that the new constable encountered in the Lancashire Constabulary was the "strictest discipline; the most proper and effectual mode of securing which is by establishing and exact gradation of responsibility from the highest to the lowest."[22] This (to working people) extraordinary commitment was taken even further by the other conditions of police service. Constables had to devote literally their "whole time" to the force and had to work and reside wherever they were assigned. Any duty missed due to illness was unpaid and, in the early years, holiday time was not set aside. The force also imposed regulations on the constable's personal life. Men were expected to avoid debt; they were each to have "a respectable suit of plain clothes," and the chief constable's permission was necessary for a policeman to marry. And the slightest misconduct could be punished by a fine and/or dismissal at the Chief Constable's discretion.[23] On paper, this was indeed the "strictest discipline." It becomes clear that in practice a sustained effort was made to enforce it.

The mid-Victorian policeman's principal daily activity involved patrolling his assigned area on foot, the beat. A constable was expected to walk twenty miles a day (covering two and one-half miles per hour) for several straight weeks. Day duty was divided into two split shifts that included a meal break and nights were done in an eight-hour block. Reports and other official business had to be handled during "free" time.[24] The Lancashire Constabulary worked shifts "round the clock" throughout the week, which was a mixture of day and night shifts, the longer shifts coming at night. Night duty was particularly stressful and many constables experienced difficulty trying to sleep during the day. Even by the 1870s rest days were allowed only every four to six weeks and the annual week's holiday was unpaid. It was the early twentieth century before a weekly rest day became common practice for constables.[25] While on their long and often tedious tours of duty Lancashire policemen were expected to exhibit courtesy, alertness, responsibility, and a great deal of self-restraint at all times. They were charged with a special watch on pubs and beerhouses, but were prohibited from entering them except in the line of duty. Drunkenness was "unpardonable" and constables were discouraged from entering local hostelries even on their own time,[26] a restriction that proved the undoing of many policemen. This summary of the kind of discipline that applied to a man's entire life while he was a policeman shows clearly that by mid-nineteenth-century standards the police represented one of the most demanding occupations. Outside the military, perhaps, only railwaymen had a comparably strict routine and such continuously long hours.[27] Even factory workers' time was their own after hours, and there was usually a day and a half's free time on Saturday and Sunday.

Long hours, a great deal of walking, and very high standards of personal comportment were not the whole story. Policemen were directly involved in preventing (by their presence) crime and protecting the citizenry, as well as apprehending offenders, great and petty. During the mid-nineteenth century the incidence of crime in Lancashire's urban areas and, through the activity of the police, the numbers of apprehensions rose very steadily.[28] The Lancashire Constabulary had to handle a large portion of this problem. It dealt with mainly petty offences, particularly drunkenness, which was by far the largest category of offense. But individual policemen found themselves heavily involved in taking people into custody. For example, in 1869 the 894 men of the Lancashire Constabulary made 33,132 apprehensions, thirty-seven per man.[29] Further, this intervention exposed the police to a problem a great deal more serious than sore feet. Policemen were frequently assaulted while on duty,[30] which made their already arduous occupation the more difficult.

This overview demonstrates that even if the constabulary offered steady work for hearty individuals, it was, even in an age of hard-working men,[31] a very difficult way to make a living. So who was it that enlisted? The personnel files of the Lancashire Constabulary, preserved in the Lancashire Record Office,[32] give us a great deal of information about individual constables during the first quarter century of the force, 1845–1870, its formative period. Besides recording general data such as name, address, age, and marital status, the files indicate a man's previous occupation and contain details of his service record. From this information it is possible to produce a social and occupational profile of the men of the Lancashire Constabulary. Knowing something about their occupational backgrounds and wage levels (tied in with their lengths of service) can provide hints about their motivations for becoming policemen. All of the men who enlisted during the years 1845 through 1870, a total of 4,357 individuals, are included in the analysis, which begins after the uncharacteristic reduction in strength of 1842.

There was an open admissions policy for entry into the constabulary.

Men who appeared capable of handling the job were hired as needs required; on average, 168 new faces each year. The Lancashire Constabulary personnel files indicate that police work was very much a young man's occupation. The mean age of a new policeman nationally during the mid-nineteenth century was 26 years.[33] Overall, the mean age of a Lancashire Constabulary recruit was 26.1 years. But the mean age declined from 27.8 in 1845–1850 to 24.8 in 1866–70. This trend was not influenced by the trade slumps that occurred during 1847–48, 1855–57 or the Cotton Famine of the early 1860s. Clearly, the very young or the middle-aged were not likely to be attracted to the very long hours and strict discipline of the police force. If new constables were generally in their twenties, they were also increasingly likely to be single men. Half of the Lancashire recruits were single, the proportion rising very steadily from about 46% in 1845–50 to 60% in 1866–70. Similar to the armed forces, a policeman's work did not lend itself very well to married life. The long shifts with rare rest days meant married men would have little opportunity to even see their families. Married men were able to have their wives live with them in the station houses. But this could cause a number of problems, particularly involving privacy. Over time the number of married men without children remained fairly steady at 13% to 15% of the recruits, before dropping below 12% during 1866–70. The numbers of married men with children declined steadily from 40% to 28%. Only during the recession of 1847–48 does it appear that there was any significant rise in the number of married men seeking employment in the constabulary. Young, single men looking for a suitable occupational role or an interim position while keeping an eye out for something better were the most likely recruits.

Recruits usually had not migrated from any great distance before enrolling as policemen, which bears out Arthur Redford's conclusions about labour migration.[34] Fifty-eight percent of the police had been born in Lancashire or Cheshire and another 25% came from other English counties that were usually adjacent or nearby Lancashire, particularly Yorkshire. The proportion of the force born in Ireland grew very steadily during the mid-nineteenth century. During 1845–55 only between 4 and 7% of the policemen were Irish, but by 1866–70 this proportion had grown to 18%. This reflects the fact that there was a large Irish community in the northwest and that the Irish were beginning to be assimilated into the general working-class population.[35]

A very useful feature of the police personnel files is the inclusion of a constable's previous occupation. Tremendous occupational diversity is represented by the men who became policemen during 1845–70. The personnel files list occupations as they were stated by the recruits and do not classify or qualify the entries in any way. Nearly 250 distinct occupations are identified. To facilitate examination while obscuring as little detail as possible, these occupations have been grouped into twenty-two job classifications. Sixty-nine percent of new constables in 1845–70 (3,017 individuals) came from four major occupational groupings: skilled tradesmen, cotton factory operatives, weavers, and general labourers who did not declare a particular occupation.

Table 1: Previous occupations of Lancashire constables, 1845–70
(Number and percent of recruits)

Occupational Group	Number	Percentage
1. Skilled trade	608	13.8
2. Cotton factory	298	6.8
3. Other textile factory	194	4.5
4. General factory operative	142	3.3
5. Labourer	1,642	37.7
6. Non-factory textiles	121	2.8
7. Messengers, porters, shop assistants	56	1.3
8. Railway worker	9	.2
9. Overlooker	29	.7
10. No occupation	7	.2
11. Weavers	469	10.8
12. Professional	29	.7
13. Domestic service	187	4.3
14. Marine	33	.8
15. Business	5	.1
16. Small business	149	3.4
17. Farmer	146	3.4
18. Clerk, bookkeeper	82	1.9
19. Industrial owner	12	.3
20. Municipal & government service	42	1.0
21. Transport	23	.5
22. Miner	70	1.8
Overall	4,357	100.0%

Nearly 14% of policemen recruited by the Lancashire Constabulary during the mid-nineteenth century came from better-paid craft occupations that had some prestige within the working class, in terms of earnings and job security.[36] Fifty-four skilled occupations, some certainly on the margins of the labour aristocracy, are represented in the sample. The most common entrants from the trades were boot and shoemakers, who comprised one of the largest occupational components of the force (3.4% of all those enrolled). Other groups with significant numbers joining the police were carpenters, joiners, wheelwrights, masons, blacksmiths, iron dressers and moulders, bakers, sawyers, cabinetmakers, and ten men classifying themselves as mechanics. Nearly 7% of the men came to the Lancashire Constabulary from cotton factories. Eighteen distinct cotton factory functions are identified, including spinners (108 or 2.5%), grinders, winders, minders, carders, and warpers. Another large group, weavers (10.8%), poses a problem of definition. Four hundred sixty-nine (10.3% of the force) constables had been weavers, but it is not always possible to know if they had been independent handloom weavers or factory weavers. Nineteen men identified themselves specifically as former handloom weavers. In the absence of precise information from the men themselves, 450 former weavers are placed within the ambit of handloom weaving, since power weaving was largely a female task in Lancashire during the mid-nineteenth century. Men from skilled trades, weaving and the cotton factories accounted for 31% (1,375 individuals) of the Lancashire Constabulary and about half of those entering from specific occupational designations.

But more than a third of the constables (37.7% or 1,642 men) came from the ranks of the largest occupational group in Victorian society, the unskilled labourers who claimed no particular line of work.[37] While some held steady positions, these men were employed mostly on a casual and seasonal basis anywhere that extra hands were needed to do unskilled, manual work. They were paid low wages and engaged on a temporary basis, which left them usually underemployed and frequently unemployed. Even though they came from the bottom rung of the working class, they were eligible for police work, where only basic literacy, attention to duty and a strong constitution were required. Among the other previous occupations represented in the Lancashire Constabulary during 1845–70, textile factory operatives, other industrial workers, servants, small businessmen, and those from agricultural occupations accounted for 19% of the policemen.

Lancashire's policemen came from the great body of the English working class and, from their personnel records, it is possible to know something about why workingmen became policemen and how they found life as constables. The decision to take a particular job could involve several considerations for a Victorian workingman. First, of course, was the overriding determinant of necessity, which was very closely related to the question of wages. An unskilled worker, particularly, was often in the position where he had to take what employment, and wage rates, he could find. But if he was fortunate enough to have a choice of positions, he was certain to favour the most advantageous wage rate. The "cash nexus" need not be the only consideration though. The permanency of the employment, working conditions and perquisites, as well as the possibility of occupational advancement (with its concomitant improvement in living standards) could also be part of the equation. The workingman contemplating becoming an officer with the Lancashire Constabulary was able to consider all of these elements, a rare opportunity at the time for any but a professional or highly skilled industrial artisan. Still, it is impossible to know if many, or any, constabulary recruits were making decisions that were part of a career plan. "Perks" and advancement were, for most, probably secondary considerations to that of wages, even though the constabulary might offer the common workingman a unique chance to both earn a steady wage and achieve modest occupational and social respectability.

Although there are gaps in our information on wage levels in nineteenth-century England, there is a substantial amount of information available from a variety of printed sources.[38] Generally, wages in the northwest of England "were high by contemporary standards; almost invariably above average and in many occupations among the highest in Britain." Good wages over a sustained period made Lancashire a relatively good place for workingmen. This favorable situation also made local policemen among the highest paid in the country.[39] In 1840 the first Lancashire policemen were started at a wage of 16s. per week. Promotion to second and first class constable brought wages up to 17s. and 18s., respectively. In 1865 the rate at appointment was 19s. 10d., and in 1868 21s. 7d. Weekly rates increased modestly through advancement in rank, if a man performed his duties satisfactorily.[40] Many occupations promised better wages than the constabulary, but police rates were consistently ahead of the wages that an agricultural labourer or an urban general labourer could expect. Police rates were also better than those paid for most cotton factory jobs. But something else distinguished police wages that could easily appeal to even a well-paid urban worker. For anyone willing to serve as a constable, decent wages were paid the year round. Labourers were often underemployed and skilled men, while earning a good living during some parts of the year, could find themselves idle during certain seasons. Police work knew no such interruptions.

Police wages, while decent and steady, were not strictly comparable to those in other occupations. Those earning lower or similar wages were probably working shorter weeks than the constables. Other industries worked longer, but wages for skilled men in a foundry or on a building site were higher. Lancashire's policemen could expect to work ten to twelve hours on a seven-day basis, a work week of seventy to eighty-four hours. By the 1860s rest days were possible only every four to six weeks.[41] Clearly, some of the advantage of constabulary wage levels was eaten up by longer hours and arduous, tedious duty. In 1872 the Chief Constable of the Lancashire Constabulary, Robert Bruce, recognized the fact that police wages would have to rise in order to make the constabulary a competitive occupation. "The rate of wages, as well as the demand for workers, in other employment is increased... in these other employments there is very generally a considerable reduction in the hours of labour. . . ."[42] Many of the men who enlisted did not fully understand the nature of the commitment and attrition, for several reasons, was a persistent problem. But the constabulary data show that the decent, steady wages that were available probably attracted a large proportion of the recruits. The occupations held previously that are represented in the personnel files have been placed into three wage categories: I) those earning less than the police rate; II) those earning approximately the same rate; and III) those earning a rate higher than that offered by the constabulary.

The personnel files do not tell us anything about a number of factors that could influence these groupings significantly. Unemployment, seasonal fluctuations or other things that could determine individual earning levels are not mentioned. Further, exact information is not always available for wage rates in particular occupations and these have been placed as closely as possible. The general picture is very clear. Overall, nearly two-thirds of recruits came from occupations offering less in wages than the police. This was increasingly the case over the years. Consistently, less than 10% came from the same wage stratum. Interestingly, 28% of the men came from better paid occupations. Data isolated for years of economic recession (1847–8, 1855–7, 1861–5) show that there was not a significant departure from these general trends in those years.

Nearly three-quarters of the policemen were recruited from the lower to middle ranges of the wage spectrum. An improvement in living standards could seem a definite possibility for them, even if, later on, they decided that the demands of the occupation were too great. Also, the constabulary could be a very acceptable living if a man was between occupations and seeking a better position. Those able to earn higher wages outside the constabulary were a decreasing proportion of recruits over the years, except during the recessions of the late 1840s and mid-1850s, when there were mild increases. Dissatisfaction with their trades, temporary unemployment due to seasonal or cyclical fluctuations, a desire to place their incomes on a steadier basis, or, since most new constables were fairly young, failure to realize expected wage levels or advancement soon enough could impel these men from the

Table 2: Wages earned in previous occupations compared to police wages, 1845–70.

| | Occupational Category | | | | | |
| | I | | II | | III | |
	Number	Percentage	Number	Percentage	Number	Percentage
1845–50	494	55.4	80	8.9	318	35.7
1851–55	487	61.0	68	8.5	243	30.5
1856–60	569	64.2	64	7.2	253	28.6
1861–65	600	69.4	71	8.2	193	22.3
1866–70	617	67.3	69	7.5	232	25.3
Overall	2,767	63.5	352	8.0	1,239	28.4

higher-paid occupations to try the constabulary. After the lay-offs of 1842, the constabulary was immune to seasonal or cyclical shifts and the danger of trade decline due to industrial changes. Police wages were certainly an important inducement to enlistment for a wide variety of workingmen, usually those who would earn less outside the constabulary. But becoming a constable brought more than a secure weekly pay packet. Wages were supplemented by both fringe benefits and the possibility of advancement.

The first extra benefit that Lancashire policemen received was a suit of work clothes, a uniform. Clothing and equipment were replaced as needs required.[43] The Lancashire Constabulary uniforms distinguished the policemen from the public at large and from other police forces in the country because they were rifle green, "therein differing from all others."[44] In 1840 the Chief Constable thought that it was of the "utmost importance that in populous places the constables should be separated as little as possible when off duty," in order to enforce discipline and to prevent the men from becoming overly friendly with people living in their areas.[45] Station houses were established, the costs of which were defrayed by modest rents paid by the policemen.[46] Day rooms and kitchens were furnished and strict rules for conduct and cleanliness were enforced.[47] In an age of generally poor working-class housing, police accommodation could be an attractive feature of police work. Married men were allowed to live in station houses with their wives, as long as wives did not fight with their husbands or other officers.[48] By 1867 the Lancashire Constabulary had 112 station houses and 282 men, most of whom were married, lived in them. They represented 34% of the force.[49] Two-thirds of the force had to find their own lodgings and by 1872 Chief Constable Bruce found there was a rent problem for his men. Bruce asked the Constabulary Committee to approve an annual grant of £450 to subsidize housing for the police, both by direct grants and by renting suitable housing to be sublet to constables. The committee approved the funding to aid any constable paying more than 3s. in rent per week.[50] Between station house accommodation and rent subsidies, the constabulary offered a unique benefit to working men.

Constabulary service also brought provision for a man's future. The county constabulary act of 1840 (3 & 4 Vic, c. 88) authorized the establishment of a superannuation fund that was financed through constables' contributions, fines imposed for misconduct, fines from convictions for such offenses as drunkenness and assaults on police, and the sale of used police equipment. A constable with between fifteen and twenty years service was eligible to retire on half-pay. The minimum retirement age was set at sixty years, unless the constable suffered from some incapacity. A Lancashire constable contributed 15s. 2½d. each year to the pension fund, and higher ranks put in somewhat more.[51] To make the pension scheme more attractive to younger men, the vast body of constabulary recruits, Chief Constable William Elgee recommended in 1866 that policemen be allowed to retire after twenty years, without any age qualification. This liberalized scheme was adopted.[52] The country constabulary act also allowed pensions (up to the full amount of their pay) for men wounded while on duty, at the chief constable's discretion.[53] The statutory superannuation system did not encompass widows and orphans of constables who died while on active service during this period. The Lancashire Constabulary Committee approached the Home Office about instituting such a provision, but the Home Office could not find authorization for the step in the constabulary acts.[54] In individual cases, the Chief Constable did recommend a single grant from the superannuation fund for the family of a deceased policeman.[55] It was not a perfect retirement system, but it was still one that offered more security than most occupations open to workingmen.

There were other fringe benefits available to policemen. While 1s. per day was deducted from a man's pay when he was off duty due to illness, from the early days of the force free medical attention was provided from the constabulary rate.[56] Constables also received special allowances for executing some of their duties. For example, a policeman received 1s. for apprehending a vagrant and 2s. 6d. for other classes of offenders. Serving a summons brought 1s. and executing a warrant 2s. 6d.[57] Chief Constable Bruce pointed out in 1872, while enumerating the various constabulary perquisites, that if a man had to resign due to illness after three years of service, it had become policy to grant him a month's pay for each year's service. Likewise, if a man died after three year's service, his family received a similar grant. Acknowledging that the constabulary operated within statutory and financial limits, Bruce felt that "the members of the force have always been liberally dealt with."[58] Altogether, decent wages and a good package of fringe benefits offered a workingman an adequate standard of living and an uncommon degree of security.

A workingman also had the chance to rise through the ranks of the constabulary to a responsible and respectable position through "diligence and fidelity" on the job. During the 1840s an entry-level man was called a third class constable, but this designation was eventually dropped. By attention to duty and "efficiency" a man was, as a matter of course, promoted to second class and then first class constable, which brought pay increments. There was a limit to the number of sergeants that the force could assimilate, but the position was available to first class constables when attrition or promotion created openings. From the rank of sergeant it was possible, but much less likely, to become an inspector and then a superintendent. But minor misconduct could also cause mobility in the other direction through disciplinary demotions. Chief Constable Woodford felt very strongly that a distinct gradation of rank and pay was a "proper stimulus to exertion," so that policemen would strive to improve themselves.[59] It was always considered desirable to fill vacancies in the upper ranks from the force itself and seniority and merit were the criteria for advancement. A Home Office estimate of 1878 said that it took four to five years for a constable to reach the rank of sergeant and an additional eight to ten years to become an inspector; not a meteoric rise, but not a totally umpromising prospect for a workingman either.[60] Woodford included a prescription for advancement in his *Rules and regulations*: "Every police constable in the force may hope to rise, by activity, intelligence and good conduct. . .diligent discharge of his duties and strict obedience. . .reading, writing and the general improvement of his mind."[61]

High standards were demanded for promotion, but working satisfactorily for a number of years did make it possible. High personnel turnover in the force did open promotion possibilities for steady men. But this same attrition also meant that relatively few men were on the job long enough to take advantage of promotion opportunities. Nearly 44% of police recruits did not reach the first promotion rank of second class constable before leaving the force. This proportion was decreasing somewhat by 1866–70, but it still stood at 38%. There was a slight improvement in this attrition situation during the recessions of the late 1840s, the mid-1850s and during the Cotton Famine, which indicates that men might have been more inclined to stick with the job during hard times. An additional 14% of policemen left the force at the rank of second class constable. Reaching the rank of second class constable seems to have been the major step for a policeman, because a significant proportion of recruits did make it to first class constable. The achievement of one promotion, with a pay rise, was undoubtedly an inducement to earn a second one. Still, 32% left the force at first class constable, a trend which rose steadily until it was nearly 40% in 1866–70. During the mid-nineteenth century 349 men who reached the rank of sergeant left the force without further advancement, 8% of the force. There were many fewer men in the ranks above sergeant, which set very definite limits on promotion possibilities for sergeants. Generally, anyone who could make it to second class constable had an excellent chance of getting to first class constable, and a further 32% left at first class. For only less than half of police recruits can it be said that advancement through the ranks proved of any real value. Only 11% ever achieved a responsible position. Police wages were decent and steady. Fringe benefits, by Victorian standards, were very good and quite comprehensive. And promotion at the very least to first class constable was automatic for any steady man. So it is not surprising that many work-ingmen, from well-paid as well as lower-paid occupations, were attracted to employment with the Lancashire Constabulary.

The personnel files also contain information on each constable's length of service. Turnover was a tremendous obstacle to building a reliable, profes-sional police force. Retention improved during the mid-nineteenth century, but it certainly had not reached an optimal level. Even by 1870, more than a third of recruits did not last a year. The proportion staying with the police from one to two years hovered between 12% and 13%, but, except for the late 1850s, more than 20% lasted from two to five years. Few individuals remained policemen after the five-year mark, but those who did were very likely to make the police a career. The proportion of men serving more than ten years increased steadily throughout the period until it was one-fifth of the force by 1870. Overall, nearly three-quarters of the recruits left the constabulary within five years, but the mean length of service increased steadily from 4.5 years during 1845–55 to 5.9 years during 1866–70. While over 250 men left the force within a month of joining, 426 remained police-men for more than twenty years, twenty-five of whom served more than forty years. The longest service during this period was fifty-six years; the shortest, a couple of hours.

Table 3: Length of service among members of the Lancashire Constabulary, 1845–70.

Enrollment years	<1 yr		>1, <2 yrs.		>2, <5 yrs.		>5, <10 yrs.		>10 yrs.		Mean
	%	No.	%	No.	%	No.	%	No.	%	No.	Yrs.
1845–50	41.0	366	12.6	112	21.6	193	10.7	95	14.1	126	4.5
1851–55	40.9	326	11.7	93	23.2	185	9.9	79	14.4	115	4.5
1856–60	42.4	376	12.9	114	17.5	155	8.8	78	18.4	163	5.1
1861–65	38.8	335	12.3	115	20.5	177	6.7	58	20.7	179	5.8
1866–70	34.6	317	12.4	114	22.6	207	10.5	96	20.0	183	5.9
Overall	39.5	1720	12.6	548	21.0	917	9.3	406	17.6	766	5.2

Resignation was the principal cause of attrition. From half the departures in 1845–50, it increased steadily to over 60% by the end of the period. A smaller but still very significant source of losses was dismissal. We have seen that standards of conduct, on and off duty, were high and strictly enforced.[62] Discipline improved over time, as resignations rose, and dismis-sals became less frequent, although some resignations were probably precipitated by imminent dismissals. But fully a quarter of the policemen were dismissed during 1845–70. Drinking was, far and away, the chief reason for dismissal, and increasingly so. By 1870, 63% of dismissals involved drinking. General misconduct, neglect of duty and falsehood accounted for another 24% of dismissals. The personnel files show that there were numerous other ways for a constable to get into trouble. One constable was dismissed for stealing and smoking cigars, while another was found in bed with a fellow policeman's wife. Men who interfered with the local women, in or out of custody, were obvious candidates for the sack, but one must sympathize with the constable who was dismissed for reciting poetry in a public house while on duty. Resignations and sackings added up to 85% of the attrition. A small number died while in service and a growing proportion (16% in 1866–70) were becoming eligible for pensions.

High personnel turnover was not the sole problem of the Lancashire Constabulary. Other forces experienced similar difficulties. A less detailed analysis of the personnel register for the Preston borough police during 1860–71 produces attrition and discipline figures similar to those of the Lancashire Constabulary.[63] The Manchester city police not only had difficulty retaining recruits in the service, they were seriously under-manned.[64] A significant part of the retention question stems from the constabulary's own policies. They did not want to retain men who could not live up to strict discipline, and dismissals were summary and frequent for, sometimes, small infractions. But many more officers were likely to resign long before they could be dismissed or superannuated. The heart of the problem was a very general desire not to remain as a policeman.

Chief Constable Willis at Manchester was certain that the rigors of constabulary duties and the restrictions imposed on policemen drove men from the force and hindered the recruiting of replacements.[65] Bruce of the Lancashire Constabulary felt that service in his force was "more onerous and often attended with more risk" than policework elsewhere.[66] Many English workers, particularly skilled men, would probably be less deterred by the long hours than by the loss of independence implied by a commitment to the constabulary. Still, rates of resignation considered by previous occupation, while showing periodic fluctuations, appear to be consistently high for all significant occupational groups, varying from 50% to 66%. For example, in three of the major groupings of prior occupations (skilled trades, cotton factory workers and labourers) the percentages of resignations for the whole period are 59%, 60% and 58%, respectively. Analyzing these three groups by shorter periods, the lowest rate of resignation occurred in 1845–50 among cotton factory workers (50%) and the highest in 1861–65 among skilled men (67%). Both the cotton workers and skilled workers had resignation rates of 63% in 1866–70. Likewise, dismissals stayed pretty uniformly around 25% of those from each group, although some groups, such as general factory workers and some non-factory textile workers, showed higher dismissal rates. Men who had been in domestic service had a very low dismissal rate. Thirty-five percent of recruits during the period enrolled during the years of economic hardship, 1847–8, 1855–7, 1861–5. But except in a few isolated instances, these men had a mean length of service comparable to, and, in several cases, longer than, those who joined in better times. Some certainly returned to their former trades or went to better positions as soon as circumstances allowed, but these men were no more transitory than other recruits. Altogether, the occupational backgrounds of policemen and economic fluctuations add very little to our understanding of attrition in the constabulary.

Table 4: Reason for termination of service, 1845–70.

| | Resignation | | Dismissal | | Retirement | | Death | |
	No.	%	No.	%	No.	%	No.	%
1845–50	454	50.9	327	36.7	81	9.1	30	3.4
1851–55	462	57.9	232	29.1	82	10.3	22	2.8
1856–60	545	61.5	202	22.8	113	12.8	26	2.9
1861–65	521	60.3	181	20.9	141	16.3	21	2.4
1866–70	571	62.3	161	17.6	147	16.0	38	4.1
Overall	2553	58.6	1103	25.4	564	12.9	137	3.1

Considering the rank at which men resigned perhaps tells us more. The personnel data tells us almost nothing about individual decisions to leave the force. It is noted occasionally that a man had found a better job, or wanted to search for one at resignation. The arduous duty and discipline and the intention to leave the force at the first favorable opportunity certainly helps to explain why during 1845–70, 1,170 men (27% of all recruits) resigned without achieving second class constable. Men who joined the force during the recession periods behaved in almost exactly the same manner as the rest of the sample. Forty-six percent of those resigning left quickly and a further 51% remained in the force long enough to be promoted at least once. And we have seen that achieving the first promotion was a promising sign of a second one, a point borne out by the figures on rank at resignation.

A rise in pay was certainly some incentive to achieve promotion, but promotion carried further advantages. Rising through the ranks to become a sergeant or an inspector brought a modest advance in social status to respectability. But promotion had another, more immediate value to a workingman. Even if he thoroughly disliked the constabulary life, he might calculate that achieving a good rank, such as first class constable, and receiving a good "character" on leaving the force would be a great advantage in finding a better position outside the force. The 1,200 men (28% of all recruits) who resigned in good standing after at least one promotion for satisfactory service could expect a favorable reception in the employment market. Unfortunately, the personnel files do not reveal anything about what happened to the men after they left the force.

Table 5. Rank at resignation, 1845–70.

Rank at Resignation	All Resignations		Resignations among those enlisting during recessions 1847–8, 1855–7, 1861–5	
	No.	% of Resignations	No.	% of Resignations
No rank	1,170	45.8	444	45.9
2nd class	463	18.1	197	20.4
1st class	850	33.3	304	31.4
Sergeant	65	2.5	20	.02
Inspector	3	.1	1	.001
Superintendent	2	.1	1	.001
	2,553		967	
Total recruits	4,357		1,668	

There was probably another potent reason why nearly 60% of the police recruits resigned the force. If the long hours and discipline were not enough to drive them away, their role in the community was occupationally and socially distasteful. Police forces were viewed as alien engines of continental-style social control and repression by many English people in the early nineteenth century, and the dread of spies in radical movements (real and imagined) heightened working-class sensitivities. The "respectable" classes desired greater security for their health and, above all, their property. The constabulary commissioners reported in 1839 that one of the great advantages of uniformed police in the country would be their "general presence."[67] This presence in Lancashire was "favourably received by the respectable and orderly portion of the community."[68] In 1853 Captain Woodford actually thought the police were becoming "popular."[69] But to the working people of Lancashire the police were truly "those ogres of our streets."[70] Storch has shown that the policemen, if substantially untrained and ideologically uncommitted, nonetheless served a "missionary" role in working-class neighbourhoods.[71]

Their presence and duties brought policemen into the social lives of working people through their efforts to regulate or suppress customary social activities. This made conflict and assaults on individual constables frequent occurrences. Interference in neighbourhood life and their surveillance function created tremendous working-class distrust.[72]

Though chief constables certainly acknowledged the problem, the men who resigned from the force were the least likely to record their motivations for doing so. But it is impossible to dismiss the impact on constables of their position in the community, particularly in the formative years of the force. The men of the Lancashire Constabulary were overwhelmingly from among the working class, against whom they were principally deployed. Their general unpopularity and being rejected by their own class must have affected many recruits deeply. General dislike and abusive nicknames were tolerable punishment compared to violent assaults. Indeed, as Chief Constable Willis at Manchester wrote, it was a wonder that anyone wanted to become a constable at all. The high rates of dismissal and resignation during 1845–70 show that very few recruits were deeply committed to their missionary function, either because of individual, short-term calculations about employment opportunities, or their dislike of being in the jeopardy situation as representative of an alien class outlook. For many workingmen who became policemen, good pay and generous benefits could only be partial payment for bearing popular contempt and, too often, violence. Overt, violent opposition to the police declined during the last quarter of the nineteenth century[73] and the average length of service increased, but the life of the constable throughout the Victorian period was far from enviable.

Notes

1. I wish to acknowledge the invaluable, and patient, assistance of my friend John Haslett (Department of Statistics, University of Dublin). I must also thank Mr. R. Sharpe France and his staff at the Lancashire Record Office, Preston, for their help in enabling me to tackle the archives of the Lancashire Constabulary, and Dr. R. D. Storch for his helpful comments on an earlier draft of this paper.

2. R. D. Storch, "The plague of the Blue Locusts: Police reform and popular resistance in northern England, 1840–57," in *International Review of Social History* xx, Part I (1975): 61–90; "The policeman as domestic missionary: Urban discipline and popular culture in northern England, 1850–80" in *Journal of Social History* ix, no. 4 (1976): 481–509; W. R. Miller, *Cops and Bobbies: Police authority in New York and London* (Chicago, 1977), pp. 104–39.

3. P. J. Stead, "The new police" in D. H. Bayley, ed., *Police and Society* (Beverly Hills, 1977), pp. 74–6.

4. 2 & 3 Vic., c. 93. General accounts of the police legislation and the foundation of police forces outside of London are found in F. C. Mather, *Public order in the age of Chartists* (Manchester, 1959), pp. 96–140; E. C. Midwinter, *Law and order in early Victorian Lancashire* (Borthwick Papers, no. 34, 1968), pp. 8–11, 13–17; and T. A. Critchley, *A history of the police in England and Wales, 900–1966* (London, 1967). The latter work is a loose narrative, but it does contain useful factual information.

5. Lancashire Quarter Sessions (proceedings under the act for appointing county and district constables), 1840–51, 14 October 1839 (Lancashire Record Office [LRO], QEC/1/1).

6. LRO, QEC/1/1, 6 November 1839, 1 January 1840.

7. 3 & 4 Vic. (1840), c. 88.

8. LRO, QEC/1/1, 20 May, 13 July, 14 July 1842.

9. The letters approving individual appointments appear in the County Constabulary letter books (Public Record Office [PRO], HO 65); Midwinter, *Law and order*, 21–22.

10. *Reports of the Inspectors of Constabulary for the year ended 29 September 1857*, (House of Commons, 1857–58), p. 35, xlvii, 693.

11. *Reports of the Inspectors of Constabulary, 1871*, (House of Commons, 1872), p. 115, xxx, 115.

12. Home Office (HO) circular to Clerk of the Peace, Lancashire, 5 October 1839 (LRO, QEC/1/1).

13. Critchley, *History of the police*, pp. 146–7.

14. Ibid., pp. 147, 151; J. Woodford, *Rules and regulations for the government and guidance of the Lancashire Constabulary Force* (Liverpool, 1842), p. 24; Stead, "The new police," p. 78.

15. Critchley, *History of the police*, p. 149.

16. Ibid., p. 147.

17. Woodford, *Rules and regulations*, pp. 4–5.

18. Quoted in E. P. Thompson, "Time, work-discipline, and industrial capitalism," reprinted in M. W. Flinn and T. C. Smout, eds., *Essays in social history* (Oxford, 1974), p. 56. This same subject is addressed in the American context in H. G. Gutman, "Work, culture and society in industrializing America, 1815–1919" reprinted in H. G. Gutman, *Work, culture, and society in industrializing America* (New York, 1976), pp. 3–78.

19. Thompson, "Time and work-discipline," p. 56.

20. Ibid., pp. 57–64.

21. Ibid., p. 64.

22. Woodford, *Rules and regulations*, pp. 5–6.

23. Ibid., p. 9.

24. Finlay McKichan, "Constabulary duties: The lives of constables a century ago" in *History Today*, 30 Sept. 1980, p. 39; Critchley, *History of the police*, pp. 151, 158; J. P. Martin and G. Wilson, *The police: A study in manpower* (London, 1969), p. 22.

25. McKichan, "Constabulary duties," pp. 40, 43; Critchley, *History of the police*, pp. 151–2, 172–3.

26. Critchley, *History of the police*, p. 22.

27. Frank McKenna, "Victorian railway workers" in *History Workshop*, I (1976), pp. 26–73.

28. Harold Perkin, *The origins of modern English society, 1750–1880* (London, 1974), pp. 167–9; J. J. Tobias, *Crime and industrial society in the nineteenth century* (London, 1967). The incidence of crime in Lancashire during this period (drawing on local and Home Office sources) is discussed in W. J. Lowe, "The Irish in Lancashire, 1846–71: A social history" (Ph.D. dissertation, University of Dublin, Trinity College, 1974), pp. 214–46.

29. PRO, HO 63/23, Police returns, England and Wales, 1869.

30. See Storch, "Policeman as domestic missionary," especially pp. 502–9.

31. Raphael Samuel, "The workshop of the world: Steam power and hand technology in mid-Victorian Britain" in *History Workshop II* (1977), pp. 6–72.

32. Lancashire Constabulary, examination books, 1845–70 (LRO, PLA). An analysis of comparable data from a much smaller sample is available for the Black Country police in D. Philips, *Crime and authority in Victorian England: The Black Country, 1835–1860* (London, 1977), pp. 57–79.

33. Critchley, *History of the police*, p. 145.

34. Arthur Redford, *Labour migration in England, 1800–50*, edited and revised by W. H. Chaloner (Manchester, 1964), pp. 68–70.

35. See W. J. Lowe, "The Irish in Lancashire."

36. E. J. Hobsbawm, "The labour aristocracy in nineteenth-century Britain" in *Labouring men* (London, 1973), pp. 272–315.

37. The labourer category contains a dozen agricultural labourers and six costermongers.

38. The most recent and comprehensive study is E. H. Hunt, *Regional wage variations in Britain, 1850–1914* (Oxford, 1973). See also A. L. Bowley, "Changes in average wages in the United Kingdom, 1860–91" in *Journal of the Royal Statistical Society* lviii, Part II (1895); "The statistics of wages in the United Kingdom during the last hundred years," Parts I-IX in *Journal of the Royal Statistical Society* lxi-lxv (1898–1902); *Wages in the United Kingdom in the nineteenth century* (Cambridge, 1900); G. H. Wood, *The history of wages in the cotton trade during the past hundred years* (London, 1910); "The course of wages" in *Economic Journal* (1899); *Labour statistics: Return of wages published between 1830 and 1886*, (House of Commons, 1887), C. 5172, lxxxix.

39. Hunt, *Regional wage variations*, pp. 37, 39, 40.

40. LRO, QEC/1/1, 6 November 1839, 6 January 1847; *Reports of the Inspectors of Constabulary, 1857*, (House of Commons, 1857–8), pp. 80–81, xlvii, 738–9; Proceedings of the Constabulary Committee, February 1872 (LRO, QEC/2/4).

41. McKichan, "Constabulary duties," p. 43.

42. LRO, QEC/2/4, Robert Bruce to Constabulary Committee, 8 February 1872.

43. Woodford, *Rules and regulations*, pp. 6–8.

44. *Reports of the Inspectors of Constabulary, 1857*, (House of Commons, 1857–58), p. 35, xxxvi, 87.

45. Miller, *Cops and Bobbies*, pp. 25–7.

46. LRO, QEC/1/1, Woodford, 6 April, 29 June 1840.

47. Woodford, *Rules and regulations*, pp. 25–7.

48. Ibid., p. 27.

49. *Reports of the Inspectors of Constabulary, 1867*, (House of Commons, 1867–8), p. 87, xxxvi, 87.
50. LRO, QEC/2/4, 20 March 1872.
51. LRO, QEC/1/1, 5 April 1843.
52. LRO, QEC/2/3, W. Elgee to Constabulary Committee, 19 December 1866.
53. For examples of such awards see LRO, QEC/2/2,4, 16 June, 21 July 1847, 19 May 1869.
54. LRO, QEC/2/4, 16, 18 June 1847.
55. LRO, QEC/2/4, 21 April 1869.
56. LRO, QEC/1/1, 6 April, 30 April 1840.
57. LRO, QEC/1/1, 21 October 1841; Woodford, *Rules and regulations*, p. 54.
58. LRO, QEC/2/4, 8 February 1872.
59. LRO, QEC/1/1, Woodford, 6 April 1840.
60. Critchley, *History of the police*, pp. 154–5.
61. Woodford, *Rules and regulations*, p. 20.
62. The enforcement of strict discipline was also characteristic of the Metropolitan Police. See Miller, *Cops and Bobbies*, pp. 37–42; Midwinter, *Law and order*, pp. 26–27.
63. Preston Borough Police, Personnel register, I (Preston Central Library).
64. Chief Constable Willis to Watch Committee, October 1866 (Manchester Central Library, watch committee letter books, M70/2/2). The town of Oldham faced similar problems (Borough of Oldham, watch committee minutes, 1849–71, A-J, Town Clerk's Department, Oldham Town Hall).
65. Manchester Central Library, M70/2/2, Willis to Watch Committee, October 1866.
66. LRO, QEC/2/4, Bruce, 8 February 1872.
67. *First report of the constabulary commissioners*, (House of Commons, 1839), pp. 149–59, xix, 155–65.
68. LRO, QEC/1/1, Woodford, 6 April 1840.
69. *First and second reports of the select committee on police*, (House of Commons, 1852–53), p. 99, xxxvi, 103.
70. E. Gaskell, *Mary Barton: A tale of Manchester life* (Harmondworth, 1970), p. 438.
71. Storch, "Policeman as domestic missionary," p. 481; Storch, "Crime and justice in nineteenth-century England" in *History Today*, 30 (September 1980), p. 34.
72. Storch, "Policeman as domestic missionary," pp. 481, 502–8. Additional examples of the rough treatment that Lancashire policemen received at the hands of citizenry, particularly the Irish community, are found in *Manchester Courier*, 18 March 1846; Chief Constable Willis to Watch Committee, 28 August 1858 (Manchester Central Library, M/9/70/2/1); *Liverpool Courier*, 3 May 1848, *Oldham Chronicle*, 29 July 1854; Riot deposition, 10 October 1856 (LRO, QJD/1/238). Figures on police assaults compiled by the Home Office are found in Police returns, 1858–69 (PRO, HO 63/1-23).
73. Storch, "Policeman as domestic missionary," pp. 502–8.

The Ordeal of a "Liberal" Policy: Fuller Warren and the Gambling Controversy in Florida, 1949–1953

William Howard Moore,
University of Wyoming

Despite the officially repressive policies toward gambling in twentieth-century America, there has been widespread de facto tolerance for it. Scholarly work on the informal regulation of illegal gambling and vice has largely focused on urban machines, the police, and ethnic politics in the period prior to the Great Depression.[1] During more recent periods of rapidly expanding gambling activities, however, local regulatory structures have frequently shown signs of strain, and state, even sometimes federal, officials have been drawn into what were, in quieter days, local problems.

One such period of expansion occurred in the newly prosperous 1940s when the volume and apparent profits from illegal gambling mushroomed across the country. This growth, in turn, created explosive underworld competition and political difficulties for local and state officials. A series of police scandals in Chicago, Philadelphia, New York, and other major cities reflected the dislocating impact of the expanding illegal gambling industry on the informal regulatory structures. The highly publicized murders of a political middleman in Kansas City and of a major figure in the racing telegraph wire service in Chicago underscored the seriousness of the problem. Even in Nevada, which had legalized most forms of gambling in the 1930s, pressure was felt. Rival factions of gambling entrepreneurs sought advantages through influence with state regulatory commissions and through monopolies on the wire service necessary for large-scale book-making. Whatever the precise explanation for the gruesome assassination of Benjamin "Bugsy" Siegel in 1947, gambling rivalries were clearly at the core. Attempts by the mayors of New York and New Orleans (and by small groups in many states) to deal with the gambling problem by expanded legalization failed miserably.[2]

While professing that illegal gambling remained a local problem, a surprising number of postwar governors found themselves compelled to take action when local authority appeared to be breaking down. In Minnesota and Wisconsin, Governors Luther Youngdahl and Walter Goodland launched programs to close down all forms of gambling in their states by revoking business licenses of operations permitting wagering on their premises. Governors of other states—California's Earl Warren, Illinois's Adlai E. Stevenson, Ohio's Frank Lausche, and New York's Thomas E. Dewey—eventually intervened with state troopers or other law enforcement personnel when local officials appeared to have lost control or to be openly tolerating gambling. While most of the governors involved postured as bold defenders of public virtue, in fact most risked serious political repercussions had they not acted.[3]

No governor inherited more serious problems with the postwar gambling phenomenon than Florida's Fuller Warren. While most accounts have focused on Warren's ties to alleged underworld fronts, the available evidence suggests that the governor's difficulties were more a function of his impulsiveness, the state's excessively decentralized law enforcement structure, and a forceful anti-gambling lobby. A closer look at Warren's problems in Florida sheds light on the complexity of the gambling issue throughout the country.

Fuller Warren's dramatic rise in Florida politics obscured serious personal and administrative inadequacies. Born in 1905 in a small fundamentalist hamlet in the rural panhandle of Florida, young Warren worked as a field hand, errand boy, salesman and auctioneer. His frustration when, at the age of twelve, he was unable to serve as a page in the state legislature bespoke an early, consuming political ambition. A handsome and compelling public speaker, he interrupted his undergraduate studies at the University of Florida to win a state house of representatives seat from his native Calhoun County. After obtaining a law degree from Cumberland University in Tennessee, he moved to Duval County in 1929. There he established his practice and served on the Jacksonville City Council. Overwhelmingly elected to the lower house from Duval County in 1939, Warren ran a surprisingly strong third in the gubernatorial race the following year. Wartime service as a naval gunnery officer in the Atlantic precluded a statewide campaign in 1944, but Warren kept in close contact with voters through a variety of newspaper articles and columns. Although he advocated a harsh peace (including the systematic sterilization of German men), Warren lauded Florida's politically liberal, internationalist Senator Claude Pepper, called for attacks on disease, ignorance and monarchies, and advocated a redistribution of wealth.[4]

Warren planned another try for the governorship after the war. While continuing his weekly column, he became the state's most sought-after public speaker. By mid-1948, he claimed to have delivered over three thousand speeches, "one or more in nearly every inhabited place in Florida." Warren delighted in overstatement; he advised would-be speakers to refer to an opponent not as a "cad" but as a "lying, libidinous, lecherous libertine." His bombastic, alliterative, adjective-filled speeches became his political trademark and endeared him to his natural constituency in rural north Florida.[5]

Despite his contention that the purpose of oratory was "sound, not sense," Warren gradually developed a comprehensive program for the state that permitted him to appeal also to the rapidly growing urban areas in the south. Calling for reapportionment of the state legislature, establishment of a central state purchasing agency to cut costs, flood control, and aid to cities, he also promised to veto any general sales tax bill. He advocated state aid in modernizing Florida's citrus export industry, and he proposed a road building program and removal of cattle from highways as steps to promote industry and tourism. He promised to become a salesman for the state, to convert his remarkable speaking talents and showmanship to Florida's advantage.[6] Warren's personal following and populistic platform gave him sufficient statewide appeal to win in Florida's peculiarly decentralized, factionalized political environment. Aided by the Pepper forces and the state's labor leaders, Warren capitalized on his opponent's alleged ties to the outgoing Caldwell administration and captured the governorship in 1948.[7]

Despite success with parts of his platform, Warren's lack of legislative and administrative expertise stymied much of his program and led to early disappointment among his followers. Impulsive and thin-skinned, the governor invariably met charge with countercharge and tried to arouse support with dramatic, if essentially hollow, gestures. In 1949, for example, when the legislature rejected his plan to raise state revenues to cover a deficit, Warren sought to bring public pressure on the lawmakers by mortgaging his car and delaying payment of his official salary.[8]

No issue he inherited, however, brought Warren more difficulty than the perennial problem of public gambling. Florida's experience with gambling had consisted historically of unofficial tolerance punctuated by occasional reform outbursts. For most of the twentieth century, the exclusive Bradley's gambling house in Palm Beach had attracted the cream of American and European society and wealth. In Tampa, particularly among the Cuban population, *bolita* (a variation of the illegal numbers game), had been an institution for over sixty years. Colonel E. R. Bradley, the *bolita* operators, and hundreds of less celebrated local gambling entrepreneurs throughout the state had achieved varying degrees of toleration by providing contributions to local politicians, loans to influential businessmen and newspapers, and charitable donations. A variety of legalized gambling proposals was put forward during the interwar period as Miami and south Florida grew as tourist meccas. Hoping to lure tourists and alleviate the effects of the Great Depression, the state legislature legalized parimutuel betting on horse and dog races in 1931, using part of the state's tax revenue from it for support of aged indigents and dividing the rest among the county governments. In 1935 Florida launched an abortive two-year experiment with legalized slot machines. There was no other important legalization; but the total volume of illegal gambling undoubtedly increased greatly in the 1930s and 1940s, straining informal local regulatory structures.[9]

By the time Warren took office, a fairly precise rationale for toleration had developed among wide segments of the state's population. Particularly in the vacation areas of the south, but elsewhere as well, a substantial body of opinion maintained that gambling, whether legal or illegal, was essential to the tourist industry. A persistent theme, dating back at least to the 1920s, held that vacationers would go elsewhere if gambling opportunities were not readily available. Support for wide-open towns became an element in the boosterism that pervaded many non-gambling as well as gambling elements in the state.[10]

More than in most states, an intense localism characterized both politics and the gambling issue in Florida. Local business and political leaders favored illicit gambling operated by local figures and informally regulated by local law enforcement officers. The kind and degree of gambling supposedly could be tailored to local traditions, tourists, and social needs by local control. A measure of local pride accompanied local control of illegal gambling. The most explosive charge that could be made was that sinister outside gangsters, unresponsive to local needs, were moving into the area, bringing corruption and violence, displacing local control, and ultimately draining the area of gambling's supposed financial benefits. In Florida, as in most of the country, the archetype of the outside gangster was rooted in the highly publicized gang wars of Chicago in the 1920s; repeatedly, Capone gangsters were alleged to have designs on both the state's legal racetrack betting industry and the informal local systems.[11]

Localism clearly implied home rule and a passive attitude on the part of state officials. While home rule traditionally protected illegal gambling in Louisiana, Arkansas, and other states, the exceptional decentralization, even atomization, of Florida politics gave it particular strength there. Although the governor had the constitutional right to suspend county sheriffs if they tolerated or protected gambling, to do so would almost surely alienate the local power structure in resort areas. In a number of cases in the 1940s, the state senate reinstated sheriffs suspended by the governor, and the voters reelected them. Governor Millard Caldwell adopted a policy of suspending only after the official in question had been indicted; he refused to remove one sheriff for mere "stupidity and ineptitude," and he rebuked a Dade County minister for trying to shift responsibility for law enforcement away from apathetic or tolerant local voters and onto him. Home rule enabled governors to avoid political hazards and local voters to opt for a liberal policy on gambling. Between 1936 and 1948 the successful gubernatorial candidates pledged their support of home rule, the liberal policy, and protection of the tourist industry from outside racketeers.[12]

The unprecedented economic growth of the greater Miami area in the immediate postwar years created a situation that would eventually entangle Fuller Warren in the gambling controversy. Broward County, including Fort Lauderdale and Hollywood, had become the center of a series of large casino operations and other gambling activities, some of them owned by veteran Sheriff Walter Clark. Dade County encompassed some twenty-six separate municipalities, including Miami and Miami Beach, and an extensive unincorporated area policed by the controversial Sheriff Jimmy "Smiling Jimmy" Sullivan. Miami Beach and its many new fashionable hotels had emerged as "the richest single plum in the field of illegal gambling in America." For protection of the extensive off-track bookmaking in Miami Beach's hotels, an estimated $1,000,000 was paid annually to law enforcement officials, who had become mere "tools of the gamblers." A local bookmaking syndicate, the S. & G., had won much local support with charitable and political contributions and police payoffs, but its influence was being challenged by outside hoodlums who sought entry into the business. Political power was of the essence in this situation; as much as $90,000 was reportedly spent to elect councilmen whose annual salaries were only $3,000. The explosive conditions in Miami Beach alarmed a number of citizens. In 1949 a young reformist lawyer, Melvin Richard, was elected councilman on an anti-gambling platform, threatening all of the lucrative illegal operations.[13]

In Miami, plush gambling conditions contributed to a running power struggle that virtually paralyzed the police department. While contending interests offered financial rewards for the chance to operate unmolested, police factions jockeyed to exploit the illegal business. Lieutenant C. O. Huttoe, sometime head of the vice squad in charge of the suppression of gambling, had rivals who staged "insurgent raids" when regular graft payments were interrupted. The byzantine intrigue involving Huttoe and his enemies led to almost constant dismissals, reinstatements, and investigations. The police rivalry ultimately engulfed the city fathers, and it led to one police faction's attempt to frame the city manager and mayor in a Newport, Kentucky, disorderly house.[14]

Alarmed at the seeming breakdown of local law enforcement due to illegal gambling, a Dade County grand jury in May 1948 advocated the legalization of off-track bookmaking by the state. Invoking the precedent of Prohibition, the grand jury feared the situation would continue to disintegrate until the control of government fell into the hands of gambling gangs. The grand jury proposed that a series of off-track stations, licensed by the State Racing Commission, collect bets and channel them through the existing parimutuel machinery. Although generally rejected by civic and religious leaders, the recommendation apparently had much appeal. Press reports suggested that support for legalization was also growing in Tampa, Fort Lauderdale, and Key West.[15]

Whatever support expanded legalization might have had in south Florida slowly dissipated before a group of upper middle- and upper-class leaders, whose new, well-financed organization focused upon local fears of outside gangsters. The key figure of this organization would ultimately be Daniel P. Sullivan, a former agent of the Federal Bureau of Investigation who had been active in kidnapping cases of the 1930s and in the investigation of alleged Japanese sabotage in the early months of World War II. On leaving the FBI in 1942, Sullivan moved to Miami as plant protection supervisor of the Consolidated-Vultee aircraft plant. In 1945 he became chief investigator for the Florida State Racing Commission and also assisted the new Thoroughbred Racing Association in suppressing illegal activities at racetracks along the East Coast. In 1947 a group of businessmen representing Miami's two major newspapers, the radio stations, a large department store, the Florida Power and Light Company, and Hialeah Racetrack secretly hired Sullivan to conduct an investigation of the infiltration of underworld figures into the Dade County area and of the general significance of mushrooming gambling activities. Stunned by the extent to which gangsters and racketeers from northern cities had become involved in local gambling, hotels, apartments, bars, and real estate, the secret businessmen's group contacted United States Attorney General Tom Clark to request a coordinated federal assault on the problem. Although the group was unable to secure an audience with President Harry Truman in Washington, former Ohio governor and Democratic presidential candidate James Cox and John S. Knight, owners of the Miami newspapers, were able to see him in Key West and obtain a promise of cooperation.[16]

Although the businessmen provided federal prosecutors with the information Sullivan had uncovered, the Truman administration never acted on its supposed promise to Cox and Knight. Given Truman's old links to

Kansas City's Pendergast machine, the President must have understood the explosive nature of the problem in the greater Miami area. Preoccupation with foreign policy crises and concern in an election year with a Democratic South already restive over possible administration incursions on the civil rights question prompted Truman to avoid such local imbroglios. On the crime issue, moreover, the chief executive and his advisers genuinely appear to have believed in local control and initiatives. Although he apparently gave the south Florida question little personal attention, Truman probably hoped that a hard-hitting speech in the area by Attorney General Clark would fulfill any promises he had given Cox and Knight.[17]

As the businessmen's group vainly sought federal intervention, members of the bar association hoped to mobilize local opinion against the liberal policy that was making Dade County into a mecca for national criminals. In early 1947 the Dade County Bar Association endorsed a report by a group of young attorneys advocating the creation of a "Law Enforcement Institute" to streamline the criminal justice machinery, focus public pressure on elected officials to enforce all the laws, and combat pro-gambling sentiment. In an attempt to enlist sluggish public opinion against the liberal policy, the bar association in 1948 sponsored two large rallies of civic organizations, one keynoted by Attorney General Clark and the other by the operating director of the Chicago Crime Commission, Virgil W. Peterson. In a nativistic speech, Clark warned of the infiltration of a roaming "criminal army of 6,000,000" into a variety of legitimate businesses. Peterson, a former FBI agent, personal friend of Daniel Sullivan, and foremost critic of legalized gambling in the country, attacked "The Myth of the Wide-Open Town" before an overflow crowd in Bayfront Park. Drawing in part from information gathered by Sullivan for the businessmen's group, Peterson argued that the liberal policy only attracted outside hoodlums who drained tourist money away from the local economy and poisoned local government. In the wake of Peterson's speech, the two local groups (the businessmen's group and the concerned members of the Dade County Bar Association) merged as the Crime Commission of Greater Miami, with Sullivan as operating director.[18]

Sullivan's access to Peterson's voluminous files, his own investigative talents, support from newspapers and radio stations, and the financial backing of the local establishment made the Crime Commission a formidable organization. A socially conservative group that spurned the use of the word *reform*, the Commission frequently linked laxity in law enforcement with general social and economic decay. The Commission, which was dominated by upper-middle-class businessmen and professionals, argued not so much for moralism as efficiency and stability in the criminal justice system. The chaotic conditions spawned by gambling in south Florida posed a threat to the orderly business and community development the Commission so much desired.[19]

In its first two years the Crime Commission concentrated its energies at the local level. In 1948 Daniel Sullivan spearheaded an investigation of Captain Huttoe and the municipal police department on behalf of the Miami city manager.[20] The Commission and its allies, however, concentrated most of their wrath on incumbent Dade County Sheriff Jimmy Sullivan, who was running for reelection. Sullivan, a genial former traffic cop and prizefighter, had drawn the fire of civic groups and grand juries for his passive attitude toward gambling and the influx of racketeers. The establishment candidate, with the backing of the local daily newspapers, contended that Sheriff Sullivan's laxity had allowed "thugs, burglars, rapists, and the like" into the county while discouraging "year-around industries and businesses."[21]

Sheriff Sullivan, speaking for the liberal policy, argued that the community was dependent upon legal racetrack gambling and that the tourist traffic necessitated that he be "tolerant to some degree" of illegal wagering; he favored the recent grand jury recommendation for legalized off-track betting. He stressed that he operated under a $25,000 surety bond and that he could not harass an alleged outside hoodlum without solid evidence that he had committed a crime. "His past record or general appearance may make him undesirable for drawing room companionship," Sullivan contended, "but unless he has violated the law he cannot be arrested. . . ." Spoofing talk of a hoodlum invasion, the sheriff boasted that there had been no "gang murders" in the area.[22]

The reelection of Sullivan in 1948 led to escalation of his battle with his critics. The Crime Commission repeatedly sought to force him to more vigorous action, both by appeals and by embarrassing exposés of gambling through the newspapers and radio stations. While claiming that he would execute any arrest warrant they might obtain through the courts or prosecutors, Sheriff Sullivan refused to risk his bond, he claimed, on the basis of their allegations. In early 1949, Circuit Court Judge Stanley Milledge appointed elisors to serve warrants, but Sullivan contested Milledge's action, and the latter's fellow jurists cautioned that his insistence might "invite chaos, revolution, and bloodshed." Despite the enormous energies the Crime Commission and its allies had invested in their fight against Jimmy Sullivan, they were frustrated at the local level. Shortly they would take their case against the sheriff to the governor, with results neither could have anticipated.[23]

Although gambling controversies simmered in Dade County and elsewhere, neither Warren nor his opponents commented on the situation

during the 1948 gubernatorial election. Initial steps taken by Governor
Fuller Warren on the gambling problem, however, indicated a good deal of
vigor, at least comparable to that of Youngdahl in Minnesota or Stevenson
in Illinois. To the applause of civic and religious leaders around the state,
Warren announced a clamp-down on the ubiquitous slot machines. While
professing himself liberal minded on local law enforcement, he nevertheless
promised to remove sheriffs, constables, or state officials tolerating the "one-
armed bandits." Fearing that the assassination of a Tampa politician–*bolita*
operator in late 1948 might be the signal of a collapse of civil order there,
the governor demanded that the Hillsborough County sheriff take immediate action to suppress the traffic and promised to ask for FBI assistance
if necessary. In 1949 Warren successfully threw his support behind a bill
designed to disrupt wire service to Florida bookmakers who took bets on
races run in the state; even the governor's legislative critics conceded that his
aid had been critical to the bill's passage.[24]

Warren also took a strong anti-gambling stand during the heated debate
over state revenue. He inherited a large budgetary deficit from the Caldwell
administration and was confronted by an acrimonious debate over how the
state government was to be financed. Important support developed among
legislators and businessmen for a general sales tax, which would place the
burden on consumers, but Warren opposed the sales tax and advocated
higher taxes on large corporations. In the midst of the controversy, a number
of legislators, with considerable public support, suggested legalized off-track
bookmaking as a new source of state funds. Finally compromising on a
limited sales tax, Warren emphatically rejected legalization proposals and
instead ordered a crackdown on bookies. Extensive off-track bookmaking
had lessened the volume of legal parimutuel betting at the track, he
announced, and hence had deprived the state of some of its much-needed
revenue. The 8 percent state take constituted the third largest source of funds
for the state government; but, in the midst of Florida's greatest tourist
season, revenue at the state's sixteen racetracks had actually fallen 7 percent.
In February 1949, Warren ordered all sheriffs and constables to halt the "tax
stealing" by bookmakers and insisted that the state beverage and hotel
commissions revoke licenses of establishments permitting off-track gambling
on their premises.[25]

Warren's verbal departures from the liberal policy on gambling became
muffled as they worked their way downward through state and county
officialdom. Although the number of applicants for the federal tax stamp
for slot machines in Florida declined dramatically in 1949, newspapers reported that the "one-armed bandits" were in full operation near Elgin Field
in the panhandle and from Hollywood to the Keys in the south. Ominous

rumors that Tallahassee officials were offering protection in exchange for shares in local slot machine profits began to appear in the Miami and Tampa press. With only brief interruption occasioned by Warren's announcements, bookmakers in Dade County and elsewhere continued to operate throughout the winter season. The intense localism of the gambling tradition in Florida, the persistent rumors that state officials were attempting to use the governor's crackdown as a tool to arrange local fixes, and the general cynicism that pervaded the gambling culture began to poison Warren's anti-gambling campaign.[26]

By reversing, even briefly, the traditional liberal policy of his predecessors, Warren allowed his name to be drawn into an undercurrent of intrigues revolving around the gambling problem. While the governor was preoccupied with the sales tax debate and other concerns, various state officials, acting with Warren's authority, jockeyed for influence. When Warren named special state investigators to work on the gambling problem, he maintained only minimal personal contact with them, and such direction as they were given came from the governor's quarrelsome assistants. Meanwhile, the new State Beverage Department Director, Louis Schott, and Jim Landon of the Hotel Commission, ordered by Warren to crack down on gambling violations, became concerned over the alleged influence on the governor of racetrack owner William H. Johnston. Rumors and counter-rumors linked almost all of these officials with attempts to organize protection systems in various parts of the state. On several occasions, acquaintances of the governor tried to invoke his friendship in order to overawe their rival gambling entrepreneurs, but there was no clear evidence that Warren knew specifically of these efforts. When the governor's orders went out to sheriffs or other officials in the porous, localized law enforcement structure, there might be a brief pause of activities out of respect or from fear of his powers to suspend or disrupt, but almost invariably there would follow a resumption of business as usual.[27]

In early 1949 the Crime Commission, vaguely aware of some of these problems but pleased by Warren's initiatives in protecting state revenues from bookmakers, sought to enlist him in their campaigns. They wanted to apprise him of their discovery of outside hoodlum influence in Florida dog tracks and to present to him their case against Sheriff Sullivan. Although office assistants tried to protect the beleaguered governor from the Miami group, the internal struggles in the administration almost provided the opportunity the Crime Commission was seeking. In mid-January, 1949, State Beverage Director Schott contacted Daniel Sullivan confidentially to obtain information on an applicant for the Miami District Supervisorship and on a Dade County hotelman with ties to New York gambling figures. Schott and Hotel Commissioner Jim Landon also asked Sullivan about the governor's friend, William H. Johnston. Sullivan presented his material on the three figures to Schott and Landon, who were so impressed that they arranged for Sullivan and themselves to meet with Warren. The governor listened to Sullivan's report on the beverage commission applicant, but shut off the discussion when Sullivan went on to the hotelman and Johnston, observing that they were not seeking state employment. Although it persisted in attempts to reach Warren, the Crime Commission was at least mildly suspicious of the governor thereafter. That suspicion was strengthened as the Commission monitored a complex intrigue taking place in the gambling community of south Florida.[28]

Circumstantial evidence and rumor suggested to the Crime Commission that the power of the governor's office was being used not to suppress Dade County gambling but expand it. One of the roving state investigators working out of Warren's office was an old friend of the chief executive, a ten-year veteran of the Jacksonville police department, W. O. "Bing" Crosby. Assigned to the Dade County area, Crosby requested the assistance of Sheriff Jimmy Sullivan's office in a series of raids on Miami Beach gambling accommodations, all involving operations of the S. & G. syndicate. For several years, S. & G. had been well-protected by the sheriff's office, but Crosby's presence—backed by the threat that the governor might suspend Sullivan if he failed to cooperate with the state investigator—neutralized the sheriff and the usually cooperative Miami Beach police.[29]

At the time the Crosby raids were taking place, S. & G. lost its vital wire service from Continental Press. Continental sat atop an extremely complicated national system of leased telephone and telegraph lines that obtained and distributed last-second changes at horse races throughout the country; access to the wire service was essential to S. & G. if it were to retain its large volume of wagering and protect itself from scheming bettors. The lucrative wire service historically had been subject to intrigue and violence, and a series of murders in the postwar years had convinced a number of knowledgeable persons, including Daniel Sullivan, that Continental had fallen into the hands of Chicago underworld figures. The suspension of service to S. & G. by elements tied to Continental, coinciding as it did with the Crosby raids, convinced both the Crime Commission and the local gambling community that alien interests were attempting to "muscle in" on the plush S. & G. operations.[30]

S. & G. resisted the incursions for several days. At one point it was able to obtain bootlegged information from another subscriber to the wire service, but Continental then halted information to the entire state. Losing money and under pressure from local gamblers to reach a settlement, S. &

G. accepted Harry Russell as a member of the syndicate, after which the Crosby raids ceased and the wire service resumed.[31]

Russell's identity and the mechanics of the "Russel muscle" became a subject of local speculation in 1949. From Chicago, Russell had been a temporary resident of Miami Beach for a number of years. He had obtained gambling concessions from the Chicago-based owners of a number of beachside hotels and had been contemplating expanding into baseball betting. Rumors developed, and were later confirmed, that Russell had been an informant to Crosby and had "fingered" some of the S. & G. establishments. Russell's entry into S. & G. appeared to have been facilitated by the raids, and he almost certainly represented elements other than himself.[32]

The coincidence between the Russell muscle and the Crosby raid, conducted under the governor's authority, drew informed speculation as to the mysterious influence of racing magnate William H. Johnston. Born in Scotland, Johnston had moved with his mother and family to Chicago when his father, who raised horses, died. In the real estate business in the 1920s, Johnston became an auditor at Sportsman's Park Racetrack outside Chicago during the Depression. Al Capone and a number of associates, including John Patton, "boy mayor of Burnham," had been involved in the racetrack, and many observers were convinced that they continued into the 1930s and 1940s to be the real owners behind a succession of fronts. Johnston worked for Edward J. O'Hare, who had reportedly purchased the various Capone racing interests in Illinois and elsewhere, until O'Hare's assassination in 1939. O'Hare's murder prompted at least three states, Illinois, Massachusetts, and Florida, to launch investigations of racetrack ownership with the goal of purging the industry of underworld influences. By the late 1940s, through a series of puzzling financial maneuvers, Johnston, who had no police record, emerged as president of the group owning Sportsman's Park and as head of four Florida dog tracks—two in Jacksonville, one in Tampa, and one in Miami. Johnston insisted that while Patton and others he had known might earlier have had "skeletons in their closets," he had always known them as respectable figures.[33]

A wealthy benefactor of Jacksonville charities and a jovial and witty conversationalist, Johnston had been a loyal friend and political contributor to Fuller Warren for fifteen years. He was a frequent visitor and occasional overnight guest at the governor's mansion, and in turn played host to Warren at one of his homes in Michigan and at his suite in the Blackstone Hotel in Chicago. Although he professed to have turned down a place on the governor's patronage committee and to be uninterested in any benefits that might come from his friendship with Warren, he had considerable influence and attracted comment in the state's newspapers.[34]

Although Johnston knew Crosby in Jacksonville and had been in contact with both Crosby and Russell during the raids, the details of the Russell muscle were too obscure to bring any immediate outcry. It would appear that Johnston, as an entrepreneur of legal racetrack betting, would benefit from the kind of crackdown on off-track bookmaking that Warren had announced. The lack of demonstrable motive in the Russell muscle case was acknowledged by the Crime Commission. Nonetheless, Johnston's background and his ties with the governor and Crosby fueled both awe and resentment within the Dade County gambling community.[35]

Mistrust of Johnston and Warren because of the circumstances of the Russell muscle turned to bitterness by the end of 1949. During the legislature's consideration of legalized gambling, Dade County bookmakers attempted to win the support of both men for bills authorizing and taxing off-track betting. Such a move would effectively replace the nebulous legal position of bookmakers with both legality and respectability; legalization would bring a more stable and predictable pattern of regulation; and the state could be expected to protect its gambling licensees against arbitrary suspensions of wire service such as had occurred during the Russell muscle. The S. & G. group, for precisely such motives, retained the attorney for Johnston's tracks to draft a legalization bill and hoped that such a move would influence Johnston and, ultimately, the governor. Raymond Craig, a native Floridian, substantial Miami bookmaker, and perennial supporter of the idea, agreed to fly to Chicago with his attorney to lobby for Johnston's support. Johnston was unenthusiastic and suggested that the bill be considered as a revenue measure only if the controversial sales tax package failed. The sales tax passed, the legalization scheme died, and Craig, who had supported Warren in 1948, became vindictive toward both Johnston and the governor. The embittered Craig and a Daytona Beach gambling figure, who felt he had also been "dealt out" after contributing to Warren's campaign, became the sources of a number of stories linking Johnston and the governor to the Russell muscle, the Chicago underworld, and statewide corruption.[36]

The gambling issue was one of several controversies that overwhelmed the inept governor in 1949. Probably even more damaging had been the marathon sales tax debate, which occupied most of Warren's attention and cost him much support. His task was made no easier by his contentious office staff, chosen less for efficiency and loyalty to him than to placate various campaign backers. Hoping to keep his campaign promise of an open administration, Warren dissipated his energies by personally handling endless individual entreaties. (During his first year in office, he received ten thousand callers, forty thousand letters, and over ten thousand long-distance telephone calls.) Working from ten to fifteen hours a day, sometimes in his office until 11 p.m. greeting visitors, Warren worked himself into a state of near collapse and spent a month in the hospital recovering from nervous exhaustion.[37]

The struggle for power within the administration became public knowledge in mid-February of 1950 when one major campaign contributor, Charles V. Griffin, broke with the governor. Griffin, head of the national Democratic Party fund-raising campaign in the state, first met Warren while both were students at the University of Florida. Griffin became a wealthy citrus grower who extended small loans to Warren and indulgently shipped Christmas fruit gifts to many persons on the governor's behalf. When Warren began his 1948 campaign, he asked Griffin to take charge of fund raising. Griffin, in turn, approached William H. Johnston, known to him at the time as an affluent racing entrepreneur, and Louis E. Wolfson, a youthful self-made Jacksonville financier who had made a fortune by reselling war surplus material. (He later ran afoul of securities laws.) Together the three men agreed to underwrite Warren's campaign. While each had expected to contribute about $25,000, campaign costs vastly exceeded expectations, and each ultimately contributed or raised over $150,000.[38]

Warren was barely in office before a fierce power struggle erupted among his three major contributors. Suspicious of Johnston, Griffin and Wolfson sought to undercut him by arranging changes in the governor's staff. Griffin apparently began to press upon the governor some of the Miami Crime Commission's doubts about Johnston. In July 1949, Griffin obtained the governor's signature on a card that designated him as "chief investigator," a title Warren understood to be purely honorary. In mid-February, 1950, when the governor continued to resist Griffin's proposed staff and patronage changes, the citrus grower publicly announced his own appointment as "chief investigator." Pained by the situation, Warren first attempted to reconcile Griffin and then fired his "chief investigator."[39]

Griffin's break with Warren brought into the open for the first time the swirling undercurrents and recriminations that in 1949 had marked the Florida gambling question. While the governor claimed that his old friend had asked that he "virtually abdicate" over the patronage quarrel in his office, Griffin's early revelations centered on two points: the size of the contributions to Warren's campaign by himself, Wolfson, and Johnston, and the supposedly baleful influence of Johnston on Warren and the gambling problem. Although state law limited a gubernatorial candidate to "knowingly" spending no more than $15,000 on his campaign, Griffin maintained that the three contributors alone had chipped in over $460,000. The $15,000 legal limit, repealed by early 1950, had been widely violated for years. Most political observers claimed that a minimum of $200,000 to

$250,000 was necessary for a viable statewide campaign, and Warren conceded that candidates kept themselves in the dark on campaign financing so they could have a "legally clear" conscience when filing the required statement on spending.[40] Nonetheless, the sheer size of contributions by these three men to Warren's campaign provoked questions as to how much the governor might have been compromised.[41]

More serious still, Griffin publicly intimated that his firing resulted from his investigation of outside gangsters' entry into Florida gambling. He suggested that Johnston, now openly linked by the press and the Crime Commission of Greater Miami with the Capone syndicate, had prevailed upon the governor to relieve him of his duties. After the firing, moreover, Warren and Griffin exchanged a series of angry and embarrassing public letters and Griffin circulated rumors that the governor had been physically intimidated by gambling elements before entering the hospital for rest in December.[42] Operating openly as Warren's "past chief investigator," Griffin wrote the chief executive to report on out-of-state mobs in Florida and on rumors linking the state beverage commission with corruption and illegal slot machine operations. He deplored the "Babylonian" scale of illegal gambling in Dade County. Griffin also charged that a quarreling, incompetent staff was obstructing any feeble attempts by the governor's office to deal with the gambling problem. In light of Warren's reluctance to intervene in the situation, the "past chief investigator" petitioned President Truman to launch a "great moral crusade" against "imported" gangsters active in the area.[43]

Although Griffin later equivocated on many of his charges, his public blasts at Warren and outside gangsters attracted the support of and emboldened the Crime Commission of Greater Miami and its allies. Local newspapers and radio stations enlisted such nationally prominent newspaper columnists and radio broadcasters as Drew Pearson, Bob Considine, and Robert Montgomery to expose the problem. In his own weekly radio program, carried by fourteen stations and entitled "The Sinister Blot," Daniel Sullivan of the Crime Commission lambasted the alleged takeover of Miami-area gambling by Chicago and New York gangsters. In March of 1950, Sullivan's program featured an interview with William Drury, a bizarre former Chicago police detective, who claimed that a national gangster confederation with worldwide ties controlled most of the nation's rackets and that many of these underworld figures had investments or homes in south Florida. The Miami *Daily News* carried a twelve-part series by Drury, further detailing the gangster invasion of the area.[44]

Increasingly suspicious of Governor Warren, the Crime Commission renewed its campaign for a federal investigation, not only into Dade County gambling, but also into organized crime throughout the country. When the Truman administration again proved unresponsive, the group shifted its support to a proposal by Tennessee's Senator Estes Kefauver for a wide-ranging congressional investigation. In league with newspaper reporters, municipal and civic organizations, and such groups as the Chicago Crime Commission, Daniel Sullivan and the Miami anti-gambling forces helped nudge Kefauver's resolution through a reluctant United States Senate in early May.[45]

Griffin's allegations and the agitation of the Crime Commission focused attention on Dade County, then in the midst of the 1950 winter tourist season. Although Miami Beach bookmaking had been disrupted during an explosive recall effort against anti-gambling councilman Melvin Richard and by the confusion over gangster influence, extensive gambling continued in the casinos and bookmaker facilities in Dade and Broward counties. In January, the Crime Commission asked Warren to suspend Sheriff Jimmy Sullivan for failure to enforce the gambling laws, but the governor, perhaps because he was stung by the problems of the previous year, had retreated to the more passive liberal policy. Noting the precedents of previous chief executives and the apparent endorsement of the liberal policy by Dade voters in the 1948 election, Warren refused to remove Sheriff Sullivan.[46]

Warren was thrown on the defensive after the Griffin defection, however, and began to seek accommodation with the boisterous Dade anti-crime forces. Having been advised by the Saint Petersburg *Times* to appoint a statewide commission on law enforcement and to replace Jimmy Sullivan with Daniel Sullivan, Warren suddenly flew to Miami to discuss the situation with the Crime Commission. Warren, looking strained and occasionally even trembling, wedged into the group's small offices with reporters, cameramen, and several disdainful officials of the Crime Commission. The governor stressed his earlier anti-gambling steps and explained that in the welter of other problems he had not fully grasped the extent of the difficulties in Dade County. Commission officials interrupted that they had been trying for "month after month, year after year" to get his attention but were never able to get past the governor's assistants. The Commission was especially scornful of Warren's refusing to suspend Jimmy Sullivan, and Daniel Sullivan lectured the chief executive on the need for a thorough investigation of "hidden" underworld ownership of Johnston's racetracks. A shaken Warren appeared receptive to the track investigation, hinted that he would reconsider his decision on Sheriff Sullivan, and tentatively offered the job to Daniel Sulivan, who emphatically rejected the overture.[47]

Warren succeeded temporarily in smoothing the ruffled feathers of the Crime Commission members. Daniel Sullivan praised the forthcoming racetrack investigation as a "milestone in Florida's march toward better law enforcement" and looked forward to confirming his conviction that Johnston was a front for Capone gangsters. The Commission was pleased by a new order the governor sent to the state's sheriffs insisting that all gambling laws be enforced, though baffled by the appearance of an aging gumshoe whom Warren sent to help Sullivan explore the local scene. Given the uncertainty of the situation and the fear that a besieged Warren might engage in wholesale law enforcement suspensions, most substantial illegal gambling operations in south Florida closed in late February and early March, the peak of the 1950 winter season.[48]

Within a month, however, Warren's inconsistent handling of the gambling issue led to condemnation throughout the state. In a statewide broadcast a week after his visit to the Crime Commission, the governor announced that any action he took on local gambling needed community support to be effective. Obliquely, he left the impression that he would suspend sheriffs only if a local grand jury had returned indictments against them. A similar policy had been popular under Millard Caldwell, but unfortunately for Warren a shift in public opinion had occurred by mid-1950.[49]

As usual, the first criticism came from the Crime Commission in Miami, which encouraged local civic groups to bombard Warren with demands for Sheriff Sullivan's ouster. In central Florida, the governor was criticized for failing to oust the sheriff of Hillsborough County (Tampa) in the wake of another gangland-style assassination. In the northern panhandle county of Okaloosa, a group of religious and civic leaders pleaded with Warren to break precedent and crack down on the ubiquitous slot machines in Crestview and Fort Walton. Warren urged Sheriff H. U. Enzor to greater vigilance, but asked for evidence of local initiative on the part of the citizens as well. In response, the Okaloosa group mobilized a mass meeting (of five hundred persons) and coordinated an attack on gambling from the pulpits of some twenty ministers, steps aimed at establishing a groundswell against Sheriff Enzor.[50] Elsewhere, civic and religious groups condemned Warren's stance; the state's Methodist ministers even demanded elimination of all racing and legal wagering in Florida.[51]

Warren's passive policy kept him under intense pressure for well over a year. In August he finally removed Sheriff Enzor but then, unknowingly, appointed to succeed him a Crestview attorney who turned out to be Enzor's son-in-law. By the following spring he had suspended five other sheriffs including those of Hillsborough and Broward counties. Only after the Kefauver Committee, aided by the Crime Commission of Greater Miami, had publicized evidence of corruption in Jimmy Sullivan's office and after a grand jury had indicted the sheriff did Warren suspend that controversial official. In mid-November the state supreme court overturned Sullivan's indictment on two legal technicalities, but the major newspapers in Tampa and Miami argued that for Warren to reinstate Sheriff Sullivan would be a "mockery" and would "slap Dade County in [the] face."[52]

While the governor struggled with the thorny suspension issue, the Crime Commission was escalating the pressure for an investigation of hidden gangster influence in Johnston's four Florida dog tracks. Soon after Warren agreed to such a probe during his February meeting with the Crime Commission, the Miami group sent him its tentative report on the ownership of the tracks. The report stressed Johnston's ties to Sportsman's Park, the original Capone track, and emphasized that the aging John Patton, a friend of Johnston and the Capones, had investments in both the Chicago and Florida racetracks. Warren demanded more specific evidence of a violation of state law. In disgust, Commission President Jack Younger and Daniel Sullivan sought to prod the State Racing Commission directly, claiming that Johnston's campaign donation to Warren violated state law prohibiting a track licensee from contributing to a political campaign. The Racing Commission eventually began a slow-moving study of all the state's dog tracks, but the frustrated Sullivan doubted its sincerity and initiated his own laborious study of the ownership of Johnston's tracks.[53]

The Crime Commission also had been able to focus much of the highly publicized Kefauver study on the Florida situation. Working from Daniel Sullivan's offices, the Senate committe explored the Russell muscle; it delved into the embarrassing campaign contributions; and, drawing upon the testimony of confidential informants such as the embittered Raymond Craig, it came to focus upon Johnston's influence on the governor. Daniel Sullivan repeatedly stressed to Kefauver the need to demonstrate that Johnston was a front whose racetrack interests were actually owned by Chicago under-world figures. By linking Warren to a Capone syndicate through Johnston, the Kefauver Committee could dramatize the problem of interstate racketeering, and Warren's critics in Florida could score a breakthrough. Although some concealed ownership (by John Patton) was easily demonstrated in Johnston's Florida dog tracks, Sullivan reasoned that the true extent of Capone mob investments in the state could be discovered only by a thorough analysis of shifting ownership in Sportsman's Park. Some revealing pieces of evidence were uncovered during Kefauver's Chicago hearings, but no compelling case was ever made to show that Johnston was in fact a front for Capone interests. His past associations in Chicago—common to many in racing at the time—and the very complexity of the charges against him, however, led many to think the case against Johnston was established.[54]

The already strained relations between Governor Warren and the Crime Commission deteriorated into personal recrimination and near crisis in March of 1951. On the basis of leaks from the chairman of the State Racing Commission, Daniel Sullivan charged that the governor had interceded with the commissioners to rescind an earlier order banning a New Jersey bookmaker from Florida's tracks. Sullivan maintained that the alleged Warren telephone call to the Racing Commission had come at the request of ranking political figures from Chicago and Washington. Members of the Racing Commission publicly denied the specifics of the charge, and the governor denounced Sullivan as a "hired liar." Warren then accused Jack Younger of the Crime Commission of having accepted a "brown envelope" from "one of Miami's most notorious gamblers" at the McAllister Hotel Bar and of seeking to prolong the verbal duel in order to keep money coming into his "cabal." An outraged Younger went before a local grand jury, vehemently denied Warren's allegation, and dared the governor to repeat his story under oath before the Kefauver Committee. Warren apparently had received a garbled report linking Younger to Raymond Craig from a professional stool-pigeon working on all sides of the tangled controversy.[55]

In the midst of this fray, the governor lit a political powder keg by reinstating Jimmy Sullivan. Warren, now committed to the liberal policy as he understood it, had evidently concluded that he had nothing more to lose in his relations with the Crime Commission. He and his staff had miscalculated, however; the outcry erupted from every influential newspaper in the state and from important national publications. Many of the state's newspapers advocated Warren's impeachment. There was especially strong support for this in the Tampa area, where a second crime commission had been formed and where the governor had further alienated the local power structure by reinstating another law enforcement official. Dade County churches and newspapers encouraged their local legislative delegation to take the lead in ousting the governor. Miami Representative George O'Kell, until recently a strong Warren backer, emerged as the spokesman for the impeachment forces.[56]

Although Warren had little support in the legislature, the reaction there was more varied and subdued than in the press. Immediately after the Sullivan restoration, the state house unanimously requested that the governor reinstate no suspended official without first presenting the case to the senate. While O'Kell gathered evidence for impeachment, Pinellas Republican William Cramer proposed the creation of a "little Kefauver Committee" and an end to all legal dog and horse racing in the state.[57] Apparently sensing that both ideas were premature, the majority awaited a series of committee hearings into the corruption charges. The committee, chaired by James Haley of Sarasota, heard Daniel Sullivan air the standard complaints against Governor Warren regarding the Russell muscle, campaign contributions, the racetrack ownership, the Racing Commission's actions, and reinstatement of Jimmy Sullivan. Hostile interrogation from Representative John Bollinger of West Palm Beach, however, made Sullivan's evidence appeared much more circumstantial than it had seemed earlier. The Haley Committee eventually found no hard evidence of "improper conduct" by "any constitutional officer of the state," although it did deplore the atmosphere in which the Racing Commission's decisions were made and noted some instances of illegally concealed track ownership.[58]

By the time the Haley Committee reported in late May 1951, the demand for impeachment had abated. O'Kell's bill—which centered on the familiar charges that Warren had knowingly underreported his campaign funds, failed to push the Racing Commission into enforcing the ownership and campaign contribution laws, disregarded evidence in reinstating suspended sheriffs, and agreed to a division of patronage spoils between his three big contributors—was defeated in the lower house by a 76–6 margin. Given conflicting testimony, the long tradition of lax campaign financing laws, and the well-established liberal policy in law enforcement, the evidence was deemed insufficient to justify impeachment.[59]

The squabble attracted a good deal of national attention, almost all of it unfavorable to Warren. On the basis of two interviews with William H. Johnston and derogatory material from the Crime Commission and the Kefauver Committee, *Collier's* magazine published a scathing criticism of Warren's supposed capitulation to the racing magnate. Senator Kefauver condemned Warren's reinstatement of Sheriff Sullivan in a public interview and in his committee's much heralded *Third Interim Report*. The Tennesseean's series in the *Saturday Evening Post* and his successful book, *Crime in America*, also sketched an unfavorable portrait of Warren.[60]

The hapless governor fought back. In response to the *Collier's* article, Warren issued a series of denials and sued the magazine, eventually winning a token settlement of $2,000, amply offset by court costs. Warren and his staff sent Florida investigators into the home states of members of the Kefauver Committee to seek evidence compromising them. Accepting half-truths from such hack journalists as Jack Lait and Lee Mortimer, the governor hurled a series of distorted questions at Kefauver and his colleagues. He even considered accusing Kefauver of having a "personal predilection" for sexual "perversion." On another occasion, an "informant" obtained a sample of a white powdery substance near Kefauver's Tennessee home; the governor sent it to a state laboratory, where it was found to be table sugar. In an attempt to silence his press critics in Miami and Tampa,

Warren forwarded to the legislature a series of anti-newspaper bills, which prompted further condemnation. By June, such reckless and erratic behavior had cost Warren the support of one of the last two dailies in the state that backed him, the *Tampa Morning Tribune*.[61]

Warren's ordeal continued into the summer of 1951 after Congress extended the life of the Kefauver Committee under a new chairman, Senator Herbert R. O'Conor of Maryland. Acting upon anonymous information, committee investigators developed research implying that Sheriff Jimmy Sullivan and his wife had obtained substantial income during his term that they never reported in tax returns. The revelation threatened to drive the sheriff from office once more and might justify calling Warren to testify under oath about the reinstatement. Sullivan resigned in mid-June. Later he faced serious tax difficulties.[62]

Sullivan's resignation took little of the pressure off Warren. Although the governor provided O'Conor with a detailed explanation of his reinstatement of the sheriff, he insisted that he was not responsible to the Senate or any federal agency for his actions. After O'Conor tried unsuccessfully to lure Warren to the committee as a voluntary witness, the senators (encouraged by the Crime Commission) issued a subpoena for him, the first ever to be served on a state governor by a congressional committee. Warren rejected the subpoena on grounds of states' rights and won important support for doing so from South Carolina Governor James F. Byrnes, a former Supreme Court justice and cabinet member.[63] O'Conor eventually dropped the matter, although he condemned the chief executive in the committee's *Final Report*.[64]

Fuller Warren retired from politics at the end of his term. Destitute upon leaving the governorship, he established a struggling law practice in Miami. He made only infrequent public appearances after a disastrous comeback race for the governorship in 1956. By the time of his death in 1973, most commentators had concluded that his road building program, promotion of the citrus and tourism industries, and financial management as governor had been surprisingly successful. These accomplishments were overshadowed, however, by the furious battles over the liberal policy during his governorship.[65]

The gambling problem that overwhelmed Warren in Florida was of national dimensions. Throughout the country, after the war, illegal gambling mushroomed, placing enormous strains on local regulatory structures and provoking much public discussion. In most states legalization proposals were put forward, but they were almost invariably defeated.

Under these circumstances, many postwar governors found themselves confronted with demands that they, as the states' chief law enforcement officers, attack the gambling problem. Dewey of New York agonized over the precedents he might be setting before dispatching state troopers into the wide-open resort of Saratoga. Describing the gambling question as his major "headache," Illinois's Stevenson grudgingly employed the state police when widespread local tolerance for slot machines threatened him politically. Youngdahl of Minnesota and Goodland of Wisconsin launched programs to revoke licenses for businesses that allowed wagering on their premises, but both men encountered bitter opposition from tourist interests in their states. Perhaps the most successful of the governors, Earl Warren of California, seized the initiative by appointing a state crime commission and deflecting public criticism onto the state attorney general.[66]

Although the pressures on Fuller Warren may have been intensified by the state's dire budgetary situation, his difficulties with gambling were similar in many respects to those faced by other governors. Throughout the state, but especially in the south, illegal gambling operations were outstripping the regulatory capacity of the informal local machinery, and outside gangsters jockeyed for influence. In the chaos, proposals for further legalization were raised, only to be beaten back both at local and state levels. Although he did not attempt to use state troopers, Warren's movements away from Florida's liberal policy were similar to the responses of Stevenson or Youngdahl.

In Florida, however, the deeply rooted decentralization of gambling and law enforcement complicated the governor's problems. Warren's threat to suspend uncooperative sheriffs, his order to revoke business licenses for operations permitting illegal gambling, and his appointment of special investigators engulfed his office in the endless cynicism, jealousies, and recriminations endemic to the localized gambling culture. By threatening suspensions of sheriffs, and then retreating from his threats, Warren became entangled in local power struggles he could neither understand nor control. More important, the naming of special state investigators almost immediately led to rumors of "fixes" involving the administration. Such stories ultimately linked Johnston to the Russell muscle, and Warren to a Capone syndicate through Johnston's campaign contribution.

The gambling and law enforcement dilemmas confronting Warren reflected the atomized political situation in Florida. Warren, like most of his predecessors, had no trusted network of contacts or confidants among local political organizations in the state. His startling lapses, such as his ignorance of the problems in Miami and his appointment of Enzor's son-in-law as sheriff in Okaloosa County, reveal the absence of ties to local sources that could provide reliable political and law enforcement intelligence. Given the inadequacy of institutional political structures in the state, sheriffs long accustomed to going their own ways largely ignored Warren's orders. Warren's combative nature, his administrative inadequacies, his tolerance for a contentious and ineffectual staff, and his aversion to alienating old friends like Johnston (after the Griffin case) only compounded his difficulties.

Despite rumors implicating Warren in wrongdoing, the evidence suggests his innocence. His naming of special investigators and his suspensions of sheriffs constituted honest, if clumsy, attempts to protect state revenues. Once he had moved from the liberal policy toward intervention in 1949, his name and office were dragged into hundreds of local power struggles involving gambling and law enforcement officials. Even in his isolation, Warren must have realized that this was happening. In the near anarchy of the situation in Florida, however, there was little he could do except posture, attack his critics, and retreat to the liberal policy by insisting on local indictments before suspensions. He might have pressed the investigation of Johnston's racetracks, but he could not completely trust the Racing Commission; and such an inquiry might have disrupted the whole racing industry, so important to state revenues. Moreover, the Kefauver Committee of the U.S. Senate, which explored the problem, established no clearcut proof that Johnston was a Capone front. The best evidence of Warren's innocence is his relative poverty on leaving office and setting up his law practice in Miami. He probably knew his office was being used but felt he could do little about it, and he appears not to have benefited financially from the situation.[67]

Warren also faced in the Crime Commission of Greater Miami a lobby far more tenacious and resourceful than confronted any other governor on the gambling issue. In alienating the Crime Commission on the Sullivan suspension and the Johnston racetrack investigation, he brought upon himself the wrath of newspapers and civic organizations throughout the state. The Miami anti-crime forces even enlisted the Kefauver Committee of the U.S. Senate. More than elsewhere, the Senate committee immersed itself in Florida politics, rehashing the Commission's case against the governor and lending it a credibility, circulation, and force it would not otherwise have had. The quarrel between the governor and his critics focused public opinion on Warren and blurred the essentially historical nature of the problems he faced. For although such skillful politicians as Adlai Stevenson and Earl Warren received more favorable attention, none of the postwar governors were notably successful in combatting illegal gambling, which continued to cause intermittent problems in many states and localities.

Notes

The author is working on a study of public attitudes and policy toward gambling in the United States since 1931. He acknowledges research funding for this project from the University of Wyoming Basic Research Grants Program and the National Endowment for the Humanities.

1. *See* especially Mark H. Haller, "Organized Crime in Urban Society: Chicago in the Twentieth Century," *Journal of Social History* (Winter 1971–72), 210–234, and Haller's "Bootleggers and American Gambling, 1920–1950," in Commission on the Review of the National Policy Toward Gambling, *Gambling in America* (Washington: Government Printing Office, 1976), Appendix 1, 102–143.

2. William Howard Moore, *The Kefauver Committee and the Politics of Crime, 1950–52* (Columbia: University of Missouri Press, 1974), [in order of text citation] 196–199, 154–155, 59; Virgil W. Peterson, *Barbarians in Our Midst: A History of Chicago Crime and Politics* (Boston: Little, Brown, 1952), *passim.*

3. Rufus Jarman, "The Governor and the Gamblers," *Saturday Evening Post,* Dec. 13, 1947, 22, 23, 56, 62; "Wisconsin Badlands," *Newsweek* (Jul. 30, 1945), 22; Earl Warren, *Memoirs of Earl Warren* (Garden City: Doubleday, 1977), 198–200; John Bartlow Martin, *Adlai Stevenson of Illinois* (Garden City: Doubleday, 1976), 442–445; Moore, *Kefauver Committee,* 107, 193.

4. David Colburn and Richard K. Scher, "Florida Gubernatorial Politics: The Fuller Warren Years," *Florida Historical Quarterly* (April 1975), 390–391, 408; Miami *Herald,* May 23, 1948; Miami *News,* Sept. 24, 1973; Fuller Warren, *Speaking of Speaking: Articles, Addresses and Other Strident Stuff* (St. Augustine: Record, 1944), 26, 56, 86–88.

5. Miami *Herald,* May 23, 1948; Fuller Warren and Allen Morris, *How to Win in Politics* (Tallahassee: Peninsular, 1949), 26.

6. *Ibid.,* 26, 52; Miami *Herald,* May 23, 30, 1948; Warren and Morris, *How to Win,* 57–61; Miami *Daily News,* May 1, 1948.

7. V. O. Key, Jr., *Southern Politics in State and Nation* (New York: Knopf, 1950), 95, 96 and *passim*; Tampa *Tribune,* May 30, 1948; Miami *Daily News,* May 16, 18, 1948; Colburn and Scher, "Florida Gubernatorial Politics," 393. Senator Pepper sat enthralled by Warren's inaugural address, delivered entirely from memory. Pepper to Warren, Feb. 28, 1949, General Correspondence Carton 19, Claude Pepper Papers, Federal Records Center, Suitland, Maryland.

8. Colburn and Scher, "Florida Gubernatorial Politics," 398–402; Miami *News,* Sept. 24, 1973.

9. Theodore Pratt, *That Was Palm Beach* (St. Petersburg: Great Outdoors, 1968), 39–56; "Final Presentment of the 1950 Fall Term Grand Jury for Hillsborough County, Florida" (filed March 30, 1951), copy in Box 127, Files of Special Committee to Investigate Organized Crime in Interstate Commerce (Kefauver Committee), RG 46, National Archives, Washington, D.C. (hereafter KCF); Miami *Herald,* August 14, 1966; Tallahassee *Democrat,* Dec. 4, 1965. So plentiful was gambling money, the Tampa grand jury concluded, that it was virtually impossible for a local politician to avoid its presence in his campaign. "Respectable and good citizens" might well be involved in the local *bolita* business.

10. Nixon Smiley, *Knights of the Fourth Estate: The Story of the Miami Herald* (Miami: Seeman, 1974), 15, 87; Virgil W. Peterson, "The Myth of the Wide-Open Town," *Journal of Criminal Law and Criminology* (September-October, 1948), 288–292; O. D. Henderson, Jr., to Senator Herbert O'Conor, June 5, 1951, Box 157, KCF. In 1928, even nativistic former Governor Sidney Catts had advocated legalizing gambling as a means of encouraging tourism in the south. Wayne Flynt, *Cracker Messiah: Governor Sidney Catts of Florida* (Baton Rouge: Louisiana State University Press, 1977), 317–330.

11. Daniel P. Sullivan testimony, *Hearing before [State] Committee on Crime Investigation in Tallahassee, April 25, 1951*, 15 (copy in Folder U-10, Fuller Warren Papers, Florida State University Library, Tallahassee [hereafter FWP]); Paul E. Jeans, *Tropical Disturbance: The Making of the Miami Tribune* (Miami: Miami *Tribune*, 1937), 3, 25, 48; James M. Cox, *Journey Through My Years* (New York: Simon & Schuster, 1946), 315–316, 323; Pat Frank and Luther Voltz, "Florida's Struggle with the Hoodlums," *Collier's* (March 25, 1950), 21; Ralph W. Mills, internal memo on "Chronological Factors Leading to Issuance of Subpoena of Fuller Warren," July 4, 1951, Box 200, KCF.

12. Key, *Southern Politics*, 478–79 n18, 171–72 n29, 202, 82; Typescript of radio speech by Fuller Warren, Feb. 28, 1950, File U-1, FWP; Miami *Herald*, May 27, 1948; Millard Caldwell to Rev. Donald Douds, Feb. 6, 1947, copy in File U-1, FWP; Warren, *How to Win*, 139. Unlike the governors of New York and Ohio, the Florida chief executive had no powers to suspend municipal law enforcement officials. Fort Myers *News Press*, July 14, 1950.

13. Frank and Voltz, "Florida's Struggle with the Hoodlums," 72–73, 78, 81; Undated typescript of news story by Ted Link, Box 115, and "Memo to Mr. Crowley," Dec., 1949, Box 42, KCF; Miami *Daily News*, Jan. 25, 1950. In 1949 an attempt by New York bookmaker Frank Erickson to establish himself at a hotel in Miami Beach at the expense of S. & G. was squelched by the Miami Beach vice squad. *Third Interim Report of the Special Committee to Investigate Organized Crime in Interstate Commerce*, Senate Report No. 307, 81st Cong., 1st sess., 32–33.

14. Ted Link, "Working Memorandum of Florida Gambling Situation," Dec. 22, 1949, Box 96, KCF; Miami *Herald*, March 9, 12, 13, 1947; Miami *Daily News*, May 7, 8, 9, 12, 1948; Memorandum, Ted Link to Estes Kefauver, Rudolph Halley, and Joseph Nellis, Jan. 17, 1951, Box 146, Memorandum on Plans for Florida Hearings, June 27, 1950, Box 37, KCF.

15. *Tampa Morning Tribune*, May 11, 12, June 5, 1948; Pat Frank and Luther Voltz, "Gamblers' Siege," *Collier's* (April 1, 1950), 72; Miami *Herald*, May 8, 14, 16, 1948; Miami *Daily News*, May 12, 1948.

16. Miami *Herald*, July 18, 1948; Miami *Daily News*, Jan. 6, 1952; Interview with Daniel P. Sullivan, Miami, Aug. 14, 1974; Smiley, *Knights of the Fourth Estate*, 237, 241–244; Daniel L. O'Connor to Matthew J. Connelly, Feb. 4, 1948, Connelly to O'Connor, Feb. 18, 1948, Harry S. Truman Papers, OF 532, File #117, Truman Library, Independence, Missouri; Daniel P. Sullivan to James M. Cox, Aug. 23, 1949, "WMIE Radio Station" File, Records of the Crime Commission of Greater Miami (hereafter CCGMR). John Clark, president of Hialeah Racetrack, once had been frightened and physically upset

by a request that he arrange for Al Capone to win a horserace bet. He was concerned about the harmful impact of off-track betting on track profit and state revenue. Smiley, *Knights of the Fourth Estate*, 237. Knight, who in 1945 proclaimed himself "the best crapshooter in the world," had undergone a change of heart on the gambling issue. While he saw no personal harm in gambling for himself, he had become convinced that it had a deleterious social impact on the community. In the new consumer-oriented, middle-class society of the postwar era, his views were a throwback to an earlier period. Jack Alexander, "Up From Akron," *Saturday Evening Post*, Aug. 18, 1945, 10–11, 39, 41, 43, 44; Smiley, *Knights of the Fourth Estate*, 240–241; Daniel Bell, *The End of Ideology: On the Exhaustion of Political Ideas in the Fifties* (New York: Free Press, 1962), 130, 133.

17. Moore, *Kefauver Committee*, 43. On at least three questions—domestic communists, civil rights, and organized crime—the Truman administration sought to diffuse public concern with rhetoric, only to be forced by events into stronger stands. The circumstances in south Florida suggest that the administration may have been following the same pattern there. On the Truman administration, *see* Richard S. Kirkendall, *The Truman Period as a Research Field: A Reappraisal, 1972* (Columbia: University of Missouri Press, 1974).

18. *Report of Conclusions and Recommendations of Committee...*, *appointed to make a Survey of Law Enforcement in Dade County* (Miami, March 12, 1947); Miami *Herald*, March 16, 17, 30, 1948; Form letter to civic organizations from president of Dade County Bar Association, March 6, G. Ralph Kiel to Peterson, June 14, Peterson to Kiel, June 21, 1948, File 1-7, CCGMR; Sullivan interview; Peterson, "Myth of the Wide-Open Town;" Miami *Herald*, July 1, 23, 30, 1948. On Peterson and the anti-legalization campaign, see Moore, *Kefauver Committee*, 35–41.

19. Melbourne L. Martin to Frank S. Wright, n.d., "Governor Fuller Warren, 1948–1950" File, CCGMR; Miami *Herald*, March 16, 1947, July 23, 1948. The composition and orientation of the Crime Commission of Greater Miami was similar to those of municipal reform groups in many cities during the progressive period and the 1920s. Less effective citizens' crime commissions arose in Kansas City, St. Louis, Philadelphia, New York, Dallas, and Gary, Indiana, during the post-World War II gambling scare. A fuller analysis of the crime commission movement will be developed in my study of public attitudes and policies toward gambling. *See* Samuel P. Hays, "The Politics of Reform in Municipal Government in the Progressive Era," *Pacific Northwest Quarterly* (October 1964), 157–69, and Mark H. Haller, "Civic Reformers and Police Leadership: Chicago, 1905–1935," in *Police in Urban Society*, ed. Harlan Hahn (Beverly Hills: Sage, 1971), 39–56.

20. Miami *Herald*, May 8, July 18, 1948, Jan. 6, 1952. Sullivan's fellow investigator and the city manager, Richard Danner, were also former FBI agents.

21. *Final Report of the Grand Jury* to Circuit Court of Eleventh Judicial Circuit, Nov. 9, 1949, copy in Box 105, KCF; Miami *Daily News*, May 2, 3, 1948; Miami *Herald*, May 22, 1948.

22. Untitled, undated typescript of news article by Ted Link, Box 119, KCF; Miami *Herald*, May 22, 1948.

23. William A. Lane to Jimmy Sullivan, Feb. 17, 1949, "Governor Warren, 1948–1950" File, CCGMR; Jimmy Sullivan to Estes Kefauver, July 6, 1950,

Box 190, Richard H. Hunt to Rudolph Halley, Aug. 7, 1950, Box 198, KCF; Frank and Voltz, "Gamblers' Siege," 72.

24. Unidentified newspaper clipping on slot machine ban and congratulatory letters to Warren in File U-5, "Statement of Fuller Warren" on Tampa *bolita* problem, Feb. 21, 1949, File U-1, FWP; Attorney General Richard Ervin testimony, *Hearings before Special Committee to Investigate Organized Crime in Interstate Commerce*, 81st Cong., 2nd sess., Pt. 1-A, 181–182 (hereafter Crime *Hearings*); Henry S. Bayard to Herbert O'Conor, June 25, 1951, C. L. Alford to O'Conor, June 30, 1951, copies in File U-1, FWP. Although they endorsed Warren's opponent in 1948, neither major Miami daily appeared disturbed by his election. They were far more hostile to Sheriff Sullivan. Miami *Daily News*, May 10, 1948; Miami *Herald*, May 27, 1948. Charges of bribery over the bookmakers' wire service bill had rocked the state legislature in both 1947 and 1949. Frank and Voltz, "Florida's Struggle with the Hoodlums," 81.

25. Colburn and Scher, "Florida Gubernatorial Politics," 398–99; Florida *Times Union,* Aug. 25, 1949; Miami *Herald*, July 6, 1949; Okaloosa *News*, Aug. 26, 1949; "Florida: Bookies vs. Budget," *Newsweek*, March 7, 1949, 24–25; Typescript of "Statement of Fuller Warren," Feb. 18, 1949, File U-1, FWP.

26. W. O. Crosby to Warren, December 13, 1949, File U-6, FWP; Tampa *Tribune*, July 15, 17, 22, 1949; Miami *Daily News*, July 17, 1949; Daniel P. Sullivan to Herbert O'Conor, July 11, 1951, Box 123 KCF. The federal government had imposed an excise tax on slot machines in 1941. Payment of the tax did not confer a legal right to operate, but it did contribute to popular confusion over the legality of the machines. Rufus King, *Gambling and Organized Crime* (Washington: Public Affairs, 1969), 87; Moore, *Kefauver Committee*, 233. In Jacksonville in early 1949 bookies openly advertised in the weekly newspapers. Frank and Voltz, "Gamblers' Siege," 73.

27. Warren to Rudolph Halley, Aug. 8, 1950, Crime *Hearings*, Pt. 1, 798–800; Memorandum re William H. Johnston by Daniel P. Sullivan, June 20, 1950, Box 123, KCF; Tampa *Morning Tribune*, April 24, 1951. For information on the use of the governor's name by acquaintances, see the classic statement of George Patton, Nov. 11, 1950, in Crime *Hearings*, Pt. 1A, 459–481, especially 475–476. Privately, from the outset Warren seems to have made his threats to suspend sheriffs with some cynicism. He supposedly told Senator Pepper that he had heard reports that political enemies of Hillsborough Sheriff Hugh Culbreath were out to get Culbreath removed, but that he would take no action on the sheriff, a Pepper friend, without first consulting the senator. Pepper to Culbreath, May 12, 1949, General Correspondence Box 3, Pepper Papers.

28. Miami *Herald*, Feb. 21, 1949; William A. Lane to Warren, Feb. 19, 1949, Dec. 30, 1948; Melbourne L. Martin to Frank S. Wright, n.d., "Governor Warren, 1948–1950" File, CCGMR; Tampa *Morning Tribune*, April 24, 1951; Daniel P. Sullivan to Herbert O'Conor, July 11, 1951, Box 123, KCP.

29. *Interim Report of Investigation in Florida and Preliminary General Conclusions*, Senate Report No. 2370, 81st Cong., 2nd sess. (1950), 12–13; W. O. Crosby testimony, Crime *Hearings*, Pt. 1, 380; Memorandum to Files re S. & G. syndicate from Downey Rice, June 26, 1950, Box 21, KCF.

30. Moore, *Kefauver Committee*, 18–19, 27–28, 93–96; New York *Enquirer*,

Jan. 24, 1949; New Orleans *States*, March 17, 1949; Memorandum to Files re S. & G. syndicate from Downey Rice, June 26, 1950, Box 21, KCF. S. & G. was licensed by the city of Miami Beach as "investment brokers." It had at least seven offices scattered through twenty blocks of the city. One member of the syndicate closely monitored "hot horses" (horses that might win at high odds) on tracks from around the country. On the basis of information on such horses, obtained through the wire service, the syndicate would adjust its odds to minimize its losses. Undated typescript "History of S. & G. Down to 1948," Box 115, *ibid.*

31.   Moore, *Kefauver Committee*, 94–95; Edward Rosenbaum testimony, Crime *Hearings*, Pt. 1, 565, 594; and Joseph Friedlander testimony, *ibid.*, Pt. 1A, 329–331, 336.

32.   Miami *Herald*, Dec. 29, 1950; Typescript for radio program by Daniel P. Sullivan, March 18, 1950, in Crime Box 3, Estes Kefauver Papers, University of Tennessee Library, Knoxville (hereafter EKP); Ben Cohen testimony, Crime *Hearings*, Pt. 1, 514–15; *Third Interim Report*, 33; Lester Velie, "Secret Mr. Big of Florida," *Collier's*, May 5, 1951, 70. The Kefauver Committee believed that Russell was a front for Tony Accardo and Jack Guzik, Chicago underworld figures, whose 1949 partnership tax returns showed a business loss attributed to S. & G. operations. *Third Interim Report*, 34.

33.   Miami *Herald*, Jan. 16, 1950; William H. Johnston testimony, Crime *Hearings*, Pt. 1, 600–609, 616–655; Memorandum to Files re Johnny Patton from Downey Rice, July 5, 1950, Box 21, Memorandum to Files re William H. Johnston, Aug. 5, 1950, Box 22, KCF.

34.   St. Petersburg *Times*, March 1, 1951; Telegram, Warren to C. V. Griffin, Nov. 2, 1948, copy to Johnston, File U-2, FWP; Velie, "Secret Mr. Big," 68; Johnston testimony, Crime *Hearings*, Pt. 1, 651, 648, 645. When Fuller Warren was married in California in the summer of 1949, Johnston hosted a reception for him. Although invited, Governor Earl Warren was steered away from the event by subordinates knowledgeable about Johnston's background. H. G. Robinson to John H. Hanson, July 25, 1950, Box 21, KCF.

35.   Johnston testimony, Crime *Hearings*, pt. 1, 642–648; "Memo to Mr. Crowley," Dec. 1949, "Governor Warren, 1948–1950" File, CCGMR; Miami *Herald*, Feb. 16, 1950; Johnston to Rudolph Halley, Aug. 10, 1950, Box 198, KCF.

36.   Ben Cohen and John Rush testimony, Crime *Hearings*, Pt. 1, 520–524, 388–390; Memorandum, Downey Rice to H. G. Robinson, June 20, 1950, Box 21, undated typescript on Albert Hubbard, Craig's attorney, Box 119, memorandum re William H. Johnston, June 20, 1950, Box 123, KCF. Craig resented S. & G. as outsiders in Dade County gambling. Craig and S. & G. sought assurances from one another that their separate spheres, Miami and Miami Beach, would not be violated in the event off-track bookmaking was legalized. Cohen testimony, Crime *Hearings*, Pt. 1, 522.

37.   Warren to Rudolph Halley, Aug. 8, 1950, Crime *Hearings*, Pt. 1, 798–800; Orlando *Sentinel*, Feb. 5, 1950; Colburn and Scher, "Florida Gubernatorial Politics," 394–398; Tampa *Morning Tribune*, Feb. 16, 1950; Miami *Herald*, Feb. 19, 1950; St. Petersburg *Times*, Sept. 27, 1973.

38. Miami *Herald*, Feb. 17, 18, 1950; Memorandum for Files re Wolfson-Griffin-Johnston contribution to Gov. Warren, June 2, 1950, Box 21, KCF; Testimony of Griffin, Johnston, and Wolfson, Crime *Hearings*, Pt. 1, 355, 597, 646–47, 653, 339–341. Wolfson had been best man at the governor's wedding. In 1949 he acquired Capitol Transit in Washington, D.C., and began to arouse the intense suspicion that would dog his career. Although not involved in racing in 1949, he bought into the industry in 1958. He later served a prison term for selling unregulated stock and was involved in a complex financial affair that culminated in the resignation of U.S. Supreme Court Justice Abe Fortas. Miami *Herald*, Feb. 16, 1950; "Nice, Quiet Life," *Time*, May 29, 1978, 60–62.

39. Griffin and Wolfson testimony, Crime *Hearings*, Pt. 1, 362, 341, 357–58; Colburn and Scher, "Florida Gubernatorial Politics," 396–397; Warren to Halley, Aug. 8, 1950, Crime *Hearings*, Pt. 1, 799; Chicago *News*, Feb. 18, 1950; Statement of Griffin, Griffin to Warren, transcript of Warren press conference, all dated Feb. 15, 1950, File U-3, FWP.

40. Chicago *Daily News*, Feb. 18, 1950; St. Petersburg *Times*, Feb. 21, 1950; Tampa *Morning Tribune*, April 30, 1950; Velie, "Secret Mr. Big," 68; Warren, *How to Win*, 156–159.

41. There were other contributions to Warren's campaign; the total may well have exceeded $600,000. Donations from local and county organizations apparently were frequently disbursed without the knowledge of either the state headquarters or the candidate. Some contributors (such as Raymond Craig) were involved in illegal gambling operations. Although no hard evidence shows that Warren knew of these gambling donations, he did know that "a wealthy Jacksonville businessman," almost certainly Johnston or Wolfson, had made a "substantial" contribution to the 1948 campaign. Senator Pepper (possibly anticipating his own 1950 reelection bid) expressed an interest in Johnston in late 1948. "Memo to Mr. Crowley," Dec. 1949, "Governor Warren, 1948–1950" File, CCGMR; Typescript of interview with Ralph Mills in Miami *Herald*, March 6, 1951, File U-1, FWP; Warren, *How to Win*, 159, 161; Telegram, Pepper to Frank Wright, Dec. 16, 1948, File Z-5, FWP. *Collier's* estimated that each of the four or five major candidates for the Democratic nomination in 1948 spent at least $500,000. Frank and Voltz, "Gamblers Siege," 72.

42. Chicago *News*, Feb. 18, 1950; Florida *Times Union*, Feb. 15, 1950; Memorandum re Wolfson-Griffin-Johnston contributions to Warren, June 2, 1950, Box 21, KCF; Griffin testimony, Crime *Hearings*, Pt. 1, 353–366.

43. Griffin to Warren, March 2, 1950, File U-3, FWP; St. Petersburg *Times*, Feb. 21, 1950; Telegram, Griffin to Truman, Feb. 16, 1950, OF 532, Truman Papers.

44. Griffin testimony, Crime *Hearings*, Pt. 1, 353–366; Telegram, Jack Younger to Griffin, Feb. 15, 1950, "Governor Warren, 1948–1950" File, CCGMR; [Miami Beach] *Morning Mail*, Feb. 15, 1950; Undated handwritten notes on Florida gambling by Ted Link, Box 96, KCF; Miami *Daily News*, Jan. 6, 1952; Tampa *Morning Tribune*, April 26, 1951; Miami *Daily News*, March 3, 5–10, 12, 13, 1950. On Drury, *see* Moore, *Kefauver Committee*, 151–152.

45. Telegrams, Younger to Truman, Feb. 16, April 10, 1950, "Governor Warren,

1948–1950" File, Younger to deLesseps S. Morrison, Sept. 28, 1949, "Chicago Crime Commission" File, CCGMR; Miami *Daily News*, March 14, 15, 1950; Kefauver to James M. Cox, Jan. 26, 1950, Daniel Sullivan to Kefauver, Feb. 28, 1950, Crime Box 2, EKP. On the pressure for a national investigation, *see* Moore, *Kefauver Committee*, 25–73.

46.   St. Petersburg *Times*, Feb. 20, 1950; Ralph W. Mills, internal memo on "Chronological Factors Leading to Issuance of Subpoena of Fuller Warren," July 4, 1951, Box 200, KCF; Telegrams, Warren to Younger, Feb. 10, 1950, Younger to Warren, Feb. 15, 1950, "Governor Warren, 1948–1950" File, CCGMR.

47.   St. Petersburg *Times*, Feb. 19, 20, 1950; Miami *Herald*, Feb. 19, 1950; Typescript "Proceedings of Conference between Governor Fuller Warren and Members of the Crime Commission of Greater Miami," Miami, Feb. 20, 1950, in File U-6, FWP. At the conference, the president of the Crime Commission told Warren that he had heard rumors that the governor himself was involved in the rackets. Warren dismissed the stories by claiming that there were also widespread allegations that the Crime Commission was being financed by one group of gangsters hoping to establish their control over the area. Such stories were in fact common. Miami *Herald*, Feb. 19, 1950; Tampa *Morning Tribune*, Feb. 26, 1950.

48.   Miami *Herald*, Feb. 26, 1950; Memorandum re Governor Warren, March 2, 1950, "Governor Warren, 1948–1950" File, CCGMR; Typescript "Statement of Fuller Warren," March 1, 1951, copy of Warren letter to sixty-seven sheriffs, Feb. 22, 1950, File U-1, FWP; Miami *Herald*, Feb. 23, 1950.

49.   Tampa *Times*, March 1, 1950; St. Petersburg *Times*, March 13, 1950; Unlabeled news clipping dated June 18, 1950, File U-8, FWP. Characteristically, Warren's office gave out conflicting signals after the February 28 radio address. A columnist in the Tallahassee *Democrat* noted that the governor had only said that he would suspend an official who had been indicted. He had not ruled out suspension *prior to* an indictment. The governor's staff clipped the article, circled in red the columnist's observation, and mailed it out to other newspapers without comment. St. Petersburg *Times*, March 13, 1950.

50.   Bradenton *Herald*, March 2, 1950; Rozella Dillard to Warren, March 16, 1950, Warren to Younger, Aug. 31, 1950, "Governor Warren, 1948–1950" File, CCGMR; Tampa *Morning Tribune*, June 6, 1950; Pensacola *News*, June 18, 1950; Tampa *Morning Tribune*, Feb. 2, 4–6, 1950. One minister claimed that he had been offered a $1,000 bribe if he would not condemn gambling during his regular radio gospel hour. *Ibid.*

51.   Tampa *Morning Tribune*, June 13, 1950; Orlando *Star*, June 8, 1950. By mid-1950 Warren became tenacious in his demands that individuals report gambling to local officials before coming to him. He upbraided a south Florida Bible class for appealing to him before complaining to the local sheriff. To underscore his point, the governor even offered small rewards for citizens swearing out warrants against persons violating gambling laws. Warren to A. D. Attom, n.d., File U-6 and "Statement of Fuller Warren," June 12, 1950, File U-1, FWP.

52.   St. Petersburg *Independent*, Aug. 5, 1950; Tallahassee *Democrat*, March 9, 1951; Tampa *Morning Tribune*, April 12, 1951, Nov. 23, 1950; Miami

Herald, Nov. 23, 1950.

53. Younger to Warren, March 22, 1950, Warren to Younger, May 24, 1950, Younger to Leo Edwards, Florida State Racing Commission, July 18, 1950, "Governor Warren, 1948–1950" File, CCGMR; Miami *Daily News*, Oct. 24, 1950; Sullivan to Kefauver, Aug. 24, Oct. 24, 1950, Box 200, KCF.

54. Memorandum re Identity of KM-1 from Downey Rice to H. G. Robinson, June 20, 1950, Box 21, Daniel Sullivan to Kefauver, Aug. 24 and Oct. 24, 1950, Ralph W. Mills, internal memo on "Chronological Factors Leading to Issuance of Subpoena of Fuller Warren," July 4, 1951, Box 200, Sullivan to Halley, Sept. 23, 1950, Box 37, KCF. Daniel Sullivan thought that, by 1950, former associates of Al Capone were operating individually in liquor businesses, night clubs, and hotel operations, but that at Sportsman's Park and the four Johnston racetracks in Florida they continued to operate as a syndicate. Sullivan to Kefauver, Oct. 24, 1950, Box 200, *ibid.*

55. Florida *Times Union*, March 20, 1951; Roy Patience to Loyal Compton, March 20, 1951, telegrams, Leo Edwards to Hoke Welch, March 18, 1951, and Patience to Welch, March 18, 1951, File U-18, FWP; Tampa *Morning Tribune*, March 22, 1951; Telegrams, Younger to Warren, March 21, 1951, Younger to Herbert O'Conor, June 25, 1951, "Governor Fuller Warren, 1951–1952" File, CCGMR; Downey Rice to Daniel Sullivan, June 20, 1950, Box 21, KCF. Preoccupied with the intrusion of out-of-state gangsters into the local gambling market, the Commission had indeed paid less attention to Craig. One informant to Warren reported that when queried about the relative neglect of Craig, Daniel Sullivan laughed off the question with the explanation, "[a] native." James J. A. Swain to Warren, March 25, 1951, File U-18, FWP.

56. Tampa *Morning Tribune*, April 10, 11, 1951. For earlier discussion of possible impeachment, *see* Roy Pennington to Dante Fascell, Aug. 22, 1950, "Governor Warren, 1948–1950" File, CCGMR. For hostile press reaction, *see* the excellent scrapbook #41 in FWP.

57. Tampa *Morning Tribune*, April 11, 21–23, 25, 1951. The Tampa Ministerial Association swung behind the new crime commission and asked area legislators to prevent the reinstatement of Sheriff Hugh Culbreath. The *Morning Tribune* endorsed the Cramer proposal. There had been a crazy-quilt pattern of groups advocating both further legalization and total repeal throughout the state in 1950. *Ibid.*, April 22, 23, 25, 1951; Florida *Times Union*, Feb. 10, 1950; Miami *Herald*, Oct. 25, 1950.

58. Tampa *Morning Tribune*, April 14, 24–26, 1951; *Hearing before [State] Committee on Crime Investigation in Tallahassee, April 25, 1951*, File U-10, FWP. The members of the Haley Committee were viewed as neither friends nor enemies of Warren. No clear pattern of membership support or opposition emerged within the legislature on the impeachment question. Tampa *Morning Tribune*, April 14, 1951.

59. Tampa *Morning Tribune*, May 26, 29, 1951. The legislature rejected Warren's reappointment of the five incumbent members of the Racing Commission and he was forced to name a new slate. The governor signed several pieces of anti-gambling legislation, but vetoed a bill proposed by the state attorney general, a political foe. New York *Times*, June 1, 2, 12, 1951.

60. "Storm over Miami," *Newsweek*, April 23, 1951, 41; Florida *Times Union*,

April 27, 1951; Velie, "Secret Mr. Big," 13, 68–71; Tampa *Morning Tribune*, April 11, 1951; *Third Interim Report*, 36; Estes Kefauver, "What I found Out about the Miami Mob," *Saturday Evening Post*, April 14, 1951, 24–25, 113–114, 116–118; Kefauver, *Crime in America* (Garden City: Doubleday, 1951), 60–73.

61. Florida *Times Union*, April 27, 1951; Miami *Herald*, Aug. 11, 1953; Photostatic copy of $2,000 check, File KK-26, and typescript of Warren press statement, May 2, 1951, File U-1, FWP; Miami *Sunday News*, Aug. 17, 1951; Various materials in Files U-21, U-23, U-27, FWP; *Crime and Law Enforcement in the District of Columbia*, House Report 324, 81st Cong., 2nd sess. (1951), 30–32; "Reporter Feud Tied to Florida Anti-Press War," *Editor & Publisher*, June 2, 1951, 10; Tampa *Morning Tribune*, May 5, 1951, and cartoons, April 11, 15, 26, 1951. Not knowing what to make of Warren's blasts at him, Kefauver asked the governor's friend, former Senator Pepper, for his confidential assessment of Warren's "frame of mind." Kefauver to Pepper, May 16, 1951, Crime Box 5, EKP.

62. Moore, *Kefauver Committee*, 210, 215–219; Memorandum, Downey Rice to Richard Moser, May 21, 1951, Box 24, KCP; Jimmy Sullivan to Fuller Warren, June 15, 1951, File U-19, FWP; New York *Times*, July 17, 1951. Sullivan died in 1969, still asserting that he was innocent. Smiley, *Knights of the Fourth Estate*, 248.

63. Miami *Daily News*, June 17, 1951; Telegrams, O'Conor to Warren, June 14, C. L. Clark to O'Conor, June 14, Loyal Compton to O'Conor, June 15, O'Conor to Warren, June 16, 1951, File U-1, FWP; Younger to Senators O'Conor, Kefauver, Hunt, Wiley, and Tobey, June 19, 1951, "Governor Warren, 1951–1952" File, CCGMR; *New York Times*, June 22, 24, 27, July 15, 1951.

64. Florida *Times Union*, June 27, 1951; *New York Times*, July 3, 20, 1951; Warren to O'Conor, June 16, 1951, Box 123, KCF; *Final Report of the Special Committee to Investigate Organized Crime in Interstate Commerce*, Senate Report No. 725, 82nd Cong., 1st sess., 76; *New York Times*, Sept. 2, 1951. The governor and his last important newspaper backer, the Fort Myers *News-Press*, argued that Warren's two predecessors, Spessard Holland and Milard Caldwell, had been as passive as Warren toward the "liberal policy" and that the volume of illegal gambling had actually declined since 1949. Paul (?) to Loyal Compton, Aug. 11, 1950, File Z-7, FWP; Ft. Myers *News-Press*, July 29, Aug. 21, 1950.

65. Miami *Herald*, Sept. 25, 1973; Miami *News*, Sept. 24, 1973; St. Petersburg *Times*, Sept. 25, 1973. The involvement of the big three in Warren's 1948 race led to the state "Who-Gave-It-Who-Got-It" campaign contribution law. Tampa *Tribune*, Sept. 23, 1973; Jack Bass and Walter De Vries, *The Transformation of Southern Politics: Social Change and Political Consequences Since 1945* (New York: New American Library, 1977), 113–115.

66. Moore, *Kefauver Committee*, 193–194; Stevenson speech, January 2, 1950, in *The Papers of Adlai E. Stevenson*, ed., Walter Johnson (Boston: Little, Brown, 1973) III, 213; Jarman, "Governor and Gamblers," 22, 23, 56, 62; "Wisconsin Badlands," 22; Warren, *Memoirs*, 198–200.

67. Miami *News*, Sept. 24, 1973; Miami *Herald*, Sept. 24, 1973. One rumor suggested that compromising photographs had been taken of Warren by

Chicago underworld figures and that these had been used to influence the governor's actions. These stories circulated in the atmosphere of bragging and posturing among rival gambling factions in Dade County. Similar stories about Senator Kefauver's 1950 Chicago crime hearings suddenly surfaced in the mid-1970s and were almost certainly groundless. Statement of George Patton, Nov. 11, 1950, Crime *Hearings*, Pt. 1A, 478. On the Kefauver story *see* William Howard Moore "Was Estes Kefauver 'Blackmailed' During the Chicago Crime Hearings? A Historian's Perspective," *The Public Historian* (Winter 1982), 5 – 28.

"An Oscar Wilde Type": "The Abominable Crime of Buggery" in Western Canada, 1890–1920

Terry L. Chapman
University of Lethbridge
Lethbridge, Alberta

To mention sex in the context of Canadian history produces a variety of responses ranging from snickers, to queries about its historical relevance, to gossipy tidbits about some prominent or not-so-prominent person's sex life. Historians generally assume that sexual matters:

> . . .exist in a water-tight compartment, almost independently of historical trends as a whole, and that it would no more throw light on the general problem of interpreting history to open this compartment than it would to study the development of, say, cooking.[1]

Such responses are unfortunate because historians are neglecting a subject which has been regarded as "the central problem" and "root of life."[2] The only sexual encounter which seems to warrant any discussion by historians is the highly visible and greatly publicized problem of prostitution in late nineteenth- and early twentieth-century Canada.[3] Although the study of prostitution enables the historian to gain some insights into attitudes towards acceptable and unacceptable sexual behaviour during a specific period of time, it does not provide a complete picture.

A few attempts have been made to place sexual matters in historical context. In 1970, Michael Bliss used the "Self and Sex" manuals advertised by the Methodist Church publishing house to form the basis for an examination of sexual ideas in Canada prior to Sigmund Freud. Six years later, Ruth Olson surveyed two Kingston newspapers, *The British Whig* and the *Chronicle*, and concluded that the crime of rape was indeed an aspect of life in Upper Canada. Then Robert Burns used an 1838 inquiry into accusations that George Markland, the Inspector General of Upper Canada, had sexual relations with several young men to write an interesting article dealing with nineteenth-century Canadian attitudes towards homosexuality. The subjects of birth control and abortion have been examined by Angus MacLaren, while Ruth Pierson has examined the control of venereal disease and the Canadian Women's Army Corps in World War Two in a 1976 article entitled "The Double Bind of the Double Standard." In the past two years, Peter Ward has studied unwed motherhood in nineteenth-century Canada, while Susann Buckley and Janice Dicken McGinnis have examined venereal disease and public health reform in Canada.[4] Studies of this nature are few, and there has been nothing in Canadian historiography to compete with Susan Brownmiller's *Against Our Will: Men, Women and Rape* or Lawrence Stone's massive book, *The Family, Sex and Marriage in England, 1500–1800.*[5]

It is well beyond the scope of this essay to examine sex in Canadian history. By limiting the years of study, however, to the thirty-year period from 1890 to 1920 and the three most western Canadian provinces, Saskatchewan, Alberta and British Columbia, this article attempts to place Canadian social and legal attitudes towards homosexuality in a historical context.

"Natural" and "Unnatural" Sex

The enshrinement by Canadians of sex and procreation within the boundaries of marriage in the late nineteenth and early twentieth centuries served to draw a rigid line between acceptable and unacceptable sexual behaviour for both men and women. Acceptable sexual activity, "natural sex," was to be confined to the marriage bed, performed in the missionary position, and condoned solely for the purpose of procreation. Conversely, those acts which were nonprocreative in intent—such as masturbation, oral sex, anal sex, homosexual contact, and even marital sex with no intention to propagate—were defined as unnatural sex. All these acts generated varying degrees of hostility, both in written law and public pronouncements, but the most repugnant form of unacceptable sexual behaviour was "the abominable crime of buggery" which was "wickedly" committed "against the order of nature."

Due to legal and attitudinal confusion over terminology, the words *buggery* and *sodomy* were used interchangeably to refer to one or all of the following activities: anal intercourse between male and female, homosexual anal intercourse, and sexual intercourse with an animal. The latter activity was also called bestiality. Whatever term was used, Canadians and Western Canadians viewed the perpetrators of all such acts as sinners, criminals, and perverts to be hated, feared, and prosecuted, while the act itself was an abomination against God, the details of which were unfit for publication.

Such thoughts were not new. They merely solidified in the last decade of the nineteenth and first two decades of the twentieth century as the need to distinguish between acceptable and unacceptable sexual behaviour became more intense in the Western Canadian experience.

Of the three acts—that is, heterosexual anal intercourse, homosexual intercourse, and sex with animals—adjudicators, legislators, and the public expressed the most concern over sexual contact between males. In fact, it was generally assumed that all sexual encounters between males, short of anal intercourse, were merely the preliminary activities before the perverse final act. During the 1890s and 1900s, Canadians in the West, as throughout the country, admitted no concept of sexual preference or the lifestyle which accompanied the choice of sexual partners from the same sex. Aversion, not understanding, was the response to such proclivities.

At the early date of 1838, George Markland, the Inspector General of Upper Canada, resigned after he was investigated for allegedly having sexual relations with young men, including several soldiers. The housekeeper of the west wing of the Parliament Buildings in Toronto, where Markland's office was located, told an inquiry conducted by the Executive Council that she suspected there were "queer doings" there. At a time when the legal penalty for such an offence was death, Markland was not even criminally prosecuted.[6] Two decades later, Father Clement Frachon, a priest of the Diocese of London and President of Assumption College in Windsor, Ontario, was allegedly caught for having "interfered" with twelve male students at the school sometime during the 1859–1860 semester.[7] And the Marquess of Lorne, who served as Canada's Governor General from 1878 to 1883, was said to have had sexual preference for males rather than females.[8]

The "Oscar Wilde Type"

If any one event forged the identity of the homosexual[9] as a sinful, immoral, and perverse person in the minds of the public and adjudicators of Western Canada, it was the publicity which surrounded the trials of Oscar Wilde during the mid-1890s in London, England. Although the words buggery and sodomy were still used interchangeably, the identification of a sodomite—a practising male homosexual—with Oscar Wilde enabled society easily to label any such person. It did not matter whether a male had committed only one homosexual act by choice or circumstance, or whether he actually was a homosexual; he was immediately identified as "an Oscar Wilde type" by Victorian and Edwardian Canadian society.

In 1895 Wilde was in the midst of a brilliant literary career. Although rumours of his sexual escapades with young men pervaded Victorian social circles, people dismissed Wilde's behaviour as the pose of an aesthete rather than as that of a practising homosexual. One person, however, was not willing to dismiss Wilde's idiosyncrasies. The Marquess of Queensberry detested Wilde's friendship with his son, Lord Alfred Douglas. Although the Marquess threatened to disown his son if he continued the association, it did not end. On February 18, 1895, four days after the opening of Wilde's play *The Importance of Being Earnest*, the Marquess left a card addressed to Wilde at his social club. On the card were the following words: "To Oscar Wilde posing as a somdomite [sic]."[10] Wilde consulted with his lawyers and decided to press charges against Douglas's father for criminal libel.[11] The ensuing trial, and two others which stemmed from this action, did much to forge the identity of the homosexual in Victorian minds.

The trial of the Marquess of Queensberry began on April 3, 1895. When questioned about letters he had written to Douglas, Wilde defended them as examples of his extraordinary literary talents. Counsel for the defence also presented evidence that Wilde associated with unsavoury members of the lower classes, most notably young male prostitutes. And when asked whether he had ever kissed a certain male servant of the Douglas household, Wilde replied: "Oh, dear, no! He was a peculiarly plain boy. He was, unfortunately, extremely ugly." He did not mention the boy's sex as a reason for not having kissed him. In his criminal suit against the Marquess, Wilde became the defendant. As a result of the damaging evidence against Wilde, Mr. Justice Henn Collins found the Marquess of Queensberry not guilty of criminal libel because Wilde had, in fact, posed as a sodomite.[12]

A few hours after the conclusion of the trial, Wilde, along with another man, Alfred Taylor, was arrested and held without bail. Although Judge Collins had noted that Wilde had posed as a sodomite, he was not charged with sodomy or attempted sodomy. Instead, both men were charged under section 11 of the 1885 Criminal Law Amendment Act, which dealt with gross indecencies committed in public or private. In effect, this section defined all male homosexual encounters short of anal intercourse as illegal acts of gross indecency. A conviction for such a charge carried the possibility of two years' imprisonment with hard labour.[13]

On April 26, 1895, the trial of Wilde and Taylor opened in London. Again, Wilde was questioned about his association with young men and, in particular, with Lord Alfred Douglas. The prosecution even attempted to get Wilde to admit that the phrase "the Love that dare not speak its name," which appeared in a poem written by Douglas, was reference to unnatural love between men;[14] Wilde discounted such claims. Although his lawyer conducted an admirable defence and Wilde was found not guilty on several counts of the charge, the jury could not agree on the verdict on other counts. As a result, Wilde was subjected to yet another trial.

The third and final trial opened on May 20. Wilde and Taylor were tried separately; the latter was tried first and found guilty. The verdict in Wilde's case was a foregone conclusion: After a few hours of deliberation, the jury found Wilde guilty under section 11 of the Criminal Law Amendment Act. When he sentenced Wilde to the maximum imprisonment term of two years with hard labour, Judge Wells stated: "It is no use for me to address you. People who can do these things must be dead to all sense of shame, and one cannot hope to produce any effect upon them. It is the worst case I have ever tried."[15] What began in April 1895 as a simple attempt to clear his name, resulted in a prison term for Oscar Wilde by May of the same year.

Consequently, in Canada as elsewhere, the sodomite was identified with Oscar Wilde and vice versa. Three years after the celebrated trials, Charles S. Clark insinuated in his work *Of Toronto the Good, A Social Study, The Queen City as It Is* that there were several Oscar Wilde types to be found in Canada. An eighteen-year-old boy told Clark that he had blackmailed a member of Canada's judiciary after he caught the judge in a compromising position with a bellboy at a hotel. Another boy told Clark about two merchants in Toronto who had reputations for accosting members of their own sex in order to have improper relations with them. Clark also noted that the unacceptable sexual practises of some of Canada's more prominent members of society could be exposed, as were those of Oscar Wilde, if the bellboys at the various hotels throughout the country chose to tell the public what they knew.[16] Once again, the concern about such matters focused on specific acts of homosexual contact rather than the overall concept of sexual preference.

A pre-World War One case in Saskatchewan reveals many of the same opinions found in Clark's brief account of the Oscar Wilde types in Canada. On May 13, 1912, Dr. A. E. Kelly of Swift Current wrote the Attorney General of Saskatchewan in Regina concerning the alleged immoral conduct of an unnamed doctor in the town. (Subsequent to these letters, the doctor's name was revealed as being C. McArthur.) Supposedly, as early as 1910, McArthur's partner had warned the medical council not to permit this man to become a doctor because he had some rather peculiar sexual habits. Several people claimed that he was "an Oscar Wilde" and had a revolting yet unnamed sexual habit with women. One woman told her husband that McArthur was known to drug women who came to him for medical examinations, and they could not attest to what happened while they were under the influence of the drugs.[17] Less than a year later, Kelly wrote the

Attorney General on the same matter. This time he referred to a certain doctor (later identified as McArthur) as a sex pervert. He also noted that several young men had informed him "They have had to make this man keep straight as he would try to get hold of their genitals."[18] It was somewhat difficult, however, for the Attorney General to take action on the information in Kelly's letters because he did not identify the mysterious doctor in print.

Nineteenth-Century Theories of Homosexuality

Perhaps the most interesting aspect of Kelly's complaint is that he, a medical doctor, displayed a lack of knowledge of late nineteenth- and early twentieth-century scholarly works on homosexual attraction. These studies which appeared in Europe, primarily in Germany, promoted congenital or pathological concepts of homosexuality and the homosexual, rather than sinful and immorality notions of sodomy and the sodomite. As early as the 1860s, a German lawyer, Karl Heinrich Ulrichs, a professed homosexual, popularized the theory of what he called the "third sex." According to Ulrichs, the male homosexual had been born with the soul of a female in a masculine body, while the reverse was true for the female homosexual. Such people constituted the "third sex." And since it was natural for them to be attracted to members of their own sex, he argued, the legal category of unnatural act or offence was incorrect. Ulrichs's theory was based on the assumption that man could not love another man unless he had a feminine soul. Similarly, a woman could not love another woman unless she possessed a masculine soul. Such an assumption, as one of Ulrichs's critics was to point out, merely begged the question.[19]

Although the basic premise of Ulrichs's theory, the congenital nature of homosexuality, would later appear in the works of other sexologists (most notably Havelock Ellis's *Sexual Inversion* in 1898), the popularity of the "third sex" idea was relatively short-lived. By 1879 it was being replaced by the medical model of homosexuality of which another German, Dr. Richard von Krafft-Ebing, was one of the leading exponents. Krafft-Ebing credited Ulrich, whose works he read in 1866, with having drawn his attention to the homosexual phenomenon.[20] Krafft-Ebing's study of homosexual love was included in his general work on sexual aberration, *Psychopathia Sexualis*, where he expounded a medical approach.

Published in 1886, *Psychopathia Sexualis* was a collection of case histories of what Krafft-Ebing classified as sexual abnormalities. Since he considered heterosexual intercourse for the purpose of propagation to be natural and normal, all sexual activities which were nonprocreative in intent were, by definition, unnatural and abnormal. Thus cunnilingus, fellatio, self- or mutual masturbation, and, of course, homosexual encounters, were considered abnormal sexual activities. Although he referred to the congenital theory of homosexuality in certain cases, Krafft-Ebing concluded that sexual perversion had its basis in some form of physical and/or mental disease. In fact, he specifically attributed homosexuality to a breakdown, possibly a hereditary defect, in the central nervous system. Thus homosexuality was no longer the byproduct of sin and immorality but the consequence of some pathology.[21]

If and when Canadians were mentioned in European or British studies on sexual matters, the discussion was usually in terms of sex education in Canada or the apparently declining birthrate of English Canadians.[22] Even one of the earliest studies on homosexuality in North America barely referred to the Canadian experience. Written by Edward Prime Stevenson under the pseudonym Xavier Mayne and published in 1908, *The Intersexes: A History of Similisexualism as a Problem in Social Life*, contained case histories of several homosexuals, including men and women. Stevenson commented:

> ...[O]f similisexual intercourse in the United States of America and in Canada, no possible doubt can exist, if the intelligent observer has resided there and has moved about in various social grades and circles of the larger cities.[23]

It is interesting to note that Stevenson had to obtain a physician's approval before he was allowed to read any European works on homosexuality, and that he later encountered severe difficulties when he tried to get his book published in the United States. (Eventually, *The Intersexes* was published in Italy.)

If the Canadian medical profession was aware of the theories and works of Stevenson, his predecessors, Ulrichs and Krafft-Ebing, and other sexologists, its membership did not take the time to comment on them in the medical journals. Generally speaking, the articles dealing with sexual matters which appeared in the *Canadian Lancet*, *Canadian Medical Association Journal*, and *Canadian Journal of Public Health* concentrated on birth control and abortion or the symptoms and treatment of syphilis.[24] Even late nineteenth- and early twentieth-century Canadian sexual advice manuals, which were usually American publications or Canadian editions of the American counterparts, did not pay particular attention to the homosexual or similisexual phenomenon. And much like the articles which appeared in the medical journals, these works extolled the virtues of sexual restraint, marriage, and procreative sex as well as the evils of masturbation. Homosexual activity was not singled out for examination but was classified as an example of a dangerous sexual perversion which was synonymous with all forms of nonprocreative sex. B. G. Jefferies and J. L. Nicholas, authors of Canada's *Household Guide* (1894) and *Light on Dark Corners, Search Light on Health: A Complete Sexual Science and A Guide to Purity and Physical Manhood* (1894) believed that all sexual perversions were actually "diseases of the will" and should not be regarded from a religious or moral standpoint. Therefore, the only way to overcome these abnormal sexual desires was through the "power of suggestion, right living, and inspirational occupation."[25]

It would appear that neither Canadian social nor medical attitudes towards homosexuality and the homosexual in the 1890s and the 1900s were greatly influenced or altered by scholarly works on the subject. It was the trials of Oscar Wilde which fixed the homosexual identity in the minds of Canadians. Male homosexual attraction was synonymous with the sodomite and the act of sodomy. Although this clarification was certainly true in terms of societal perceptions, the criminal justice system in Canada still suffered from the legal confusion over terminology which had its origin in the English common law. The written law continued to employ the ill-defined terms *buggery* and *sodomy* for homosexual encounters and sex with animals, and rarely did the specific term bestiality appear in the court records.

Definitions of Sexual Activities: English Law Precedents
Prior to the 1530s matters of sex and morality were under the jurisdiction of the English ecclesiastical courts, which had succeeded in broadening the pre-Christian concern over unnatural offences (including buggery) to include a punishment inflicted by God on the people who engaged in such activities. The first secular law to deal with buggery was enacted in 1533, during the reign of Henry VIII. The statute of 1533 made "the detestable and abominable vice of buggery committed with mankind or beast" a felony, punishable by death and loss of property; the offender was also to be denied benefit of clergy.[26] Originally this statute was to be a temporary measure lasting until the final day of the next Parliament, but in 1540 it became perpetual. Eight years later (1548), under Edward VI's rule, the penalties for the offence were reduced so that the property of the offender was no longer affected. In 1553, Mary I abolished all offences which had been made felonies since April 21, 1509, the first day of the reign of Henry VIII. Then in 1563, Elizabeth I revived in full the 1533 statute because its repeal apparently had led to an increase in the incidence of buggery throughout the realm.[27]

What exactly was "the detestable and abominable vice of buggery committed with mankind or beast"? The confusion over the legal definition of the term can be traced to the early seventeenth century, when Sir Edward Coke, then Chief Justice of the King's Bench, wrote the third part of *Institutes of the Laws of England*. He used the words buggery and sodomy interchangeably, as the title of Chapter 10, "Of Buggery, or Sodomy," suggests. In that chapter he defined buggery as:

> a detestable, and abominable sin, amongst Christians not to be named; committed by carnal knowledge against the ordinance of the Creator, and order of nature, by mankind with mankind, or with brute beast, or by womankind with brute beast.

This was somewhat different than the intent of the original 1533 statute, which appeared to include acts of heterosexual anal intercourse. A complete reading of Coke's chapter reveals that, in his mind, the word "mankind" referred specifically to males and did not include females. Thus, in one sense of the term, buggery could be committed by a male person with another male or with an animal; and in another sense, buggery could be committed by a female with a "brute beast." Thus, anal intercourse between male and female did not form any part of Coke's interpretation of buggery.[28]

Other English legal writers referred to buggery in a variety of ways. In his work *The History of the Pleas of the Crown*, Sir Mathew Hale echoed the sentiments of Coke.[29] William Hawkins replaced the word buggery with sodomy and wrote in his book, *A Treatise of the Pleas of the Crown*, that "All unnatural carnal copulations, whether with man or beast, seem to come under the notion of Sodomy."[30] Sir William Blackstone neatly sidestepped the problem of definition in the *Commentaries on the Laws of England* (1769) by not using either term. As far as he was concerned, it was "the infamous crime against nature, committed either by man or beast."[31] In the early nineteenth century, Edward East used the word sodomy in his *Treatise of the Pleas of the Crown*, defining sodomy as:

> carnal knowledge committed against the order of nature, by man with man, or in the same unnatural manner with woman, or by man or woman in any manner with beast.[32]

In 1819, William Russell quoted East's definition verbatim in *A Treatise on Crimes and Indictable Offences*.[33] Thus, since 1533 the definition of buggery had been broadened by some interpreters to include acts of heterosexual anal intercourse. Consistently, however, all the writers from Coke to Russell referred to sexual acts with animals as buggery.

Definitions of Sexual Activities: Canadian Law, Late Nineteenth Century

The confusion implanted by the English writers carried over to the Canadian setting. According to the first Canadian statute dealing with buggery (passed in 1869), the crime of buggery could be committed with mankind or animal. This was similar to the definition found in the Offences Against the Person Act passed eight years earlier in England.[34] Although the terminology was the same, the penalties were not. Anyone found guilty of committing buggery in England was liable to life imprisonment or a minimum of ten years in confinement.[35] In Canada, the maximum term of imprisonment was the same but the minimum was substantially reduced to two years.[36] Then, in 1886, the Canadian proviso for a minimum sentence was dropped.[37] Despite the differences in punishment, the English act and Canadian statute used the word buggery inclusively, that is, with mankind or animal. When George W. Burbidge's *Digest of the Criminal Law of Canada* appeared in 1890, however, the word sodomy was used as the inclusive term. This is not surprising, as Burbidge based his work on Sir James Stephen's *Digest of the Criminal Law* published in 1876. Following in the tradition of Hawkins, East, and Russell, Stephen had defined sodomy as carnal knowledge by a man with another male or woman *per anum*, or carnal knowledge of an animal. What appeared in Burbidge's *Digest* was the same, word for word.[38]

Total confusion accompanied the relevant statutes in the 1892 Criminal Code. Contained under the general category of "Offences Against Morality" and classified as an "unnatural offence," was Coke's dual usage of buggery and sodomy. Both terms were used to describe carnal knowledge "with a human being or with any other living creature" *per anum*. For example, the Code referred to the more serious offence of actually completing the act, as buggery,[39] while an attempt to perpetrate the offence was considered to be an attempt to commit sodomy.[40] Even the form of the indictment was misleading. The accused could be charged with "unlawfully, wickedly and against the order of nature" committing "that detestable and abominable crime of buggery" with another person or an animal.[41] In fact, in December 1920, the defence counsel in a Leduc, Alberta, case objected to the wording in a complaint laid against his client because it was not sufficiently specific. Alex Sowayak was charged with committing "buggery either with a human being or any other living creature" on November 5, 1920. Upon reading the depositions, it becomes obvious that it was a case of buggery with a mare, or bestiality. This particular aspect of the offence had not appeared in the charge, and thus the defence objected.[42] Although sodomy was dropped from explicit word usage in the Code by 1920 and buggery was the inclusive and exclusive term, the index to the Code reveals that sodomy and buggery were still cross-referenced.[43] The term bestiality does not appear.

Instances of Buggery, Sodomy, and Bestiality, 1890–1920

Case law during the period 1890–1920 in Western Canada clearly reflected the inconsistencies of definition found in the written law. At times buggery was used as the inclusive term and at other times sodomy was used. If reference was being made to carnal knowledge with an animal, the particular animal might be mentioned or the incident might simply be referred to as bestiality. Though never legally defined, the word *bestiality* was used in a number of instances to describe the offence. Unless the offence was clearly listed as buggery with a male, female, or animal, or as sodomy with male, female, or animal, or as bestiality, it is virtually impossible to ascertain what type of unnatural offence was committed. For example, in April 1907, a fifty-one-year-old miner in British Columbia was charged with committing "the abominable crime of buggery" with a cow, which in the strict sense of terminology actually constituted bestiality.[44] Fortunately, the gaol report in this particular case noted that some type of animal was involved; otherwise, the true nature of the offence would be lost.[45] For the most part, however, the reports do not provide such detailed information; buggery, and to a lesser extent sodomy, are usually the descriptive terms employed. Even the criminal statistics compiled by the federal government according to judicial districts are of little help because the offences are placed under the general category of "Sodomy and Bestiality."[46]

One can only speculate as to whether the Western Canadian setting in the late nineteenth and early twentieth century provided a more fertile environment for unnatural sex. What was the reality in the logging and mining communities, the railroad camps, and the threshing gangs? Historians have assumed that the predominantly single male population, characteristic of the Western frontier experience, frequently visited prostitutes.[47] While many males visited brothels and had sex with the women and young girls brought to their remote camps for such purpose, written reports such as police records, gaol reports, criminal statistics, magistrates' charge books, court cases, and even newspapers reveal that buggery, sodomy, and bestiality or attempts to commit these sex acts were also fairly common in Western Canada from 1890 to 1920.

Charges of buggery, sodomy, or bestiality, were usually made based on the report of someone who had seen the person or persons involved committing the offence. A case heard before the Wetaskiwin division of the Alberta Supreme Court serves as a good example of this phenomenon. At that time, John Harrington was charged with attempted buggery (which carried a maximum penalty of ten years' imprisonment)[48] on an eleven-year-old boy at Provost on December 31, 1914. Supposedly, the accused had given the boy seventy-five cents and pushed him into a water closet located behind a tailor shop where he had attempted to commit the offense. One witness, Frank Washburn, told the court that he saw the accused grab the boy and push him into the closet. He further stated that he heard the boy crying and, after talking to Edward Evanson, another witness, went to get the police. When the police constable, A. F. Barnes, arrived he heard no noise from the closet. Barnes opened the door and took the boy out. He found the accused with his pants down below his knees and, in the officer's own words, "I saw the penis of the prisoner and also put my hand there to make sure and found that it was erect." Harrington was arrested immediately.[49]

A similar set of circumstances can be found in the Sowayak case involving bestiality. On December 18, 1920, a complaint was laid by Constable P. W. Rawson of the Alberta Provincial Police at Leduc against Alex Sowayak, charging him with committing bestiality a month earlier. This charge was issued after Frederick Hook of Calmar told the police what he had seen on the evening of November 5, 1920. Hook said he went by the house of the accused and saw him in the barn, standing on a box, having carnal knowledge with a horse. When he confronted the accused, Sowayak denied the act. Hook did not go to the authorities until a week later, after several people told him his silence in the matter was foolish. Had Hook not happened into the barn during the time the offence was allegedly committed, Sowayak's actions would have gone undetected and no charge would have been made.[50]

In one particular case in British Columbia, the police went so far as to place themselves in the position of being the third party witnessing the offence. As a result of the tactic, Delip Singh was charged with attempting to commit buggery on a fifteen-year-old boy on July 20, 1918. The facts of the case were as follows. Delip Singh asked the boy to go for rides with him on a couple of occasions. Apparently the boy became suspicious of the accused's intentions and told his father. The father then went to see the police and told them what he and his son suspected. The police encouraged the boy to see him one more time. Instead of going for a drive, Singh and the boy went to the stable owned by the boy's father where, unbeknown to the accused, two policemen were hiding in the loft. Once there, the accused suggested unnatural sex which amounted to buggery, gave the boy fifteen cents, spread out a blanket, told him what to do, unbuttoned his pants (the accused's), and grasped the boy. At that moment, the policemen grabbed Delip Singh and found that he had an erection. They immediately charged him with an attempt to commit buggery. He was subsequently convicted on October 24, 1918, by County Court Judge Cayley. When the appeal case was heard in November 1918 at Vancouver, counsel for the defence contended that up until the time the police revealed themselves, the actions of the accused merely constituted "preparations" and not an attempt to commit the offence. The five judges hearing the appeal unanimously ruled that an attempt had been made to commit buggery; the conviction was thus sustained.[51]

There were instances of unnatural sexual behaviour that went unrecorded, either because the courts did not recognize them to be such or because no complaint was registered with the authorities. Some of the written law provisions for cases of serious sexual assaults against females (rape and carnal knowledge), for example, were applied in cases involving unnatural sex. It was widely thought that no one under the age of fourteen could commit rape or buggery.[52] In 1898 a conviction of an eleven-year-old boy for committing an "unnatural act" on a seven-year-old boy was overturned by a Nova Scotia appeal court because the accused was supposedly incapable of committing the act.[53]

Legislation passed in 1841 stipulated that in cases of buggery, rape, and carnal knowledge of young girls, there was no need to prove emission to prove carnal knowledge; proof of penetration to the slightest degree was all that was necessary.[54] But unlike rape and carnal knowledge of females under fourteen where consent or lack of it was an issue, consent was of no importance in cases of buggery. In fact, even consenting married adults who engaged in anal intercourse were liable to prosecution under the strict sense of the law.[55] Obviously, the issue of consent was irrelevant in cases where animals were involved.

Whereas women were expected to raise a "hue and cry" immediately after they had been assaulted, the situation was somewhat different in buggery cases. Since consent was inconsequential, it naturally followed there was no need to register a complaint at the first reasonable opportunity.[56] If two people, whether they were two males or a male and female, were consenting parties to the act, then it was unlikely that they would report themselves to the authorities. Even if a wife did not consent, she would not press charges against her husband, for implicit in the marriage contract was the idea that a woman was subject to her husband's sexual whims. As in the case of consenting adults, it is hard to imagine that a person who indulged in bestiality would turn himself or herself over to the police.

For the most part, therefore, it is difficult to obtain any factual information about this type of offence. There are very few cases of buggery and bestiality in the published law reports, especially for the years 1890 to 1920 in Western Canada. The Delip Singh case of 1918 is the only one to appear in published form. Although listings of the offence and, at times, the vital statistics of the offender are available from other sources, no further information is given. Most of the cases and the factual data surrounding them are locked in the unpublished and as yet uncatalogued criminal court cases processed through the various provincial supreme and district courts, and they are by no means complete. A file might only contain the name of the accused, the complainant, the nature of the offence, and the date it was allegedly committed. Such information is no better than what was provided in the annual reports of the federal and provincial police, the gaol and penitentiary reports, or procedure books.

Attempts to cross-reference the cases mentioned in the legal sources with reports in the Western Canadian newspapers are for the most part futile. The papers displayed an aversion to mentioning cases which involved any form of unnatural sexual activity. When one does find an account in the media, it reinforces the idea that such encounters were considered to be "detestable and abominable." For example, the Medicine Hat *Weekly Times* of May 23, 1895, had front-page coverage of a case in Regina where three men appeared before Inspector Starnes and Justice of the Peace Henry Le Jeune on charges of committing sexual acts "of an unnatural character." Under the caption "HORRIBLE CRIME AT REGINA: Arrest of Prominent Citizen in Connection with a Most Revolting Offence," the paper reported that one of the men was a prominent member of society and a manager of a large dry goods, grocery, and wholesale liquor firm in Regina. The information was obtained from two boys, who allegedly witnessed the incident through a window.[57] In another instance, the August 9, 1906, issue of the Edmonton *Journal* noted that two men had been charged "with heinous offences of character unfit for publication," and the courts were closed for the hearings.[58]

Punishment

Whether the offence was called buggery, sodomy, or bestiality, it is evident that in the eyes of the public and the written law, homosexual encounters and sex with animals were nauseating and repulsive acts committed against God, nature, and society, while the offender was a horrific sinner and criminal. Despite such notions, the available information suggests that the judges rarely resorted to the maximum penalty of life imprisonment for buggery or the ten-year maximum for attempted buggery. During the late nineteenth and early twentieth century the penalties for a buggery or sodomy conviction ranged from shorter sentences of six, twelve, eighteen, and twenty months to longer sentences of two, three, five, six, ten, and fifteen years.[59] In one instance, a fifteen-year sentence with hard labour was imposed on two single men in British Columbia, aged twenty-eight and twenty, who were found guilty of buggery on June 29, 1891.[60] Another case tried at the November 23, 1891, sitting of the Assizes court at Victoria, saw two men, one twenty-five years old and the other thirty-five years old, sentenced to fifteen years' imprisonment after being found guilty of committing sodomy.[61]

When the offence was specifically referred to as bestiality, the courts still appeared to be reluctant to hand out the maximum penalty under the law. On February 7, 1898, for example, Charles Harris was sentenced to five years' imprisonment by Judge Spinks at Kamloops for bestiality.[62] During World War One, a Russian man was sentenced to two years and three months with hard labour by a judge at Fort St. George for a similar offence.[63] In the Alex Sowayak case, which involved a charge of bestiality, Sowayak was found not guilty by Justice Scott of Wetaskiwin district of the Alberta Supreme Court on February 14, 1921.[64]

Although the law made no provision for whipping to be part of the punishment for a buggery/sodomy or bestiality conviction, on at least one occasion a dose of the lash accompanied a term of confinement. On June 6, 1912, a judge at New Westminster sentenced Allan Wilson to three years' imprisonment plus twelve lashes. The New Westminster gaol prisoner list referred to Wilson's crime as buggery.[65] The record keeping in this case and in others is somewhat suspect, however. For example, a conviction for the undefined act of gross indecency or indecent assault on a male carried the punishment of being whipped.[66] Therefore it is quite possible that Wilson's crime was one of these two particular offences, mistakenly recorded as buggery.

At times, people charged with buggery or sodomy were convicted of attempted buggery or sodomy, which carried a lesser penalty.[67] For example, Henry Crannon was charged with committing buggery with another male at Banff, Alberta, on April 15, 1908. Although the evidence suggests that the offence was completed *in toto*, the presiding judge at the June 2, 1908, sitting of the Calgary district court found Crannon guilty of attempted buggery and sentenced him to three years in prison.[68] A few years later, Robert Wilson was charged with sodomy but was found guilty of attempted sodomy. He was sentenced to six months with hard labour for his crime.[69]

A similar range of sentences is evident in those cases where a person was originally charged and subsequently convicted for attempted sodomy or buggery. Shorter sentences ranged from three to twelve months with hard labour while longer terms of imprisonment included two, three, five, and the maximum of ten years.[70] In one case heard in January 1898, the defendant who pleaded guilty to a charge of attempted buggery at Fairview, British Columbia, was sentenced to five years' imprisonment. Although, or because, he had admitted his guilt, the maximum penalty was not given.[71] When Sam Davis pleaded not guilty on a similar charge before the Calgary division of the Alberta Supreme Court on May 21, 1912, however, he was found guilty and sentenced to ten years.[72] Despite the overwhelming evidence of two eye witnesses, one of them a police officer in the Harrington case, Judge W. Walsh sentenced the accused to three years' imprisonment on February 23, 1915, for attempted buggery.[73] Once again, the judges in Western Canada exercised their powers of discretion.

Even though the offence and the offender were thought to be detestable, wicked, and despicable, at times the criminal justice system exercised its prerogative of mercy much as it did in cases involving sex assaults against females. For example, a sixty-year-old man who had been sentenced to two years' imprisonment on November 13, 1889, for committing an "unnatural offence" received an official pardon on September 21, 1891.[74] Two men who received fifteen-year sentences upon conviction for sodomy on November 12, 1891, had their sentences commuted to seven years with remission for time served on December 7, 1895.[75] In a rather peculiar combination of crimes, a twenty-two-year-old man was sentenced to four years' imprisonment on February 20, 1903, for robbery with violence and attempted sodomy. On August 10, 1906, his sentence was commuted, provided that his relatives took him home and looked after him.[76] Three years later, a man serving a prison term of between two and five years in the Manitoba Penitentiary was released on a ticket of leave. In this case, the person had served a little over half of his sentence before he was released.[77]

Conclusion

The very fact that prison terms were given for sex acts which were thought to be unnatural suggests that law and society possessed little conception of sexual activity due to circumstance or preference. In the late nineteenth and early twentieth centuries unnatural sexual activity threatened traditional concepts of married love and procreative sex. Consequently, unnatural sex had to be socially and legally condemned.

Classified as among the most unnatural of all the forms of unnatural sexual activities, homosexual encounters between males were viewed as sins against God, crimes against nature, and offences against society. The public's attitudinal confusion over what was buggery or sodomy was somewhat alleviated with the trials of Oscar Wilde. As a direct result, the perpetrator of homosexual activities between males was a sinful, immoral, and criminal sodomite. But this narrow classification was not expressed in the written criminal law or used by the criminal justice system. In the legal sense of the terms, buggery or sodomy still referred to heterosexual anal intercourse, homosexual anal intercourse, and sex with animals. Despite the continued use of generalizations by the law, the person who committed the crime of buggery or sodomy was still a sinner and a criminal. However, the equating of Wilde with a sodomite to produce the label "an Oscar Wilde type" in 1895 did not result in any noticeable increase in the sentences meted out by judges in Western Canada.

The existence of homosexual relationships and sex acts which were nonprocreative in intent seemed to threaten the very foundations of a society based on married love and procreative sex. Consequently, society made few attempts to come to some understanding of the Oscar Wildes in Canada, particularly those in the West. Instead they were feared and despised by society and persecuted and prosecuted under the law. Scholarly works did little to change these perceptions. Acceptable sexual activity had to be protected and attempts were made to eradicate or at least to severely restrict unacceptable sexual behavior. In spite of the social and legal restraints, homosexual activity did not dissipate. It continued to exist surreptitiously alongside the traditional and prevalent sexual morality.

Notes

1. Gordon Taylor, *Sex in History* (New York: Harper Row, 1970), 4.
2. George Seldes, ed., *The Great Quotations* (New York: Lyle Stuart, 1960), 861.
3. *See*, James Gray, *Red Lights on the Prairies* (Toronto: Macmillan, 1971) and Judy Bedford, "Prostitution in Calgary, 1905–1914," *Alberta History* (Spring 1981):1–11.
4. Michael Bliss, "Pure Books on Avoided Subjects: Pre-Freudian Sexual Ideas in Canada," *Historical Papers* (1970): 89–108; Ruth Olson, "Rape — An 'Un-Victorian' Aspect of Life in Upper Canada," *Ontario History* (June 1976): 75–79; Angus McLaren, "Birth Control and Abortion in Canada, 1890–1920," *Canadian Historical Review* 59 (September 1978): 319–40; Ruth Pierson, "The Double Bind of the Double Standard: V. D. Control and the CWAC and World War II," *Canadian Historical Review* 62 (March 1981): 31–58; Robert Burns, "'Queer Doings': Attitudes Towards Homosexuality in Nineteenth Century Canada," *Body Politic* 29 (December 1976/January 1977): 4–7; Peter Ward, "Unwed Motherhood in Nineteenth-Century English Canada," *Historical Papers* (1981): 34–56, and Janice Dicken McGinnis and Susan Buckley, "Venereal Disease and Public Health Reform in Canada," *Canadian Historical Review* 63 (September 1982): 337–54.
5. Susan Brownmiller, *Against Our Will: Men, Women and Rape* (New York: Bantam Books, 1975) and Lawrence Stone, *The Family, Sex and Marriage in England, 1500–1800* (New York: Harper and Row, 1977).
6. *See*, Burns, "'Queer Doings,'" 4–7.
7. Proposed History Projects, Canadian Gay Archives, Toronto, Ontario, no. 40.
8. Ibid., no. 28

9. Although the author does not refer specifically to the Canadian situation, the evidence indicates that the Wilde trials were extremely important in forming Canadian perceptions of homosexuality. Bert Hansen, "The Historical Construction of Homosexuality," *Radical History Review* (Spring/Summer 1979): 68.

10. History records this misspelling.

11. Brandf Aymar and Edward Sagarin, *A Pictorial History of the World's Greatest Trials from Socrates to Eichmann* (New York: Bonanza Books, 1977), 193–98.

12. Ibid.

13. Jeffrey Weeks, *Coming Out: Homosexual Politics in Britain, from the Nineteenth Century to the Present* (London: Quartet Books, 1977), 6.

14. The poem was entitled "Two Loves."

15. Aymar and Sagarin, *The World's Greatest Trials*, 199. The judge also stated: "[T]he crime of which you have been convicted is so bad that one has to put stern restraint upon one's self to prevent one's self from describing, in language which I would rather not use, the sentiment which must rise to the breast of every man of honour who has heard the details of these two terrible crimes."

16. Charles S. Clark, *Of Toronto the Good, A Social Study, the Queen City as It Is* (Toronto: Toronto Publishing Co., 1898), 90.

17. Dr. A. Kelly to the Attorney General, 13 May 1912. File #518, Immoral Conduct, K Case Files, Saskatchewan Provincial Police, Attorney General Papers, Saskatchewan Archives Board [hereafter SAB].

18. Dr. A. Kelly to the Attorney General, 10 March 1913. SAB.

19. Hubert Kennedy, "The 'Third Sex' Theory of Karl Heinrich Ulrichs," in *Historical Perspectives on Homosexuality*, ed. Salvatore Licata and Robert Petersen (New York: Haworth Press and Stein and Day, 1981), 103–13. Ulrichs did not use the term homosexual in his studies. He referred to a heterosexual male as dioning and a homosexual male as urning. Similarly, dioningin and urningin were used in reference to their female counterparts. The word homosexual was used by K. M. Benkert.
    Ibid., 107–8.

20. Richard von Krafft-Ebing, *Psychopathia Sexualis*, trans. Dr. Wedeck (New
21. York: Putnam's, 1886). For a discussion of Krafft-Ebing and his theories, *see* John Lauriten and David Thorstad, *The Early Homosexuals Rights Movement, 1864–1935* (New York: Times Change, 1974); Vern Bullough, "Homosexuality and the Medical Model," in Vern Bullough, *Sex, Sin and History* (New York: Science History Publications, 1976), 173–85; Havelock Ellis, *Sexual Inversion*, Vol. ll of *Studies in the Psychology of Sex*, 2d ed. (Philadelphia: Dairs, 1918).

22. *See*, e.g., Ellis, *Sexual Inversion*, and his *The Task of Social Hygiene* (Boston: Houghton Mifflin, 1912), 253. In the latter work, Ellis refers to sex education in Ontario for children above the age of ten.

23. Xavier Mayne, *The Intersexes: A History of Similisexualism as a Problem in Social Life* in Lauriten and Thorstad, *Early Homosexuals Rights Movement*, 36.

24. *See*, McLaren, "Birth Control and Abortion in Canada." Also, an examination of the indexes of the periodicals mentioned in this text reveals that very few

articles appeared on the subject of homosexuality.

25. Vern Bullough, "Homosexuality and Its Confusion with the 'Secret Sin' in Pre-Freudian America" in Bullough, *Sex, Society and History*, 112–25. *See also*, Bliss, "Pure Books on Avoided Subjects," 89–108.

26. 25 Henry VIII, c. 8.

27. In order of their appearance in the text, the statutes dating from 1533 were as follows: 32 Henry VIII, c. 3; 2–3 Edward VI, c. 29; 1 Mary, c. 1 and 5 Elizabeth, c. 17. A similar discussion of the statutes can be found in Alex Gigeroff, *Sexual Deviations in the Criminal Law: Homosexual, Exhibitionistic, and Peodophilic Offences in Canada* (Toronto: University of Toronto Press, 1968), 15, fn.4.

28. Sir Edward Coke, *The Third Part of the Institutes of the Laws of England* (New York and London: Garland, 1979). For an interpretaton of Coke, *see*, Gigeroff, *Sexual Deviations in the Criminal Law*, 7–12.

29. Hale stated that a woman could be found guilty of buggery with an animal under the statute. Quoted in Gigeroff, *Sexual Deviations in the Criminal Law*, 10.

30. William Hawkins, *A Treatise of the Pleas of the Crown*, 8th ed. (London, 1824) 1, p. 357.

31. William Blackstone, *Of Public Wrongs*, vol. 4 of *Commentaries on the Laws of England* (Oxford, 1769), 215–16.

32. Edward East, *A Treatise of the Pleas of the Crown* (London, 1803), 1, p. 480.

33. William Russell, *A Treatise on Crimes and Indictable Offences* (London, 1819), 1, p. 815.

34. "Whosoever shall be convicted of the abominable crime of buggery, committed either with mankind, or with any animal." Canada, *Offences Against the Person Act* (1861), 24 Victoria, c. 100, s. 61; Canada, *Statutes of Canada* (1869), c. 20, s. 63.

35. Canada, *Offences Against the Persons Act* (1861), 24–25 Victoria c. 100, s. 61.

36. Canada, *Statutes of Canada* (1869), c. 20, s. 63.

37. Canada, *Revised Statutes of Canada* (1886), c. 157, s. 1.

38. According to Stephen, "Every one commits the felony called sodomy, and is liable upon conviction thereof, to penal servitude for life as a maximum, and to penal servitude for ten years as a minimum punishment who (a) carnally knows any animal; or (b) being a male, carnally knows any man or any woman (per anum)." James Stephen, *Digest of the Criminal Law* (1876), c. 18, Article 168, p. 115; George Burbidge, *Digest of the Criminal Law of Canada* (1890; Toronto: Carswell, 1980), c. 19 Article 213.

39. Canada, *Criminal Code of Canada*, 1892, 55–56 Victoria, c. 29, s. 174.

40. Canada, *Criminal Code of Canada*, 1892, 55–56 Victoria, c. 29, s. 175.

41. During the late nineteenth and early twentieth centuries, every indictment issued for the crime of buggery and attempted buggery included these words.

42. Supreme Court Records [hereafter SCR], Criminal (Wetaskiwin) File #1662, Case: R. v. A. Sowayak (1920), buggery.

43. Canada, *Criminal Code and Other Selected Statutes of Canada*, with the Amendments passed up to the end of the second session of Parliament, held in 1919 (Ottawa, 1920). The listing for sodomy in the index reads "see buggery," p. 39.

44. Provincial Archives of British Columbia [hereafter PABC], Attorney General

Papers, Inspector of Gaols, Nanaimo Gaol, Record of Prisoners, vol. 1 (Nov. 1893–Feb. 1911), p. 100. On May 6, 1915, Mark Kulick was sentenced to two years and three months' imprisonment with hard labour by Judge Calder at Fort St. George for the crime of bestiality. No mention was made as to the type of animal. PABC, Attorney General Papers, Inspector of Gaols, New Westminster Gaol, vol. 7 (June 1914–Oct. 1917), p. 49.

45. See, the discussion of the Sowayak case, below. Although the ensuing case occurred a few months after the last year of this study, it serves as yet another example of the problem. On July 8, 1921, John McEwan of Vancouver, British Columbia, appeared before the Wetaskiwin District Court on the following charge: "With a certain heifer calf, wickedly and against the order of Nature did have a venereal affair, and then and there unlawfully, wickedly, and against the order of nature, with the said heifer calf, did commit and perpetrate, the detestable and abominable crime of Buggery." District Court Records [hereafter DCR], Criminal (Wetaskiwin), File #1750, Case: R. v. J. McEwan (1921), buggery.

46. The federal statistics for the years ending 1890–1920 can be found in Canada, Sessional Papers. The number of the paper changed in each volume of these collected papers.

47. See, Gray, Red Lights and Bedford, "Prostitution in Calgary."

48. "Everyone is guilty of an indictable offence and liable to ten years imprisonment who attempts to commit the offence mentioned in the last presiding section." This referred to section 174 of the Criminal Code, in which was addressed the crime of buggery. Canada, Criminal Code, 1892, 55–56 Victoria, c. 29, s. 175.

49. SCR, Criminal (Wetaskiwin), File #1004, Case: R. v. John Harrington (1914), attempted buggery. Although Harrington pleaded not guilty, he was found guilty by a judge alone and sentenced to three years' imprisonment.

50. Ibid., File #1662, Case: R. v. Sowayak (1920), buggery. See also, DCR, Criminal (Wetaskiwin), File #1750, Case: R. v. J. McEwan (1921), buggery. A complaint was made against McEwan charging him with buggery with a cow after the owner of the cow noticed there was something wrong with it. Upon giving a statement in which the accused admitted his guilt, he was sentenced to a prison term of two years less one day by Judge William Lees on August 2, 1921.

51. R. v. Delip Singh, 26 B. C. Law Reports (1917–1919), 390–96.

52. William Tremeear, The Criminal Code and the Laws of Criminal Evidence in Canada (Toronto: Canada Law Book Co., 1902), Part 13, s. 174, p. 126.

53. R. v. Hartlan, 2 Canadian Criminal Cases (1898).

54. Canada, Consolidated Statutes of Canada (1859), "An Act for consolidating and amending the Statutes in this Province relative to Offences Against the Person" (1841), 4 and 5 Victoria, c. 27, s. 18. The following year, an act stipulated that a conviction for assault with intent to commit rape or with the intent to commit "the abominable crime of buggery" could result in up to two years in another place of confinement. Canada, Consolidated Statutes of Canada (1859), "An Act for better proportioning the punishment to the offence, in certain cases." (1842/43) 6 Victoria, c. 5, s. 5.

55. "Unlike rape, sodomy may be committed between two persons, both of whom consent, and even by husband and wife." Tremeear, Criminal Code, 126.

56. However, in the late 1920s the Ontario court of appeal overturned a conviction
     on a charge of rape because the boy did not make his complaint until one
     month after the offence had allegedly occurred. This was much like the
     arguments which were used in cases involving sexual assaults against women.
     R. v. Elliot, 49 *Canadian Criminal Cases* (1928), 302. Case is mentioned in
     Gigeroff, *Sexual Deviations*, 103.
57. Medicine Hat *Times*, 23 May 1895, p. 1.
58. "Serious Police Charges," Edmonton *Journal*, 9 August 1906, p. 4.
59. E.g.: a six-month sentence was imposed on J. Storm by Police Magistrate
     Williams at Vancouver on November 30, 1907 (PABC, Attorney General
     Papers, Inspector of Gaols, New Westminster Gaol, vol. 5 (October
     1895–October 1910), n. p.). J. Evans received a twelve-month sentence for a
     buggery conviction on June 21, 1906. (Ibid.). G. Strickland received eighteen
     months' imprisonment (Ibid., vol. 7 (June 1914–October 1917), p. 20). E.
     Woons received an eighteen-month sentence on April 4, 1912 (Ibid., Victoria
     Gaol, List of Prisoners under sentence in Victoria Gaol, vol. 17 (November
     1910–1914), p. 95). DCR, Criminal (Wetaskiwin), File #1750, Case: R. v. J.
     McEwan (1921), buggery. The accused received a sentence of two years less one
     day. On July 27, 1899, John Bow was sentenced to three years' imprisonment
     (PABC, Attorney General Papers, Inspector of Gaols, New Westminster Gaol,
     vol. 5 (October 1895–October 1910), n. p.). Five-year sentences were popular
     in 1908, 1911, 1912, and 1914 (Ibid., n. p., Ibid., vol. 7 (June 1914–October
     1917), pp. 1 and 3). In Vancouver during September 1910, Judge McInnes
     sentenced a man to ten years in prison (Ibid., vol. 5 (October 1895–October
     1910), n.p.).
60. Ibid., Victoria Gaol, Record and description list of all prisoners received in
     Victoria Gaol, vol. 12 (November 1890–February 22, 1910), p. 8.
61. Canada, *Sessional Papers*, "Criminal Statistics for the year ended September
     30, 1896," vol. 30 (1897), Paper 8d, pp. 244–45.
62. PABC, Attorney General Papers, Inspector of Gaols, New Westminster Gaol,
     Return of Prisoners Confined, vol. 5 (October 1895–October 1910), n. p.
63. Ibid., vol. 7 (June 1914–October 1917), p. 49.
64. SCR, Criminal (Wetaskiwin), File #1662, Case: R. v. Sowayak (1920), buggery.
     See also, DCR, Criminal (Wetaskiwin), File #1750, Case: R. v. J. McEwan
     (1921), buggery. *See above*, note 55.
65. PABC, Attorney General Papers, Inspector of Gaols, New Westminster Gaol,
     Return of Prisoners Confined, vol. 6 (November 1910–May 1914), p. 123. *See
     also*, John Wheaton's punishment for a buggery conviction on October 2,
     1906, twenty lashes (Ibid., vol. 5 (October 1895–October 1910), n. p.).
66. Canada, *Revised Statutes of Canada* (1906), c. 146, s. 206 and Canada,
     Criminal Code of Canada (1892) c. 29, s. 260.
67. The maximum penalty for attempt to commit sodomy/buggery was ten years'
     imprisonment. Canada, *Criminal Code of Canada* (1902), s. 175 and Canada,
     Criminal Code of Canada (1906), s. 203.
68. DCR, Criminal (Calgary), File #10a, Case: R. v. H. Crannan (1908), buggery.
     The accused was sentenced to three years' imprisonment for attempted
     buggery.
69. PABC, Attorney General Papers, Inspector of Gaols, Nanaimo Gaol, List of
     Prisoners under sentence in Nanaimo Gaol, vol. 2 (February 1911–August

1914), pp. 58–60. The prisoner had been committed to trial on December 30, 1912.

70.   *See*, for example, the following cases: On June 4, 1906 Frank Clarke was sentenced to three months' imprisonment by Police Magistrate Williams at Vancouver (PABC, Attorney General Papers, Inspector of Gaols, New Westminster Gaol, Return of Prisoners Confined, vol. 5 (October 1895–October 1910)). Bram was sentenced to six months by Judge Howay at New Westminster in September 1917 (Ibid., vol. 7 (June 1914–October 1917), p. 110). On September 16, 1915, a man was sentenced to twelve months' imprisonment (Ibid., p. 59). *See also*, SCR, Criminal (Wetaskiwin), File #1004, Case: R. v. J. Harrington (1914), attempted buggery, sentenced to three years' imprisonment.

71.   PABC, Attorney General Papers, B. C. Provincial Court (Fairview), Police Charge Book, vol. 1 (1897–1908), p. 76.

72.   SCR, Criminal (Calgary), File #85, Case: R. v. S. Davis (1912), attempted buggery.

73.   Ibid., Criminal (Wetaskiwin), File #1004, Case: R. v. J. Harrington (1915), attempted buggery.

74.   Canada, *Sessional Papers*, "Criminal Statistics for the Year Ended September 30, 1891," vol. 25 (1892), Paper 7e, Table 7, "Pardons and Commutations," n. p.

75.   Canada, *Sessional Papers*, "Criminal Statistics for the Year Ended September 30, 1896," vol. 31 (1897), Paper 8d, pp. 245–46. Both men were serving their sentence in the Manitoba Penitentiary.

76.   Canada, *Sessional Papers*, "Criminal Statistics for the Year Ended September 30, 1906," vol. 41 (1906–1907), Paper 17, Table, 7 "Pardons and Commutations," n. p.

77.   Canada, *Sessional Papers*, "Criminal Statistics for the Year Ended September 30, 1909," vol. 44 (1910), Paper 17, Table 7, "Pardons and Commutations," n. p.

Criminal Justice History in Canada: A Brief Survey of Work in Progress

J. G. Woods

Solicitor General Secretariat, Ottawa

This review of research in progress is restricted to studies of the Canadian experience. It does not include the work of Canadian scholars such as Michael Ignatieff, J. M. Beattie and David H. Flaherty, to name only three, who are examining the justice history of other countries.

Productive interest in Canadian criminal justice history is so recent that, as yet, there is not a single comprehensive published historical account of any aspect of the criminal justice system. There are no Canadian equivalents to Barnes and Teeters, McKelvey, O. Lewis, W. D. Lewis, Roth, Jacobs or others who have written on the penitentiary; no Pickett, Hawes, Mennel, Platt or Schlossman on juveniles; no Lane, Fogelson, Richardson, Haller, Walker, Miller, Greenberg or Johnson on police; no Monkkonen, Gurr or Block on crime. Only in the field of juvenile justice is there the beginning of an adequate treatment, by Richard B. Splane and Neil Sutherland, although for neither author was that the major objective.[1] There is reason for optimism, however. About fifty Canadian scholars working in the field have been identified to date. Over the next decade we may expect a substantial number of significant monographs and other publications dealing with this neglected area of history.

There is, of course, a substantial body of Canadian writing which is historical in content, but it consists for the most part of popular accounts which have made no impact on académe or on the criminal justice system. This creates a minor problem of classification. The existing literature could be divided according to the criteria suggested by Cyril Robinson for American material (with the exception that there is an important French rather than "Southern" dimension to Canadian history), but there would be too few significant items in each category to make discussion worthwhile. The same may be said of division by period: New France, 1600–1759; British North America, 1760–1867 (Pre-Confederation); Canada, 1967–present (Post-Confederation); although important changes in the criminal justice system occurred at each stage. For these reasons, the division employed in the discussion below will be by broad topic: criminal justice system; law and law reform; courts; crime; police; penitentiaries and parole.[2] The discussion and alphabetical listing which follows it are based on indications of the specific and continuing research in Canada on Canadian criminal justice history, as drawn from questionnaires of 1980 with revisions to 1982.

Criminal Justice System

In Quebec, André LaChance (Université de Sherbrooke) has published monographs on the royal institutions of justice in New France and on the use of the official executioner and is now studying crime and punishment in Colonial Quebec before 1759. Douglas Hay (Warwick University) is working on crime and justice after the imposition of English law, focusing on the Court of King's Bench. André Morel (Université de Montréal) is studying the acceptance by the French of English law. Pierre Tremblay (Université de Montréal) is looking at crime and social control in Quebec from 1850 to 1914, with particular attention to social elites.

Louis Knafla (University of Calgary) is writing generally on criminal justice in the British North American colonies before 1867. Knafla also is working on the development of criminal justice on the Northwest frontier, as is Thomas Thorner (Mount Royal College). Charles Talbot (University of Ottawa) is examining the administration of justice in nineteenth-century Ontario. Brian Granger et al. (University of Regina) have written a history of adult corrections in Saskatchewan. Ezzat Fattah and others (Simon Fraser University) are preparing a history of adult corrections in British Columbia, and Jeff Taylor (independent researcher) is writing a history of juvenile justice in Manitoba. Robert Gaucher's (Sheffield University) topic is "early state formation and the Canadian criminal justice system."

Law and Law Reform

Rod McLeod (University of Alberta) has published on the evolution of the criminal law and continues to work in that area, as does W. F. Bowker (University of Alberta). P. B. L. Reedie (federal Department of the Solicitor General) has completed a study of the treason and sedition laws. John D. Blackwell (Queen's University) is examining judicial reform in pre-Confederation Ontario. Desmond Brown (University of Alberta) is writing on the origins of the Canadian criminal code of 1892. Yvon Dandurand (federal Department of Justice) has analyzed the 1892 Code and subsequent amendments to illuminate the criminalization of behavior, especially gaming, during the twentieth century. Lucie Lemieux (Université d'Ottawa) is analyzing the influence of Ontario on the drafting of the federal Juvenile Delinquents Act of 1908. Simon Verdun-Jones (Simon Fraser University) has paid particular attention to the development of the legal defense based on the insanity of the defendant. Michael Jackson (University of British Columbia) is working on a study of the use of solitary confinement as a penal sanction. Terry Chapman (University of Lethbridge) is researching morals offenses in western Canada for the period 1890–1930. Thomas Thorner's work on "Law and Lust in the Biblebelt" is forthcoming. David Flaherty (University of Western Ontario) is editor of two volumes of legal history, sponsored by the Osgoode Society.

Courts

Fred Armstrong (University of Western Ontario) has been involved for some time in a study of Justices of the Peace in Ontario before 1841, especially those who also were administrators. Kenneth Johnson (Trent University) is examining the jail registers and conviction data in two Ontario counties, for the period 1845–1867, to identify the relationship between attitudes toward crime and penal institutions. David Williams, an attorney who has published on Matthew Baillie Begbie, the controversial first Chief Justice of British Columbia, is working now on a study of the trial of Gun-A-Noot, a famous Indian outlaw. Hamar Foster (University of Victoria) is studying Commissions of Assize and significant trials in nineteenth-century British Columbia. William Wylie (Parks Canada) is analyzing the civil courts in Ontario, 1789–1812.

Crime

Popular accounts of crime and criminals abound, but there has been little scholarly work. J. M. Beattie (University of Toronto) has written on crime and public attitudes in Ontario in the first half of the nineteenth century, as have J. D. Blackwell and John C. Weaver (McMaster University). Thomas Thorner has published on crime in Alberta between 1878 and 1930. Brian Granger (Statistics Canada) is working now on a study of the "Barnardo Boys," English waifs who were shipped to foster homes in Canada and who often were blamed for crime in general in the late nineteenth century. J. B. Debo (Simon Fraser University) has undertaken a study of crime patterns in British Columbia, 1890–1920.

Police

The historical literature on policing, popular and scholarly, probably exceeds all other historical writing on Canadian criminal justice topics. Unfortunately, almost the entire output deals with the Royal Canadian Mounted Police. There is little new work dealing with municipal or provincial police forces. Philip Stenning (University of Toronto) has recently been working on the development of police commissions in nineteenth-century Ontario and on the legal status of the police in Canada. Patricia Bégin (Carleton University) is studying the development and role of police unions. Allan McDougall (University of Western Ontario) is studying policing and justice in Ontario after 1841. Stanley Horrall (Royal Canadian Mounted Police) is writing on the RCMP during the period 1886–1917.

Penitentiaries and Parole

Although nothing of substance has yet been published, a good deal of work is being done on the subject of the penitentiary. William Calder (Government of Alberta), Donald Wetherell (University of Alberta), and Christopher Norman (Queen's University) have examined the penitentiary as an institution, the efficacy of rehabilitation programs, and the political and social issues germane to the first great public inquiry into the penal system. Their work focuses on the Kingston Penitentiary (Ontario), opened in 1835. Richard Zubrycki (federal Department of the Solicitor General) is studying federal correctional policy for the period 1930–1970. J. D. Scott (independent researcher) has begun a history of the British Columbia Penitentiary, which was opened in 1878 and was decommissioned in 1980. Brian Palmer (Simon Fraser University) has been studying worker opposition to penitentiary industries. Sheila Lloyd and Graham Parker (Osgoode Hall Law School) are preparing a history of parole since the passage of the Ticket of Leave Acts in 1899. This latter work is being underwritten by the National Parole Board.

It is expected that these related studies will inform the Federal Corrections History Project, which is the most ambitious criminal justice research inquiry underway in Canada. Gerald Woods is the Principal Investigator of this project, which is being undertaken by the Department of the Solicitor General of Canada. A number of sub-projects are underway. Rainer Baehre (Mount St. Vincent University) is examining the development of the penitentiary in the four Atlantic provinces prior to 1880. Christopher Curtis (Parks Canada) is doing the same for British Columbia and Peter Orr (McGill University) for Quebec. Sheila Lloyd (federal Department of the Solicitor General) is studying the female inmate in federal institutions since 1835. Michael Whittingham (York University) studied the role of commissions of inquiry and the influence of voluntary associations on correctional reform since 1867. The sub-project reports will be published as they are completed. A comprehensive narrative synthesis will be based on the sub-projects.

Two additional studies, a documentary history and a bibliography, are in progress. Most of the relevant documents (since 1600) have been collected, but annotation has not begun. The bibliography is at the proofreading stage. Although less than perfect, the bibliography will identify thousands of source documents and should prove valuable to Canadian researchers.

Other Areas

The Department of the Solicitor General has published three other annotated criminal justice bibliographies, dealing with criminology, the costs of crime, and policing. Catherine Sheppard has written on legal resources at the Archives of Ontario. James Whalen has been active in increasing the justice holdings of the Public Archives of Canada and in encouraging their use by researchers. The Canadian Historical Atlas, Volume II, will include a section on social welfare and crime. The Dictionary of Canadian Biography puts considerable emphasis on significant lawmakers, judges and lawyers. Simon Fraser University has undertaken a project to collect copies of all Canadian theses and dissertations which deal with criminal justice, broadly construed. A film by Charles Wilkinson, dealing with penitentiary history, is in the final stages of production. The film was funded in part by the federal Department of the Solicitor General. Criminal justice history courses are becoming more common in Canadian universities, and attention to history is more common in criminology texts.

Summary

At present there is little published scholarly work on the justice system, except for the Royal Canadian Mounted Police and, to a degree, juvenile justice in English Canada. The scant existing work tends to be descriptive rather than theoretical, particular rather than general. A great deal remains to be done.

It appears, however, that a solid academic and intellectual foundation for justice history will be laid during the next few years. Catherine J. Matthews and Russell C. Smandych (Robarts Research Library, Toronto) have begun to prepare an annotated bibliography of post-1867 secondary sources on Canadian criminal justice history. At least four associations—the Society for History and Law, the Osgoode Society, La Société pour l'histoire du contrôle sociale, and the Canadian Criminal Justice History Association—encourage teaching, research, and writing on justice topics. Several conferences specifically directed to justice history have been successfully organized, and further meetings are planned. A decade from now, there should be a much richer literature and a great many more research inquiries to report.

Notes

1. Richard B. Splane, *Social Welfare in Ontario, 1791–1893, A Study of Public Welfare Administration* (Toronto: University of Toronto Press, 1963) and Neil Sutherland, *Children in English Canadian Society* (Toronto: University of Toronto Press, 1976).

2. Under the Canadian system, the *Criminal Code* is a federal statute enforced by the provinces, which are responsible for the administration of justice, *i.e.*, policing, juvenile justice, prosecution and sentencing, and incarceration for less than two years. The Royal Canadian Mounted Police is a federal force enforcing other federal statutes, but serves—under contract—as the provincial police in eight of the provinces and in about two hundred municipalities. The National Parole Board is responsible for inmates in federal prisons and for inmates in provincial jails where the province has not created a provincial parole board. Inmates sentenced to more than two years are held in federal institutions.

APPENDIX
Researchers and Projects

Professor Fred H. Armstrong
  Department of History
  University of Western Ontario
  London, Ontario N6A 5C2

The magistrates of Upper Canada, 1784–1841.

Professor Rainer Baehre
  Department of History
  Dalhousie University
  Halifax, N.S.

Gaols and penitentiaries in Upper Canada; lunacy law and asylums; paupers, poor relief, and the socio-economic etiology of crime during the 1837 rebellion.

Mr. J. Patrick Boyer
  Ste. 1602, 7 Jackes Avenue
  Toronto, Ontario M4T 1E3

Commissions of inquiry into Canadian penal conditions.

Ms. Patty Begin
  Department of Sociology/Anthropology
  Loeb Building
  Carleton University
  Ottawa, Ontario K1S 5B6

Police unions.

Mr. William A. Calder
  15104 73rd Street
  Edmonton, Alta. T5C 0N2

The Federal penitentiary system in Canada, 1867–1899.

Ms. Terry L. Chapman
  History Department
  University of Lethbridge
  Lethbridge, Alberta T1K 3M4

The history of moral offences in western Canada.

Mr. Christopher Curtis
  164 Hopewell Avenue
  Ottawa, Ontario K1S 2Z5

Penal institutions in British Columbia prior to the opening of the Federal penitentiary at New Westminster.

Professor Yvon Dandurand
    Départment de Criminologie
    Université d'Ottawa
    Ottawa, Ontario K1N 6N5

Le Processus de Criminalisation Formelle au Canada, 1892–1975; and La Criminalisation du Jeu au Canada depuis 1892.

Professeur Alfred Dubuc
    Université du Québec à Montréal
    Case postale 8888, Succursale "A"
    Montréal, P.Q. H3C 3P8

L'historie du Droit; les relations entre l'historie socio-économique du Canada et, les événements politiques d'une part, et, d'autre part, l'activité legislative, judiciaire et policière.

Professor Ezzat Fattah
    Department of Criminology
    Simon Fraser University
    Burnaby, B.C.

Provincial corrections in British Columbia since Confederation.

Mr. Robert Gaucher
    Apt. 5
    4 Howick Street
    Ottawa, Ontario

Early state formation and the Canadian criminal justice system.

Mr. Brian Grainger
    2833 Angus Street
    Regina, Sask. S4S 1N7

Adult corrections in Saskatchewan, 1905–1975, with an introductory chapter dealing with the Territorial period prior to 1905 (with O. Driedger and S. Skinner).

Dr. Douglas Hay
    Department of History
    Memorial University
    St. John's, Newfoundland

History of crime and criminal justice in Quebec.

Mr. S. W. Horrall
    RCMP Historian
    Room G-314
    1200 Alta Vista Drive
    Ottawa, Ontario K1A 0R2

The Royal Canadian Mounted Police, 1886–1917.

Professor Michael Jackson
Faculty of Law
University of British Columbia
Vancouver, B.C.

Solitary confinement as a penal sanction, with special reference to Canada.

Mr. Kenneth W. Johnson
University Archivist
Trent University
Peterborough, Ontario K9J 7B9

Computer analysis of the gaol register and court of general sessions records of
convictions for selected years, 1845–1867, for the United Counties of
Northumberland and Durham (Canada West).

Professor Louis Knafla
Department of History
University of Calgary
2920-24th Avenue N.W.
Calgary, Alta. T2N 1N4

Current work includes: History of Canadian criminal justice; early development of
criminal justice in the Northwest, c. 1850–1907; and in Alberta, 1907–1920;
comparative studies of criminal justice.

Professeur André La Chance
Departement d'histoire
Faculté des Arts
Université de Sherbrooke
Sherbrooke, P.Q. J1K 2R1

La criminalité et la répression pénale au Canada au XVIIIe siècle.

Ms. Sheila Lloyd
293 Maclaren Street
Ottawa, Ontario K2P 0L9

History of the origins of parole (for the National Parole Board).

Dr. Catherine J. Matthews
Centre of Criminology
University of Toronto
Toronto, Ontario M5S 1A1

Bibliography of Canadian criminal justice history since 1867.

Professor Allan K. McDougall
Department of Political Science
University of Western Ontario
London, Ontario N6A 5C2

Policing, police policy, and the administration of justice.

Professeur André Morel
  Faculté de Droit
  Université de Montréal
  Montréal, Québec H3C 3J7

Acceptance of English law in Quebec after 1760.

Mr. W. Christian Norman
  12-550 Platt's Lane
  London, Ontario N6G 3A9

The early years of the provincial penitentiary at Kingston, and the Commission of Inquiry into its management, 1835–1851. The founding of the prison, the controversies of the 1840s and 1850s, the Commission of Enquiry of 1849 and the Select Committee of 1850.

Professor Bryan Palmer
  Department of History
  McGill University
  Montreal, Quebec H3C 3G1

Kingston mechanics and the rise of the penitentiary, 1833–1836.

Professor Graham Parker
  Osgoode Hall Law School
  York University
  Downsview, Ontario M3J 2R5

History of the Canadian Criminal Code; historical antecedents of the Canadian Ticket-of-Leave Act.

Ms. Penny Reedie
  Statistics Division
  Solicitor General of Canada
  340 Laurier Avenue West
  Ottawa, Ontario

History of the treason and sedition laws in Canada.

Dr. Russell C. Smandych
  Centre of Criminology
  University of Toronto
  Toronto, Ontario M5S 1A1

Bibliography of Canadian criminal justice history since 1867.

Ms. Alice Switocz
  4116 Côte des Neiges, Apt. 1
  Montréal, Québec H3H 1X1

The development and implementation of the Canadian ticket-of-leave system, 1899–1925.

Professor Charles Talbot
Department of Criminology
University of Ottawa
Ottawa, Ontario K1N 6N5

Provincial corrections in Upper Canada and Ontario.

Mr. Jeff Taylor
Box 33
Snowflake, Manitoba R0G 2K0

History of juvenile justice in Manitoba.

M. Pierre Tremblay
Departement de Criminologie
Université de Montréal
C. P. 6128
Montréal, Québec

Contrôle du crime au Québec (1850–1914). A. Contrôles officiels de la criminalité:...criminelles en fonction du modèle Wilkins-Ditton concernant les cycles temporels du contrôle de la criminalité; B. Elite pénale et idéologie du crime.

Professor Simon Verdun-Jones
Department of Criminology
Simon Fraser University
Burnaby, B.C.

History of the plea of insanity.

Professor John C. Weaver
Department of History
McMaster University
Hamilton, Ontario L8S 4L9

Crime in the Gore District (Ontario), using court records for the period 1816–1851.

Professor Donald Wetherell
Department of History
University of Alberta
Edmonton, Alta. T6G 2H4

The rehabilitation of criminals in Canada, 1869–1915.

Mr. James Whalen
State and Military Section
Public Archives of Canada
395 Wellington Street
Ottawa, Ontario K1A 0N3

Archivist responsible for the reference service dealing with the records of the Department of Justice and the Department of the Solicitor General. Will assist researchers interested in these areas.

Mr. Michael D. Whittingham
Research Division
Police Research Section
Solicitor General Canada
340 Laurier Avenue West
Ottawa, Ontario K1A 0P8

Impediments to correctional reform in the nineteenth and twentieth centuries; correctional royal commissions within theory of knowledge framework; sociohistorical influences on criminological theory and practice.

Dr. J. G. Woods
Research Division
Solicitor General of Canada
Ottawa, Ontario K1A 0P8

Federal corrections history.

Mr. William Wylie
602 Surgenor Street
Cornwall, Ontario K6J 2H4

The civil courts of Upper Canada, 1789–1812.

Mr. Richard Zubrycki
Box 774
Richmond, Ontario K0A 2Z0

History of Canadian Federal Penitentiaries, 1930–1970.

Book Reviews

Robert C. Palmer, *The County Courts of Medieval England, 1150–1350.*
Princeton, N.J.: Princeton University Press, 1982. xvii + 360 pp. $35.

This unusually important book is the first satisfactory history of the English
medieval county courts. Earlier scholars were doubtless deterred because
few county court rolls have survived, although not quite as few as was previously thought. Dr. Palmer has supplemented them by searching for county
court cases and references in a wide range of administrative and legal records. The number of cases that he cites from the De Banco rolls alone rep-
resents a prodigious amount of work. The result is a convincing picture of
the workings of the courts and their officials, which operated not in isolation but in constant interaction with both lesser and superior jurisdictions.

The underlying theme of the book is that until the reign of Edward I
the county courts were an essential and vital part of an integrated legal system. That integration was fostered, in part, by the personnel of the county
courts. Until the mid-thirteenth century the sheriffs (the presiding officers)
were frequently either experienced in the central administration or as
justices, or had been sheriffs in other counties. They were therefore able to
ensure that the developing legal system was adopted uniformly throughout
the country. They were ably assisted in that by the "seneschals" and bailiffs
of the county barons, who acted as pleaders and gave all judgments in the
county courts and many of whom also had considerable experience as
attorneys in the court of common pleas.

If Dr. Palmer overstates the importance of this small band of men as
the earliest professional lawyers, it is understandable since he is the first to
appreciate it. The county courts of the early thirteenth century were far
from being amateur bodies relying on the county gentry (the suitors), but
were, as Dr. Palmer's work attests, highly sophisticated and professional
institutions. Their procedures and processes formed a strong link with the
rest of the legal system. On the one hand, the county courts had supervisory

powers over the other local courts, including seignorial courts by means of tolt; on the other, their own cases were frequently removed to the court of common pleas, by *pone* if begun by writ or by *recordari* if begun by plaint, and issues in cases begun in the common pleas were often referred to the decision of juries in the county courts. Only after the Hundred Rolls inquiry was the jurisdiction of the county courts seriously limited, and after 1285 issues from the common pleas were determined instead at *nisi prius*. On the civil side, the county courts of the later Middle Ages were largely restricted to lesser cases of trespass and debt, and they became removed from the mainstream of the legal system.

These arguments, and much more, Dr. Palmer has painstakingly constructed from a myriad of detailed cases. He argues lucidly and is the more persuasive because he prints much of his evidence in his footnotes in the form of transcripts. It is impossible to say that on no point will he remain unchallenged, but any doubters will be committed to doing even more research than Dr. Palmer himself. This reviewer must limit himself to less basic criticisms.

It is true that the county courts were not of the first importance for crown pleas and the prosecution of crime, at least after 1215. Nevertheless, appeals of felony were normally begun in them and have not been so exhaustively treated elsewhere as to justify their relegation by Dr. Palmer to a short appendix. Again, writs of exigent could be executed and outlawry promulgated only in the county courts, and that remained their most important regular function. This function also deserved greater emphasis. In short, there is an imbalance between the treatment of civil pleas on the one hand and crown pleas, crime, and exigent and outlawry on the other, which could be misleading and is unfortunate for it would have been interesting to have Dr. Palmer's estimate, however tentative, of the relative amount of time the county courts devoted to each.

It is also unfortunate that Dr. Palmer chose one abnormal county, Cheshire, from which to illustrate his basic distinction between "judges" and suitors, and concentrated on another, Lincolnshire, with its intermediate tier of courts between county and hundred, in his discussion of county offcials. He clearly realised that his use of the word "judges" for those who rendered county court judgments was far from happy, and he produced no good reason for preferring "seneschals" to the commonly accepted "stewards." It is also eccentric to call the ridings of Yorkshire and Lincolnshire "trithings." Particular care should have been taken in this book with the spelling of county court venues and legal institutions, yet Crawley and Morpeth are consistently called Crowley and Morpath, and Gray's Inn appears only as Grey's or Greys Inn. The bibliography and index contain more errors and inequalities than one would expect from so meticulous a scholar, although few are seriously misleading. Such blemishes, however, are minor ones which do not detract from a remarkable achievement.

R. F. Hunnisett
Public Record Office, London

Sung Tz'u. *The Washing Away of Wrongs: Forensic Medicine in Thirteenth-Century China*. Edited and translated by Brian E. McKnight. Ann Arbor: Center for Chinese Studies, University of Michigan, 1981. $6.

The Washing Away of Wrongs is a manual written in the thirteenth century, during the Sung Dynasty, on how to conduct inquests. It gives elaborate instructions not only on how to determine cause of death, but also on protocol. It preceded Western guides to conducting postmortems by several centuries. Revised and reprinted, it remained a standard reference work for Chinese oficials through the Ch'ing Dynasty in the nineteenth century.

McKnight has done a masterful job of translating the work and of annotating the translation. In addition, he has written a thoughtful introduction, placing the work in the context of Chinese legal practice and comparing Chinese investigation of death to European counterparts.

This reviewer is not schooled in medicine. Much less than McKnight am I qualified to assess the reliability of the techniques prescribed for preparing and examining dead bodies. As McKnight suggests, it might well be worth pathologists' time to study whether thirteenth-century Chinese investigators have something to add to the contemporary repertoire of techniques for conducting postmortems. The section of the manual on resuscitating the near-dead (which the manual characterizes as "restoring life" to dead persons) might prove equally informative to present-day medical practitioners. But its value to medical science aside, the work offers a wealth of insight into the metaphysics of law and legal investigation in dynastic China.

Students of law and crime in my country today are preoccupied with giving "just deserts" to offenders. By and large, our writings on the subject provide only a superficial idea of what just deserts are and why they ought to be given. Implicit in *The Washing Away of Wrongs* is an extraordinarily sophisticated notion of legal retribution.

The title of the book is revealing. *Hsi-yuan chi-lu* literally means "compendium on cleaning grievances." *Yuan*, the Chinese character for "grievance" or "wrong," contains the character for "hare" or "rabbit" under that for "roof," signifying having a pest in one's domain. And so, by conducting inquests, Chinese officials were perceived as helping to clean up society by putting people in their proper places. The way to cleanse wrongs is further illuminated by the title of a short imitation of this work, published soon after it: *P'ing-yuan lu. P'ing* means "to establish balance" (and also signifies "peace"). In the Chinese cosmology, the *yin* or evil force of grievances could be set right by the *yang* of punishing offenders in precise measure to the harm they had done. Chinese officials thus maintained a proper balance between natural forces of social order and disorder. By responding to grievances with punishments in kind, Chinese officialdom might succeed in erasing the grievances, as the title of another short copy of *The Washing Away of Wrongs, Wu-yuan lu—There-Are-No Grievances*—indicates.

High stakes rested on the ability of officials to make the punishment exactly fit the crime. Officials represented the Emperor, who in turn personified the dynasty. Insomuch as the government remained *yang* in response to the *yin* of social disorder, the dynasty survived. But when officials lost their mastery of social order, it was a law of nature that the dynasty would lose its "mandate of heaven," or fall. The legitimacy and indeed the existence of the dynasty rested on the infallibility of fitting punishments to crimes. There was no such thing as burden of proof in this system. Officials had to determine the full truth in exhausting detail and respond accordingly. When, for instance, someone had died of wounds inflicted by a group, the official had to determine which offender had struck *the* fatal blow; what kind of weapon, if any, had been used; and, within a margin of days, how long ago the blows had been struck, before it could be determined which offender, if any, should be sentenced to death. The magistrate who failed to solve a crime and bring an offender to justice within a prescribed period was liable to punishment himself. And if a later inquest or trial or review of punishment determined that an official had set or executed an undeserved punishment, the official would also be punished in due measure. This preoccupation with making punishment infallible has carried over to the present. According to the recently enacted Communist Chinese Law of Criminal Procedure, the absolute truth of guilt or innocence of the person charged with a crime must be determined before a decision is made even about an arrest; and where a crime has occurred, an arrest must follow a restricted period of investigation.

The dynastic system of punishment was so elaborately designed that three levels of execution were provided within the realm of capital crimes alone—from strangulation to beheading to slicing—with every death sentence to be reviewed by the Emperor personally.

The Chinese did not confuse "responsibility" with deserving punishment, as we do. "Responsibility" was instead reserved for notions of what people, including officials, had to do to help reorder the social world. Thus, the accused was not stripped of personal power but was enjoined to help set matters straight. The accused had a duty to confess, and, according to McKnight, was also commonly assigned the duty of caring for injured persons, under the assumption that he or she had the greatest stake in averting a capital offense.

With so much resting on proper punishment, and with homicide the most serious of disorders, it was deemed vital that inquests be promptly and meticulously conducted. It was the official's responsibility to use right reason to get the job done and to provide detailed records for higher review. Medical practitioners had no role to play, except to be examined in possible cases of malpractice resulting in death. This puzzles McKnight. I suspect the exclusion resulted from another Chinese premise about natural order—that those who deserved to rule did so with their minds over subjects who worked with their hands.

The Chinese attitude toward medical practice is not so peculiar. When one pauses to reflect, it is anomalous that we in the United States have raised a class of manual laborers, surgeons, to exalted social status. As one would expect from the Chinese concept of the natural order, the examining magistrate did not touch the bodies. A special class of manual workers was retained for this job. The official would tell the worker what to do, and the worker would call out loud what he or she felt and saw. And in the process, the symbolism of "washing" had its physical counterpart, for good scientific practice demanded that the corpse be washed and soaked before being examined. On the other hand, again in keeping with Chinese notions of bodily integrity, the manual nowhere suggests that bodies had to be cut open to determine the cause of death. Bodily orifices could be penetrated under special circumstances. Otherwise, the only violation of the body's integrity recommended was to insert a silver needle into the throat or abdomen in cases of suspected poisoning.

A part of the ritual of inquests was concerned with how to assemble parties to the "grievance," a ritual elaborately designed to elicit truth. The family of the victim, the accused, if any, and village leaders all were to witness the autopsy and then were to be questioned in one another's presence. Prior consultation among all participants was to be avoided. Those present were to sign the copies of the official's account of the inquest.

Beyond examination of the corpse, the manual is filled with tips on how to examine the scene of the death and how to use informants. Allegories of good detective work are interspersed throughout.

The book also conveys what kinds of social disorder and death were prominent. Suicide by hanging was common, and so was homicide made to look like suicide. Corpses were often burned in fires. Drowning was commonplace, but so was homicide from other causes made to look like drowning, and drowning occurred not only in lakes and rivers but in wells. Servants and women were commonly beaten, sometimes to death, sometimes to the point of suicide. Death from natural causes or from suicide was sometimes made to look like homicide in order to get one's enemies into trouble. (As might be expected, falsely accusing someone of a crime was as serious as committing the crime itself.) Physical abuse of prisoners was a major problem, requiring that some officials investigate others. (For one thing, with all the pressure to convict the guilty, magistrates were prone to torture the accused into confessing, or the complainant into attesting to a false accusation.) The manual makes clear that confessions alone were insufficient evidence to support conviction and punishment, but surely they helped. And in the Sung Dynasty, after trial and sentencing, the accused had to sign acknowledgment of guilt, or else a new trial was required.

W. I. Thomas wrote a theorem now famous among sociologists: "Things that are defined as real are real in their consequences." The author of *The Washing Away of Wrongs*, Sung Tz'u, had retired from officialdom early, in part because of the clash between his uncompromising integrity and official corruption. Of course officials took bribes to exonerate citizens, and of course officials were generally loath to acknowledge that a death requiring an inquest had occurred. Sung Tz'u's exhortations to diligence and propriety are a cry of impotence and frustration over the unwillingness of officials to risk being punished themselves by an uncompromising legal apparatus.

By contrast, in my own society today, all the incentives encourage officials to discover wrongdoing and pursue wrongdoers. This extends to medical examination. (For example, the examiner in Hamilton County, Ohio, considerably increased the homicide rate in the 1960s by making autopsies routine in cases such as those of bodies in cars or in bathtubs or of children being brought for emergency treatment, where previously, autopsies had been sporadic.) By contrast, the incentives in China rewarded a failure to find homicide in particular and crime generally. Everyone from the magistrate to the accused to the complainant stood to lose when a case came to official attention.

At a higher level, the odds of a regime's survival were strengthened by making the punishment fit the crime; they became even better if the crime did not occur in the first place. The greater the propriety with which the

Emperor and his officials ruled, the more nearly perfect would be the social order among the Emperor's subjects. If officials who went unpunished found no crime to report, among a set of officials who had a stake in believing in governmental infallibility, then there must in reality be no crime, and the dynasty was indeed faring well.

How much happier we Americans might be if we structured our legal system to discourage rather than to encourage the finding of crime. With less reason to fear crime, we might leave our homes more freely and circulate in the streets in greater numbers, making streets safer. With less reason to doubt our private capacity to prevent crime, we might intervene more readily to achieve the result, as the Chinese today are renowned for doing. As this American reads and considers *The Washing Away of Wrongs*, he is struck by how much centuries of Chinese tradition might have to teach us about structuring a legal system to persuade ourselves that we give just deserts to offenders, and in so doing contain crime. For further inspiration, we could look to another side of Chinese tradition, represented in the Taoist exhortation of Lao Tzu: "More restrictions mean weaker people; more weapons mean a troubled state; more cunning means many surprises; more laws mean more violators."

The Chinese have been wrestling with problems we ourselves face and have wrestled long and thoughtfully. Opportunities to read Chinese history are usually instructive. *The Washing Away of Wrongs* is a case in point.

Harold E. Pepinsky
Indiana University

Alan Macfarlane and Sarah Harrison, *The Justice and the Mare's Ale: Law and Disorder in Seventeenth-Century England*. New York: Cambridge University Press, 1981. xiv + 238 pp. $19.95.

Alan Macfarlane's latest book focuses upon the years 1680 to 1684 and the area of Westmorland, East Cumberland, Northern Lancashire, and Western Yorkshire. His principal sources are the depositions taken in criminal trials and the personal papers of Daniel Fleming, a Westmorland J.P. Depositions, frequently destroyed because they were not documents "of record," were informal, pre-trial examinations of suspects and witnesses. Fleming's papers include rough copies of depositions and about six thousand letters to and from him. Macfarlane provides extensive extracts from these interesting and uniquely preserved documents.

Macfarlane begins by discussing two contrasting views of the history of England from about 1450 to 1750. One view is that law and order were established during the late Middle Ages. The other argument is that endemic violence was eradicated much later, possibly not until the period between 1700 and 1850. Although Macfarlane never explicitly states which view he accepts, the last paragraph in the book suggests the former view.

To test the validity of the two views, Macfarlane dissects the alleged crimes of William and Henry Smorthwait and their accomplices. In 1683 the Smorthwait brothers and four others were indicted for burglary, robbery, coining (counterfeiting), and clipping (cutting metal off the edges of coins to make additional currency). The evidence is uncertain, but possibly as many as eight of sixteen bills of indictment were rejected by the grand jury. The petty jury found only one person guilty—of pickpocketing. But during the summer of 1684 the Smorthwaits and their confederates were again indicted. This time the charges were six burglaries, several cases of pickpocketing, and seven thefts of fourteen or fifteen animals. The most serious charge was wounding a defender of his property. The Smorthwait brothers were hanged in 1684; surviving evidence on some of their collaborators indicates that they died peacefully in bed much later.

The introduction leads the reader to expect that Macfarlane will document endemic violence in northern England. But his case study does the opposite. Law and order prevailed: witnesses appeared at assizes; juries decided guilt or innocence; authorities in the four northern counties cooperated; letters went back and forth between justices of the peace and petty and high constables with a speed that makes us envious; and travellers filled the highways without much fear of becoming crime statistics.

Macfarlane concludes by citing research on violence and brutality in late seventeenth-century China, eighteenth- and nineteenth-century France, and nineteenth- and twentieth-century Sicily. He claims that insecurity and violence prevailed in these peasant societies because they were in transition from peasant/feudal to capitalist/modern society. The four-county area of northern England was extraordinarily tame compared to these three peasant societies because, as Macfarlane notes that he has argued elsewhere (*The Origins of English Individualism*), "from at least the thirteenth century England has not had any peasants" (p. 199). With the exception of this statement in the book's final paragraph, there is no explanation of why Macfarlane's findings differ from those of researchers cited in the introduction who portray seventeenth-century England as violent and brutal.

The book is not consistent with the quality that we have come to expect from Macfarlane. Introductory and concluding arguments are not clearly presented. Too often the reader is left guessing whether Macfarlane is describing the opinions of others or his own, although this book was written to support his earlier research on individualism. Also, "suspected," "alleged," "accused," and "reputed" appear infrequently. Macfarlane is inadequately critical of accusations cited in depositions. For example, he convicts individuals on vague recollections related late in 1684 about an alleged burglary early in 1676. About another reputed offense he casually states, "The evidence is interesting, whether true or invented" (p. 72). And one might question his argument that it is acceptable to generalize from sensational cases, such as the Smorthwaits', because only sensational cases contain sufficient information to allow conclusions about the level of violence. Presumably, then, we may generalize about violence in the U.S. by dissecting the unique Charles Manson murders in California in 1969.

Macfarlane leaves many questions unasked. Because the Smorthwaits do not fit the sociologists' stereotype of violent peasants, Macfarlane concludes that they and their contemporaries were not peasants. Were the Smorthwaits representative of seventeenth-century offenders? Should only violent offenders be labeled peasants? Are violence and lawlessness the same, as Macfarlane implies? Are the 1680s representative of the period 1450 to 1750? Would not a test of the level of pre-Civil War violence yield a more trustworthy conclusion about peasants and violence? Is post-Restoration Westmorland representative of England, as Macfarlane assumes?

The book contains a brief but useful glossary, four maps, fourteen illustrations, and four appendices including one on the method of counterfeiting coins. The argument that quantifying indictments at quarter sessions and assizes will yield an unrepresentative count of actual illegal actions is well supported in this book. There is also an excellent description of the legal process at the assizes. As an annotated work, though not presented as such, the book is excellent; as a work containing effective arguments demonstrating an understanding of the complexity of crime and the limitations of the data, it fails miserably.

Walter J. King
Northern State College,
South Dakota

Iain A. Cameron, *Crime and Repression in the Auvergne and the Guyenne.* Cambridge: Cambridge University Press, 1982. xvi + 283 pp. $37.50.

This monograph, a study of two regional units of the national police force (a mounted constabulary based throughout rural France), provides a model for investigating criminality. In contrast to many similar works, the writing possesses considerable power and grace. Second, the author, Iain Cameron, has uncovered an impressive array of sources, thus avoiding the most common methodological pitfall in examining this kind of subject. So often the paucity of information has left scholars with only a single source whose meaning might be ambiguous. Reports on crimes, for example, may reflect either police perceptions or criminal behavior or the two in combination. Cameron's exhaustive research permits the relatively accurate evaluation of sources. One must add that he also avoids methodological difficulties by not pushing his evidence too far. Third, Cameron's book is an exemplary work on criminality because it not only illuminates the police and the policed but also adds to a broad understanding of the period under consideration.

The main thrust of *Crime and Repression in the Auvergne and the Guyenne* improves our comprehension of the eighteenth-century French monarchy. The description commences in 1720, the year the French government endeavored to modernize and strengthen the constabulary, or in French, the *maréchausée*. The government's motives included the desire to extend its authority, the need to control an increasingly destitute and potentially restive population, and the wish to provide reliable justice. Despite these seemingly compelling motives, the central administration contributed little money to the reform, and these constables had to make do on very little despite some improvements over the century. Cameron charts the effect of such changes up to 1790 in two rather different provinces—the developing Guyenne and the backward Auvergne. He finds that the financial limitations notwithstanding, these officers performed their duties diligently. As police, they normally worked hard to discipline rural areas; and in their judicial role, they seem to have been remarkably fair. One cannot judge their work by a reduction in the incidence of crime, of course, since the changes in the *maréchausée* were insufficient to counteract the problems of the time. But, by all contemporary accounts, the constables served very well. This portrait is as vivid as any we have of the strengths and weaknesses of the eighteenth-century monarchy in the provinces. Unfortunately, Cameron speculates little about the meaning of his case study. This proves regrettable since, in my view, the author could marshall his conclusions to reinforce an important diagnosis of monarchical problems: the facade of efficient government accompanied by the inability to shape developments.

The author's other main focus, the characteristics of certain varieties of crime, further facilitates our grasp of the Old Regime. Cameron's information on the *maréchausée* illuminates three common forms of law-breaking— theft, violence, and riot. His methodological care allows him to use the data

on the constables to describe the criminals as well. His findings are somewhat disparate, but most important, he argues that his evidence indicates
that some alteration is necessary in the accepted views about the balance
between crimes against property and people. While most scholars conclude
that the former came to eclipse the latter, Cameron's work on the Auvergne
suggests this shift lacked uniformity. Others may wish to investigate this
significant finding.

Although Cameron subordinates his specific examples to the general
framework outlined above, these vignettes of common men and women
contribute independently to Old Regime history. For some time, historians
of this period have inquired into the life of the population at large. More
recently, they have shifted their attention from schematic, generally quantitative, assessments to detailed characterizations of individuals. In Cameron's
book, scholars will encounter a whole host of richly textured personal
portraits, created by the author from the varied source at his disposal. In
fact, it would have been desirable had Cameron focused somewhat on these
incidents in order to explain clearly the way that such specific situations
themselves provide insights into the society of eighteenth-century France.

Cameron ought to have exploited his findings more carefully for their
implications; however, the dominant theme I wish to strike is the excellence
of this book. Its methodological care, its writing, its research, and its arguments mark it as one of the best recent monographs on eighteenth-century
France.

Jack R. Censer
George Mason University

R. F. Hunnisett, ed. *Wiltshire Coroners' Bills 1752–1796.* Wiltshire Record
Society, XXXVI: Devizes, 1981. liv + 239 pp.

With this substantial volume Dr. R. F. Hunnisett, already well known for his
monograph *The Medieval Coroner* (1961), and two volumes of medieval coroners' records, *Bedfordshire Coroners' Rolls* (Beds. Hist. Rec. Soc. XLI) and
Calendar of Nottinghamshire Coroners' Inquests (Thoroton Soc. Rec. Ser.
XXV), extends his work on the history of the coroner into the Early Modern
period. His latest offering maintains the meticulous editorial standards of
the earlier publications, and it is entirely appropriate that the volume should
be dedicated to Professor R. B. Pugh, President of the Wiltshire Record
Society, who over the years has also built a formidable reputation for exact

scholarship, crisp, detailed writing, and a deep commitment to the study of local records.

In a short introduction, Dr. Hunnisett explains that the coroners' bills calendared in this volume originated in the statutory provision of 1752 (25 Geo. II, c. 29) which allowed coroners to claim expenses for holding inquests on dead bodies. Those fees were to be paid out of the county rates; and in order to establish their entitlement to payment, coroners regularly presented their bills at quarter sessions. "The typical bill lists and summarizes in chronological order, the inquests held by the coroner since the submission of his previous claim. . . .The summaries exclude some details which were in the formal written inquests, but since hardly any inquests survive the bills are an unrivalled source for the activities of the eighteenth-century coroner and for the types of death which came within his jurisdiction, as well as throwing much incidental light on social and economic conditions" (pp. xxx-xxxi). The records calendared in this volume comprise 144 bills listing 2,779 inquests held by Wiltshire coroners between 1752 and 1796. Most are brief items recording the date and place of the inquest, the name of the deceased, the cause of death, the distance traveled by the coroner to hold the inquest, and the total amount claimed. Where the coroner's verdict resulted in a criminal trial, the editor has, very usefully, added the verdict and sentence from the assize records of the Western Circuit (PRO, ASSI 23). Access to the mass of information contained in the calendar entries is facilitated by a superbly detailed subject index which, among other things, breaks down the various causes and locations of death.

Taken as a whole, the inquests constitute a graphic reminder of the hazards of a rural life which changed little between the Middle Ages and the end of the nineteenth century. Death at the feet or horns of farm animals, under falling walls, trees, carts, hayricks, barns and quarries, in rivers, ponds, ditches, wells, fords, tubs and fish hatcheries, and in falls from haystacks, haylofts, ladders, trees, horses, carts and coaches, constantly recur. Inclement weather accounted for more than one hundred deaths during the period: eight were attributed to harsh weather in February 1762; a further eight died from exposure in the severe winter of 1767/68; and a "tempestuous wind" in early March 1781 resulted in at least two fatalities. It is perhaps hardly surprising that excessive drinking was on several occasions cited as the cause of death and that more than two hundred men and women in this period are recorded as having committed suicide. The incidence of infanticide (fifty-six verdicts) also points to the realities of early-modern rural life, although a consistently high acquittal and pardon rate at assizes suggests that by the eighteenth century the psychological, social, and economic pressures underlying that crime were widely understood. Forensic medicine, on the other hand, was still in its infancy. Although all of the Wiltshire county coroners during this period had medical qualifications, their examination and diagnosis was often superficial ("no marks of violence; natural death"), and less than one-quarter of the natural deaths were attributed to specific causes. But occasionally they did conduct autopsies (#899, 950, 1077, 1081, 1281), and the result—particularly in cases of suspected poisoning—was usually conclusive. The holding of autopsies and the mention here of three murderers who were sentenced at assizes to dissection and anatomization after execution illustrates the fumbling and unpopular attempts being made in the eighteenth century to advance medical knowledge and the strong connection between the histories of surgery and crime.

The coroner's most obvious connection with crime lay, of course, in his power to initiate criminal prosecution through a verdict of murder or manslaughter. The Wiltshire bills include more than seventy cases in which a coroner's inquest led directly to trial for homicide. The coroner was also obliged to hold an inquest on anyone dying in gaol (although his expenses in such cases were not to exceed £1) and the exercise of that function, too, yields both statistical and qualitative evidence which is of considerable interest to students of historical crime. Inquests were held on at least 139 deceased prisoners, three of whom were found to have committed suicide (#1680, 2233, 2654). An inquest (#1557) held in Devizes prison in 1787 on an emaciated prisoner attributed his death to inclement weather and lack of sustenance, adding that the daily allowance of a twopenny loaf was "a very short and scanty one, inadequate to and insufficient for the support and maintenance of the body of any man." As a result, the prisoners' allowance was increased (p. li).

Although intriguing vignettes abound, a reviewer (following the editor himself) must resist the temptation to dwell on particular inquests. In a journal devoted to the history of criminal justice, however, few reviewers of this rich and impeccably presented material could resist quoting, in conclusion, two poignant entries:

1763   9 Apr. 1791. Whitley Common. William Watson: found dead at dawn on the Common. He had got up before day on hearing a thief repeating his depredations in stealing faggots from a pile on his premises, pursued the thief in the dark, and received a blow in his head which instantly killed him.

1783   26 June 1791. Whitley Common in Melksham. Mary Watson, the unhappy widow of the above William: at the time was very much affected by the sudden and melancholy loss of her husband, and ever since, being in the same house with no company, was almost continuously possessed by lowness of spirits, despair, and despondency; at length in the night of 24 or morning of 25 June she threw herself into a well in her garden and was instantly suffocated; lunacy.

Copies of *Wiltshire Coroners' Bills* are obtainable from M. J. Lansdown, 53 Clarendon Road, Trowbridge, Wiltshire, England, price £10 to non-members, excluding postage.

J. S. Cockburn
University of Maryland

Antoinette Wills, *Crime and Punishment in Revolutionary Paris*. Westport: Greenwood Press, 1981. xxi + 227 pp. $32.50.

The fire during the 1871 Commune destroyed most Paris court records dating from the Revolution. The proceedings of six courts that existed from March 1791 to August 1792 survived, however. The revolutionaries had provisionally established these to assist the newly created departmental courts in handling both the backlog of the pre-revolutionary juridical system and the influx of new cases. According to Antoinette Wills, these six tribunals tried most criminal cases in Paris during their year and a half of existence, and she takes their documents as the base of her study.

Wills utilizes the rather straightforward proceedings of the six courts to answer a very broad and perplexing question: how successfully were progressive Enlightenment ideas on justice translated into functioning institutions and into improved conditions for individuals? In her answer, Wills describes the philosophes' belief that ameliorations of judicial structure and process would lead to a fair system that would deter crime. They supported, among other reforms, jury trial, the presumption of innocence, rehabilitation as well as punishment, equality before the law, the abolition of torture, and an end to jurisdictional ambiguities. At the same time, intellectuals noted that poverty also generated crime. The National Assembly accepted the entire Enlightenment critique, but, recognizing its inability to abolish economic misery, it nevertheless reorganized the judicial system according to the ideals of the century. These legislative initiatives led to significant changes in the courts, for the elected judges pushed legal reform and passed judgment consistent with Enlightenment concerns. In the confusion of the early Revolution, some traditional procedures persisted, but overall the courts measured up to expectations. Nonetheless, Wills's analysis of prosecutions in the provisional courts in 1791 (the year with the best data) suggests that the judicial improvements did not dampen crime. Absolute numbers of accusations jumped. Occupation, age, sex, and habitat of defendants and type of offense changed only slightly from pre-1789 figures. Furthermore, the prosecuted participated in much the same subculture as they had earlier. These individuals tended to float from residence to residence, to drink heavily, to belong to gangs, and to be largely ignorant of political questions. According to Wills, then, the efforts of reformers scarcely altered the pattern of crime. She notes in passing (what revolutionaries and philosophes also posited despite their optimism about court reform) that these changes could not reduce crime that sprang not only from the judicial system but also from poverty.

Although Wills's question—how efficacious were Enlightenment procedures—works to integrate her findings, the query itself deserves some scrutiny. Some investigators may view it as dated. Influenced by anthropologists, historians have come to believe that they may better recapture the past by evaluating ideas as part of a system of belief than by focusing on whether such beliefs later produced desired results. Hence, scholars today would ask not how Enlightenment conceptions of justice worked during the Revolution, but how they fitted within a general framework for comprehending the world. Even assuming the utility of examining how well court reforms operated, the question remains whether 1791 provides a suitable year for evaluation. The penal code's provisions for punishments (which might deter potential criminals) had not even been installed. Even if in force, more than a year would be necessary before procedural change would alter criminal patterns. In fact, a reliable test requires a lengthy chronological sample. The author notes this point once but usually ignores it. Furthermore, Wills may not be answering her question directly because checking improvements in the judicial process by examining people actually detained and brought to trial may not be the same as checking by investigating typical criminal behavior. The accused constituted a select group: those suspects whom the police wanted to and could arrest rather than a representative sample of miscreants. Consequently, even if judicial alterations affected criminals, shifts in their behavior would not necessarily appear proportionately in arrest records. Wills is sensitive to this problem but she tends only to note it rather than to cope with and offer solutions to it. In the end, practically, she overlooks the difficulty. Perhaps some estimate of the motivations and resources of the police would indicate, at least tentatively, the relationship between the accused and the group of lawbreakers. These three problems— equating the accused with the typical criminal, the traditional nature of Wills's inquiry, and the brevity of the data base—may indicate that the author should have selected a question other than the impact of contemporary ideas about justice.

Despite these reservations about the book's overall structure, individual sections prove rewarding. Wills provides a helpful summary of Enlightenment beliefs and an excellent account of the legislative debates on justice. Also, even given that the accused may not adequately represent the criminal element, an examination of the subculture of defendants illuminates the world authorities believed beyond the pale. Wills's investigation into this area is superb: lively, imaginative, and very well organized. Even readers of the works of Richard Cobb will find new insights. These contributions make her book very useful.

Jack R. Censer
George Mason University

David Jones, *Crime, Protest, Community and Police in Nineteenth-Century Britain*. London, Boston and Henley: Routledge and Kegan Paul, 1982. 247 pp. $32.

David Jones, already known for his work on rural protest and Welsh criminality, expands his range here to touch on virtually every point at issue among social historians of British crime and law enforcement. His views on these issues seem generally sensible to this reviewer, although their impact is somewhat lessened by certain persistent weaknesses of presentation.

Crime, Protest, Community and Police in Nineteenth-Century Britain is actually a collection of seven loosely related essays, some of them previously published in different form. "Setting the Scene: Contemporary Views and Historical Perspectives" opens the volume with a survey of the relevant social history, largely English and Welsh, but with some reference to foreign studies. In the course of summarizing work done and yet to be done, Jones indicates the point of view which informs his own pieces: that the records of criminality must be treated with caution, that there is as yet no simple or encompassing explanation of criminal behavior, but that economic change and its consequences for class relations account for at least some of the shifting patterns of the nineteenth-century crime "rate." The focus, here, almost as much as the materials, is characteristically British. In fact there is more than a touch of parochialism in the conclusion that "most social historians, including the present one, still see modern crime as rational behavior, closely related to the character and will of the ruling class and the defence and priorities of the capitalist system" (p. 31). Observers of the American experience, certainly, cannot be counted as subscribing to any single model, even one as broad as this. The kaleidoscopic nature of our society, the prominence of ethnic as a surrogate for (or distraction from) class conflict, and indeed the very difficulty of defining "ruling class," have often kept us from seeing whatever patterns may exist. What saves Jones from the opposite danger, of simple reductionism, is his own awareness of the problem, his insistence upon qualification, complexity, and a sense of irony.

Three of his essays deal directly with the issues of class, protest, and the politics of defining criminality in the countryside. For an American reader the most interesting and easily comprehensible of the three is "The Poacher: A Study in Victorian Crime and Protest," if only because poaching in the British sense is so unfamiliar a crime and the law which defined it so blatant an example of class legislation. It appears, too, that despite centuries of denial, opinion in the English countryside about the "ownership" of various critters differed only in degree from that in, say, Pennsylvania. Poachers were easily the most popular of "criminals"; opposition to the game laws, universal in some areas, was widespread everywhere and not uncommon even among the aristocracy; the new rural police were often forbidden to risk local goodwill by pursuing violators. In general, of course, the level of nineteenth-century criminal violence in England was by American standards remarkably low. But the ferocity displayed by bands of resolute men, when encountered by minions of the landlord class, provides a striking exception. If the nineteenth century did not witness the virtual warfare described by Hay and Thompson for the previous century, it does appear that only Lady Chatterley could love a gamekeeper at any time. Jones describes the often bitter isolation of these men, who were frequent victims of murderous assault and suicidal depression. Only with a dramatic change in legislation toward century's end, coupled with the general "pacification" of the population remarked by all observers, did these skirmishes quiet down.

The one thing missing in the account here is crucial, however; that is, a clear demonstration of the depth of the alienation expressed by the poaching phenomenon. Clearly the law was unpopular, perhaps much in the same way as was Prohibition in the United States, a situation which had at least some of the same potential for fostering class resentment. It remains impossible to tell whether the "typical" poacher—and Jones points out they were a varied lot—was any more rebellious than the typical visitor to a speakeasy, or whether his "crime" was wholly encapsulated. To suggest that "Significantly, the major explosions of unrest in the countryside...were preceded by sudden increases in the number of recorded poaching offenses" (p. 64) may, of course, be to indicate nothing more than nervousness on the part of the local aristocracy, occasioned by wholly unrelated indices of discontent.

Jones is fully aware of this and parallel problems in interpreting criminal returns, which are indeed the focus of his essay on "The Vagrant and Crime in Victorian Britain: Problems of Definition and Attitude." The issue here is not, however, the official measurement of vagrancy so much as attitudes toward it. The British Poor Laws, although often circumvented locally in ways described here in detail, still did not easily allow for the American practice of cutting back the workhouse population during periods which taxpayers as well as indigents felt as "hard times." The Home Office, then, could piece together reasonable estimates of the size of the "tramp" phenomenon. What could not be settled was the nature of the beast—that is, whether vagrants were primarily migrant or unemployed working folk, at least potentially, or rather members of a dangerous class, perhaps even a hereditary one. Here and elsewhere Jones is persuasively skeptical about the notion of a hereditary criminal subculture, which when not simply a romantic fancy was in effect a device which allowed the establishment to minimize the uprooting effects of the nineteenth-century economy. His own collective portrait of British vagrants fits most recent American findings that the men were more miserable than menacing. Harsh treatment by the authorities, even harassment through the criminal code, reflected local hostility toward all outsiders, as well as an increasingly felt need for discipline and control. The tramp, like the drunk and the prostitute, was an obvious affront to Victorian values. While Jones makes some attempt to distinguish between the generally repressive instincts of the "leaders of the local community" (p. 207) and the "generosity of working people, especially women" (p. 208), he also indicates that there is virtually no direct evidence about popular as distinct from institutional reaction to the tens of thousands of homeless Britons who wandered the countryside each year.

One of the crimes often attributed to these vagrants is the subject of the third of Jones's rural pieces, on "Arson and the Rural Community: East Anglia in the Mid-Nineteenth Century." If the evidence about poaching-as-protest is equivocal, and if vagrancy was a defeated rather than militant response, there can be no doubt about the significance of arson. Apart from a very few cases of insurance fraud, this crime "second only to murder" in its capacity to terrify, was clearly—if "rational behavior" at all—an expression of resentment toward the landlord class. The attempt to fix blame on tramps, outsiders, follows naturally from Jones's analysis; agricultural labor remained the largest single occupational category in Great Britain, and widespread local disaffection would be very hard to face, or to explain to reforming critics.

Jones is very good at describing the conditions which drove many to set houses, barns, and ricks aflame. Social grievances—he cites especially resentment against Poor Law administrators, and the introduction of professional police—often fueled basic economic complaints such as the employment of outside casual labor or persistently low wages. There are some discrepancies in the account: we are told both that "the laboring population rarely indulged in violence or looting at the scene of fires" (p. 43), while "on a good number of occasions working men came to jeer, cut hoses. . . and increasingly in Suffolk, to steal dead animals and property" (p. 48). And as so often in the interpretation of criminality, some of the evidence is decidedly ambiguous—as the fact that fires were concentrated heavily in areas which employed migrant (or "vagrant") labor. Still, the analysis is generally persuasive, and Jones ends with the observation that legal forms of protest replaced illegal, over time, as coolly nonconformist labor leaders succeeded the hotter heads of yore.

The intrinsic interest of this and indeed all three rural chapters is unfortunately undermined by Jones's writing in a language which, if not quite private, is perhaps something like Welsh. The charge of parochialism may, of course, cut both ways, and any historian may be held responsible for knowing the ins and outs of poor law and licensing administration, or of the "famous Ground Games Act of 1880," details of which the author assumes. But I must admit that I did not find it "revealing," as promised and otherwise unexplained, that ". . .the bulk of the incendiarism occurred in a rectangle bound by Mildenhall and Debenham in the west and east, and by Garboldisham and East Bergholt in the north and south" (p. 46). And it is odd, if also oddly reassuring, to imagine a readership which recognizes otherwise obscure Welshmen of the later nineteenth century as "notorious" wifebeaters or "famous" drunkards (p. 198).

The landscape is far more familiar in the three chapters which Jones devotes to urban criminality. "The Conquering of China: Crime in an Industrial Community, 1842–64" is a case study of the way in which the vice district of a Welsh boom town was assaulted, with some success, first by a corps of professional police and then by a regiment of reformers armed with "bourgeois ideology," pamphlets, and brass bands. In "Crime in London: The Evidence of the Metropolitan Police, 1831–92," Jones refines an oft-told tale with the help of the Metropolitan Police Criminal Returns, a major source unaccountably overlooked by David Peirce and other predecessors. "Crime and Police in Manchester" describes and interprets the criminal returns for that progressive city much as he and others have done for the metropolis.

There are problems of presentation in all of these chapters, notably the somewhat slapdash use of numbers. Jones believes that criminal statistics are "best used for comparative purposes" (p. 93), although he himself rarely provides the kind of comparisons between places which might lend perspective. We are repeatedly given quantitative impressions in place of figures, or told that, *e.g.,* "70 percent of apprehensions were made in six town wards" (p. 150), without any total for the wards. Jones in fact knows how to deal with numbers in theory, and his analysis of the strengths and weaknesses of various official sources is generally shrewd; perhaps it is here that we suffer from the plaint in the preface: ". . . many footnotes, tables, and graphs have been excised for reasons of economy."

Despite these annoyances and the fact that Jones has nothing dramatic to add to our knowledge of urban criminality, he does have something useful to say. If crime in Manchester does not turn out to be much different from that in other places, the analysis is helpful, in part, for that reason. Here and elsewhere Jones is particularly good at documenting the way in which shifting official priorities affected the rates especially of morals and status offenses, once the battle for the streets had been won. The themes first sounded in the introductory chapter are developed throughout, as Jones gently questions J. J. Tobias's account of a hereditary criminal class, Gatrell and Haden's insistence on a tight connection between political protest and criminal activity, David Peirce's oversimplification of the changing relations between crime and the economic cycle. The tone is modest, tentative, and open-minded as Jones manages simultaneously to suggest new interpretations, challenge old ones, establish the data, and remind us of how far we have to go.

Roger Lane
Haverford College

Virginia Berridge and Griffith Edwards, *Opium and the People*. New York: St. Martin's Press, 1981. xxx + 370 pp. $25.

Opium and the People includes a wealth of statistical information and tosses out a good many thought-provoking concepts. After briefly defining the various forms of narcotics, the authors provide a history of the use of opium and its derivatives in England during the nineteenth century. By 1800 opium was one of the mainstays of the medical profession and was the most common form of self-medication. Solid opium and laudanum, a tincture of opium, were readily available in pharmacies and neighborhood shops. For a good part of the nineteenth century, import statistics show that the annual usage amounted to about three pounds of opium per 1,000 population.

Despite these statistics, the use of opium was not considered a social or moral problem, nor is there any evidence of any major social or public health problems connected with it. At worst, opium addiction was considered a bad habit.

That opium addiction came to be considered a disease, the authors attribute, in part, to efforts by physicians and apothecaries to bolster their professional standing. The new attitude among medical professionals was supported by concerned public health authorities, who observed deaths from overdoses and the excessive dosing with opiates of working-class infants. The outcry against opium was primarily at the so-called stimulant use of it by the working class. The grim, impoverished lives of the workers and their lack of medical care were completely overlooked as factors in opium use. That certain elements in the middle class used opium strictly for pleasure was politely disregarded.

By the end of the nineteenth century, opium was no longer central to medical practice, and its popular use was declining. There was more concern about it, however, for society was preoccupied with addiction as a disease. Even today the precise definition of addiction is not clear, and in 1900 the various explanations for it were a mixture of medical science and prevailing moral beliefs. Moral insanity, the explanation for drug addiction in previous years, was replaced by the term psychiatric disorder; the study of eugenics lent credence to the old concept of hereditary dispositions, and to these was added a physiological explanation. Influenced by American developments, the treatment of addicts became a medical specialty—but a specialty with as many theories as psychiatry.

This period witnessed an opium scare based on the supposed threat from opium dens and the hypothetical threat from morphine injections. The scare was fanned, too, by a more pronounced reaction in the United States. In America, narcotics use was equated with minorities, the lowest economic groups, foreigners, and bolsheviks. This scare helped give the medical profession a firm grip on treating addicts on an individual basis. The role of social and cultural factors in inducing and controlling the use of narcotics was completely ignored.

The final section of the book compares the drug problem of the nineteenth century with that of today. It points out that the casual use of opium has been replaced by the equally casual use of analgesics and tranquilizers, and suggests that the fear of the working-class use of opium for pleasure has been replaced by the fear of a pleasure-seeking rebellious youth. Interestingly, David Musto's *The American Disease*, published about ten years ago, arrived at many of the same conclusions. My one criticism is that the chapters tend to be separate essays, and there is some repetition.

Nonetheless, the authors have produced an intriguing and perceptive book.

John Daffy
University of Maryland

Albert B. Hess and Shigeyo Murayama, *Everyday Law in Japanese Folk Art*. Aalen, Germany: Scientia Verlag, 1980. 61 pp. + 70 plates. $29.50.

The Japanese government has been astute in using popular visual media to promote public awareness of and compliance with customs, rules, and regulations. The Ministry of Justice, for example, sponsors annual programs under the aegis of "A Movement Toward a Brighter Society," which include meetings, speeches, pamphlets, and posters.[1] Popular cartoons (*manga*) are much utilized to keep the public aware of expected conduct.[2] That such an approach to public information campaigns has deep roots is demonstrated by *Everyday Law in Japanese Folk Art*, the principal feature of which is a series of seventy plates showing the details of an 1878 woodcut poster, privately published, illustrating Kyoto[3] police regulations governing public conduct.[4] The poster clearly was intended to apprise Kyoto residents of the norms they were expected to follow when the regulations went into force in 1879 and of the fact that police authorities would enforce the regulations.[5] Those regulations, however, were not unique to Kyoto, but instead were promulgated pursuant to central government policy allowing the institution of prefectural police regulations.[6]

Although the core of the book is the series of plates showing in detail the text of the regulations and illustrations for each of them, the authors have provided brief chapters on Japanese history and the development of law and legal institutions in Japan, criminological observations on popular attitudes toward crime control there, and woodblock prints as an important Japanese art medium with mass appeal. These brief discussions are particularly helpful for those without much acquaintance with Japanese law and art; the authors have included a representative bibliography for those who wish to delve more deeply into art, history, and law in Japan.

The plates themselves show clearly the public information functions they were intended to fulfill. The text of each regulation includes both the *kanji* (Chinese character) text and *yokogana*, the syllabary characters (*kana*) placed to the side of a *kanji* to show its pronunciation. The latter are no longer used with a population almost one hundred percent literate, but were essential when many citizens knew only *kana* and a sprinkling of *kanji*.

Moreover, all the illustrations are of a *genre* nature certain to have promoted lay identification with both offenders and victims.

A dweller in an American metropolitan area, and particularly New York City, is struck by the extent to which the Kyoto authorities endeavored to prevent offensive conduct against which modern American city legislatures continue to struggle. True, throwing sandals into trees (plate 55) or misconduct concerning kite-flying (plate 33), hunting areas (plate 36), fish traps (plate 37), irrigation systems (plates 39–41), hedges (plate 42), bamboo or trees (plate 44) or household nameplates (plate 19)[7] have no contemporary American urban counterparts. But it is easy to identify with civic concerns over speeding (plate 1), vehicles interfering with or endangering pedestrians (plates 3, 5), unlicensed vehicles (plate 8), improper parking (plates 4, 6), fare-gouging (plates 7, 47), fare-jumping (plate 48), and admission fee avoidance (plate 58), littering (plate 9), urinating in public places (plate 14), improper waste scavenging (plates 12–13), unlicensed vendors (plates 66, 68), businesses conducted on sidewalks (plate 60), misrepresentations of governmental status (plate 65), begging (plate 18), disorderly activities affecting the public (plates 21, 69), gambling games likely to fleece the innocent (plate 57), graffiti (43) and dog control (plates 30–32). There is a major difference, however: a western visitor to Japanese cities and towns today sees relatively few of these forms of misconduct, while in New York the problems appear to burgeon, whatever the efforts at enforcement.

In sum, this is a helpful and an amusing volume footnoting an important phase in the modernization of Japan. For an American urban dweller, moreover, it confirms the adage that the more things change, the more they remain the same—in the United States, if not in Japan.

B. J. George, Jr.
New York Law School

Notes

1. *See*, Tanigawa, "Public Participation and the Inegrated Approach in Japanese Rehabilitation Services," in *Criminal Justice in Asia: The Quest for an Integrated Approach*, ed. B. George (UNAFEI, 1982).

2. In 1983, for example, subway posters to encourage maximum use of seating showed a bird, with western hat, suit, and briefcase, looking in vain for a place to perch on a telephone line monopolized by chattering pairs and trios of birds or birds with bundles, etc. The technique is not unknown in the United States, and sometimes has been used with great success, e.g., the "Smokey Bear" campaign to prevent forest fires and "McGruff, the Crime

Dog" posters to promote crime prevention techniques.

3. Kyoto was the capital of Japan until the fall of the shogunate and the restoration to power of the Emperor Mutsuhito in 1868. At that time, the emperor moved the imperial household to Edo (the seat of the *bakufu* government during the shogunate) and renamed that city Tokyo (eastern capital). *See generally,* George, "The Japanese Judical System: Thirty Years of Transition," *Loyola of Los Angeles Law Review* 12 (1979): 807, 808–09. The publication featured in the reviewed work, therefore, illustrated regulations implemented early in the restoration period.

4. *Kai'i Zaimoku Nanaju Kajo* Seventy Regulations Concerning Minor Law Violations) (1879).

5. Page 33, plate 70. Police enforcement powers continued until 1945, but were abrogated with the promulgation of the present 1946 Constitution, art. 76(1), which vests the entire judicial power in the Supreme Court and inferior courts established by law.

6. Pages 31–32. Kyoto, Osaka, and Tokyo then had, and continue to have, equivalent authority to a prefecture (*ken*).

7. The regulation prohibited damaging for personal amusement street and house numbers, signposts, and like objects, but the illustration showed the removal of a plate bearing a householder's name. The authors note that such plates traditionally have been appropriated by students who believe they bring good luck during examinations. The reviewer recalls that, when living in a district adjacent to Kyoto University in 1956–1957, he gave up replacing such signs because students especially prized foreigners' nameplates.

Lawrence M. Friedman and Robert V. Percival, *The Roots of Justice.* Chapel Hill: University of North Carolina Press, 1981. 335 pp., tables, notes, index.

The Roots of Justice is a history of crime and punishment in Alameda County, California, for the period 1870–1910. Perhaps the most laudable feature of the book is Friedman and Percival's blending of quantitative and qualitative methodology. They collected numerical data from arrest blotter, court records, and prison log books. Then they used information from newspapers and other documents to pump life and meaning into agency statistics. The integration of the two methodologies resulted in an informative and interesting narrative.

Another notable aspect of the book is the authors' analytic dissection of the criminal justice system. Arguing that the system was arranged in "layers," they depict criminal justice as though it were a layer cake: show trials involving lurid murders or crimes with political overtones were at the top; ordinary burglaries, thefts, and assaults handled in Superior Court were in the middle; and public-order crimes were at the bottom. Each layer is described in minute detail so that the reader is afforded a clear picture of how each part of the system worked. Special emphasis is given to identifying the sequences and timing of changes that occurred in each part. The professionalization of criminal justice work, for example, is traced over the duration of the period studied and within police, court, and correctional organizations.

Deficiencies in *The Roots of Justice* are linked to Friedman and Percival's treatment of eight central points. First, the authors posit that serious crime (murder, armed robbery, rape, and burglary) was on the decline in Alameda County in the late nineteenth century. This position is supported both by arrest statistics from Alameda County and by other historical research. Friedman and Percival fail, however, to raise the question of why serious crime decreased.

Second, Friedman and Percival aver that lawyers, judges, and laypersons were the chief role players in the administration of justice. Alternative hypotheses are never examined; in particular, the authors fail to outline relations between criminal justice, politics, and business. Instead, they treat the criminal justice system as a "closed system," implying that outside social forces (with the exception of community sentiments or values) have a negligible impact on criminal justice process and policy.

Third, Friedman and Percival contend that the primary role of the police was order maintenance. The authors note that most arrests were for drunkenness, brawling, public hell-raising, and vagrancy; most of those arrested were workingmen. Did the police "repress" the working class as Marxists claim? The authors suggest the data are "too dry and mute" to answer this question. Nonetheless, they make reference to the police arresting striking ironmolders on vagrancy charges in 1890, guarding railroad property during the great railway strikes of 1894, using vagrancy as a weapon against tramps in 1883, and mounting a campaign against the Chinese in the 1870s and 1880s. Here the authors should have dug deeper into newspaper accounts of these events in order to ferret out the social-historical roots of tramping, striking, and other "problems" handled by the police. As for the so-called "Chinese problem," Friedman and Percival attribute a police crackdown on gambling by Chinese persons to "prejudice." An important, yet unanswered question is, "Did unemployment, competition for jobs, and other socioeconomic conditions undergird the racism expressed in police actions?"

Fourth, Friedman and Percival document the fact that property felonies were much more common than felonies of personal violence in cases in Superior Court. As the authors concede, "protecting private property was what felony justice was all about" (p. 149). In discussing this point, the authors show how the system became less adjudicative and more administrative. This happened when the rise of plea bargaining was coupled with the demise of trial by jury. The authors succinctly summed up the increasing crime control orientation of the system between 1900 and 1910 by stating that the public came to think that trials were unnecessary since police and prosecutors had already "tried" most cases anyway.

Fifth, Friedman and Percival maintain that ebbs and flows in sentencing were tied to reforms in correctional law. Good time credit, probation, and parole laws were among the most significant reforms. Again, pertinent substantive questions were not raised. One such question is, "What caused the reforms?"

Sixth, the authors perceptively argue that the sensational show trials taught important moral and legal lessons. In other words, these well-publicized cases showed the law in action the way it was supposed to be and also reminded the citizenry of the location of moral boundaries. Although the authors do not address the issue, it seems fitting to ask whether these cases also serve the larger purpose of legitimating the entire legal order. To the extent that the public became informed about these cases and perceived justice, equality, and fairness to be present in the processing of these cases, this was probably true.

Seventh, Friedman and Percival found very few appeals were made from Alameda County, and defendants did poorly on appeals. The reasons for the very limited number of appeals are unclear. The administrative philosophy of judges and other criminal justice functionaries no doubt contributed to a tendency not to critically scrutinize the judicial process.

Eighth, Friedman and Percival take the position that prisons were functional for this time period because they reassured the public that lawbreakers would be punished. Here more specificity would have enhanced the authors' discussion. Did all social classes and occupational groups gain increased feelings of security and moral certainty or was it primarily the elite who felt more protected from "dangerous classes?" Using vague terms like "society" or "public" does not help to answer this query.

All of the flaws discussed stem from the authors' violation of the historiographic rule of placing the unit of analysis within a socio-temporal context. In dealing with any phenomenon, it is necessary to relate that phenomenon to historically unique social, economic, political, and cultural factors. *The Roots of Justice* is lacking in this regard: it is more a "serial" than a social history. As this review has attempted to demonstrate, the book is characterized by tunnel vision in which the narrative consists principally of data directly relating the crime and punishment. Missing is a systematic examination of the social origins of criminal justice. For this reason, the authors discovered few, if any, actual "roots" of justice.

Dennis E. Hoffman
University of Nebraska at Omaha

Submissions, Subscriptions, and Professional Notes

Notes on submissions:

The general rule guiding authors and editors is that submissions should follow as closely as possible the formats of the most recent publication. Therefore, previous volumes of *Criminal Justice History* should be consulted for guidance.

Submit two copies—original and xerox or good xeroxes, the original made with a good ribbon. Submissions should be carefully proofread by authors.

Double-space throughout—text, indented quotations, and end notes. No part of a typescript should be single-spaced. Margins should be at least 1¼ inches, or 32 millimeters, on all sides.

Use text and end notes; no footnotes. End notes should be in a separate section (but with continuous pagination) following the end of the text. End notes should be numbered in the margin to the left of the first line of the particular note, a period following the number. (Do not hang end note numbers above the line, nor omit periods; this should be done only with note numbers in the text.)

Use upper and lower case throughout. Do not capitalize or underline titles or subtitles of the essay text. (If special emphases are desired, convey them in the covering letter.) The abbreviations *cap*, for capitals, and *ital*, for italics, may be written at appropriate places in the left margin if the author is convinced they are necessary. Use quotation marks for quotation marks; do *not* use apostrophes as quotation marks, except, of course, around a quotation within a quotation. Originally foreign phrases now common in English usage should not be underlined.

If there are tables, charts, graphs, or other illustrations, they should be submitted camera-ready and on separate sheets. A space may be left in the text with indication of the specific matter that belongs there. In general, however, it will be simplest and most feasible for illustrative material to be grouped in an appendix following the text, with text references to each item by number.

In end notes, the first citation of a source should be complete. Later citations of it should use short titles (not "op cit."). "Ibid." is acceptable.

Sensible abbreviations of sources often referred to, after the first full citation, are acceptable and desirable.

Editorial correspondence and sub-missions on the United States:

Submissions on countries other than the U.S.A.:

Professor Henry Cohen
Department of History
Loyola University of Chicago
820 N. Michigan Avenue
Chicago, Illinois 60611 U.S.A.

Professor Louis Knafla
Department of History
University of Calgary
Calgary, Alberta
Canada T2N 1N4

Books for review, proposals to review, and reviewer registrations should be sent to the appropriate review editor:

U.S.A. and Canada:

Other areas and transnational:

Professor Eugene Watts
Department of History
Ohio State University
Columbus, Ohio 43210
U.S.A.

Professor James Cockburn
Department of History
University of Maryland
College Park, Maryland 20742
U.S.A.

Subscriptions

Subscriptions at $49.50

Criminal Justice History
Meckler Publishing
520 Riverside Avenue
Westport, CT 06880

Professional notes

Criminal Justice History plans a register and notes on research in progress to acquaint readers with current trends and allow persons doing related research to make contact. Researchers are requested to forward information as follows, using separate pages for each project:

1. Name
2. Address
3. Telephone

4. Discipline(s)
5. Short title of research project, specifying book, article, or other
6. Description or abstract (separate attachment preferred)
7. Stage of preparation and expected date of completion

If more than one research project is in preparation use separate pages for each. Forward to:

Professor Cyril D. Robinson
Crime Study Center
Southern Illinois University
Carbondale, Illinois 62901 U.S.A.
(618) 453-5701